Religion in America

ADVISORY EDITOR

Edwin S. Gaustad

EVIDENCES

OF THE

AUTHENTICITY, INSPIRATION

AND

CANONICAL AUTHORITY

OF THE

HOLY SCRIPTURES

BY THE

REV. ARCHIBALD ALEXANDER, D.D.

ARNO PRESS

A NEW YORK TIMES COMPANY

New York · 1972

Reprint Edition 1972 by Arno Press Inc.

Reprinted from a copy in
The Wesleyan University Library

RELIGION IN AMERICA - Series II
ISBN for complete set: 0-405-04050-4
See last pages of this volume for titles.

Manufactured in the United States of America

Library of Congress Cataloging in Publication Data

Alexander, Archibald, 1772-1851.
    Evidences of the authenticity, inspiration, and
canonical authority of the Holy Scriptures.

    (Religion in America, series II)
    1. Apologetics—19th century. 2. Bible—Evi-
dences, authority, etc. I. Title.
BT1101.A56 1972   220.1   70-38431
ISBN 0-405-04052-0

EVIDENCES

OF THE

AUTHENTICITY, INSPIRATION

AND

CANONICAL AUTHORITY

OF THE

HOLY SCRIPTURES

ENGRAVED BY SARTAIN. — THE ORIGINAL BY NEAGLE

A. Alexander

EVIDENCES

OF THE

AUTHENTICITY, INSPIRATION

AND

CANONICAL AUTHORITY

OF THE

HOLY SCRIPTURES

BY THE

REV. ARCHIBALD ALEXANDER, D.D.

Prof. of Theology in Theological Seminary at Princeton.

PHILADELPHIA:

PRESBYTERIAN BOARD OF PUBLICATION.

ADVERTISEMENT.

THIS edition of the EVIDENCES has been enlarged by
the addition of one-fourth part of the volume, and
contains nearly twice as much matter as was included in the first editions of the work. The parts which
have been added to the preceding and to the present
edition are the chapter on "the necessity of Divine
Revelation;" a new chapter on prophecy, relating
.o Nineveh, Babylon, and Tyre; the chapters on
Inspiration; and the whole of what relates to he
Canon of the Old and New Testaments. This last
is an abridgment of the volume which the author
published on the CANON; of which work two edi
tions have been given to the pu lic.

CONTENTS.

CHAPTER I.

PAGE

The right use of reason in religion, ... 9

CHAPTER II.

It is impossible to banish all religion from the world, and if it
were possible, it would be the greatest calamity which could
befall the human race, ... 17

CHAPTER III.

If Christianity be rejected, there is no other religion which can
be substituted in its place, at least no other which will at all
answer the purpose for which religion is desirable, ... 24

CHAPTER IV.

Revelation necessary to teach us how to worship God acceptably—the nature and certainty of a future state—and especially, the method by which sinners may obtain salvation, ... 34

CHAPTER V.

There is nothing improbable or unreasonable in the idea of a
revelation from God, and consequently nothing improbable or
unreasonable in such a manifest divine interposition, as may
be necessary to establish a revelation 61

5

CHAPTER VI.

Miracles are capable of proof from testimony, ... **65**

CHAPTER VII.

The miracles of the Gospel are credible, ... **89**

CHAPTER VIII.

The rapid and extensive progress of the Gospel, by instruments so few and feeble, is a proof of divine interposition, ... **118**

CHAPTER IX.

Prophecies respecting the Jewish nation which have been remarkably fulfilled, ... **130**

CHAPTER X.

Prophecies relating to Nineveh, Babylon, Tyre, &c., ... **132**

CHAPTER XI.

Prophecies respecting Messiah—predictions of Christ respecting the destruction of Jerusalem, ... **159**

CHAPTER XII.

No other religion possesses the same kind and degree of evidence as Christianity : and no other miracles are as well attested as those recorded in the Bible, ... **69**

CHAPTER XIII.

The Bible contains internal evidence that its origin is divine,. **186**

CHAPTER XIV.

PAGE

The Scriptures of the Old and New Testament were written by the inspiration of God; and this inspiration, however it may be distinguished, was plenary; that is, the writers were under an infallible guidance, both as to ideas and words; and yet the acquired knowledge, habits, and peculiar dispositions, of the writers, were not superseded, ... 222

CHAPTER XV.

The inspiration of the books of the New Testament, ... 235

CANONICAL AUTHORITY OF THE BOOKS OF SCRIPTURE.

CHAPTER XVI.

The importance of ascertaining the true canon of Holy Scripture, ... 245

CHAPTER XVII.

The care with which the books of the Old Testament were preserved—their canonical authority—the sanction given to these books by the Saviour and his apostles—and the method of ascertaining what books were in the canon at the time of Christ's advent, ... 249

CHAPTER XVIII.

The books denominated aprocryphal have no just claim to a place among the canonical Scriptures of the Old Testament, 258

CHAPTER XIX.

Canon of the New Testament—method of settling it—testimony of the Church—constitution of the canon—whence these books derive their authority—solicitude of early Chris-

^{AGE}

tians to obtain these books—their care o distinguish them
from others—autographs, &c., ... 266

CHAPTER XX.

I'estimonies in favour of the canonical authority of the books
of the New Testament, ... 278

CHAPTER XXI.

Canonical authority of Paul's Epistles, ... 287

CHAPTER XXII.

The canonical authority of the seven Catholic epistles, and of
the book of Revelation, ... 295

CHAPTER XXIII.

Recapitulation of evidence on the canon of the New Testament, 303

EVIDENCES OF CHRISTIANITY.

CHAPTER I.

THAT it is the right and the duty of all men to exer
cise their reason in inquiries concerning religion, is a
truth so manifest, that it may be presumed there are
none who will be disposed to call it in question.

Without reason there can be no religion: for in
every step which we take, in examining the evidences of revelation, in interpreting its meaning, or in
assenting to its doctrines, the exercise of this faculty
is indispensable.

When the evidences of Christianity are exhibited,
an appeal is made to the reason of men for its truth;
but all evidence and all argument would be perfectly
futile, if reason were not permitted to judge of their
force. This noble faculty was certainly given to man
to be a guide in religion, as well as in other things.
He possesses no other means by which he can form
a judgment on any subject, or assent to any truth;
and it would be no more absurd to talk of seeing
without eyes, than of knowing any thing without
reason.

It is therefore a great mistake to suppose that reli
gion forbids or discourages the right use of reason.
So far from this, she enjoins it as a duty of high
moral obligation, and reproves those who neglect to
judge for themselves what is right.

It has frequently been said by the friends of reve
lation, that although reason is legitimately exercised

in examining the evidences of revelation, and in
determining the sense of the words by which it is
conveyed; yet it is not within her province to sit in
judgment on the doctrines contained in such a divine
communication. This statement, though intended to
guard against the abuse of reason, is not, in my opinion, altogether accurate. Without reason we can
form no conception of a truth of any kind; and when
we receive any thing as true, whatever may be the
evidence on which it is founded, we must view the
reception of it to be reasonable. Truth and reason
are so intimately connected that they can never with
propriety be separated. Truth is the object, and
reason is the faculty by which it is apprehended,
whatever be the nature of the truth, or of the evidence by which it is established. No doctrine can
be a proper object of our faith which it is not more
reasonable to receive than to reject. If a book, claim-
ing to be a divine revelation, is found to contain
doctrines which can in no way be reconciled to right
reason, it is a sure evidence that those claims have
no solid foundation, and ought to be rejected. But
that a revelation should contain doctrines of a mysterious and incomprehensible nature, and entirely
different from all our previous conceptions, and, considered in themselves, improbable, is not repugnant
to reason; on the contrary, judging from analogy,
sound reason would lead us to expect such things in
a revelation from God. Every thing which relates
to this Infinite being must be to us, in some respects,
incomprehensible. Every new truth must be different from all that is already known; and all the
plans and works of God are very far above and
beyond the conception of such minds as ours. Natural religion has as great mysteries as any in revelation; and the created universe, as it exists, is as
different from any plan which men would have conceived, as any of the truths contained in a revelation
can be. But it is reasonable to believe what by our
senses we perceive to exist; and it is reasonable to
believe whatever God declares to be true.

In receiving therefore the most mysterious doctrines of revelation, the ultimate appeal is to reason:
not to determine whether she could have discovered
these truths; not to declare whether considered in
themselves they appear probable; but to decide whether it is not more reasonable to believe what God
speaks, than to confide in our own crude and feeble
conceptions. Just as if an unlearned man should
hear an able astronomer declare that the diurnal
motion of the heavens is not real but only apparent,
or that the sun is nearer to the earth in winter than
in summer, although the facts asserted appeared to
contradict the senses, it would be reasonable to acquiesce in the declarations made to him by one who
understood the subject, and in whose veracity he
had confidence. If then we receive the witness of
men in matters above our comprehension, much
more should we receive the witness of God, who
knows all things, and cannot deceive his creatures by
false declarations.

There is no just cause for apprehending that we
shall be misled by the proper exercise of reason on
any subject which may be proposed for our consideration. The only danger is of making an improper
use of this faculty, which is one of the most common
faults to which our nature is liable. Most men profess that they are guided by reason in forming their
opinions; but if this were really the case, the world
would not be overrun with error; there would not be
so many absurd and dangerous opinions propagated
and pertinaciously defended. In one sense, indeed,
they may be said to follow reason, for they are guided by a blinded, prejudiced, and perverted reason.

One large class of men are accustomed, from a
slight and superficial view of the important subject
of religion, to draw a hasty conclusion, which must
prove in the highest degree detrimental to their
happiness. They have observed, that in the modern as well as ancient world, there is much superstition, much imposture, much diversity of opinion
and variety of sects, many false pretences to Divine

inspiration, and many false reports of miracles and prophetic oracles. Without giving themselves the trouble of searching diligently for the truth amidst the various contending claims, they draw a general conclusion that all religions are alike; that the whole affair is a cheat, the invention of cunning men who imposed on the credulity of the unthinking multitude: and that the claims to Divine Revelation do not even deserve a serious examination. Does right reason dictate such a conclusion as this? If it did, and we were to apply it to all other concerns, it would make a sad overturning in the business of the world. Truth, honesty, and honour might, on these principles, be discarded as unmeaning names; for of all these there have been innumerable counterfeits, and concerning all of them an endless diversity of opinion.

A second class, who profess to be men of reason, pay more attention to the subject of religion; but their reason is a prejudiced judge. They listen with eagerness to all that can be said against revelation. They read with avidity the books written against Christianity, and but too faithfully treasure up every objection to religion; but her advocates never obtain from them a fair hearing. They never inquire whether the arguments and objections which appear to them so strong, have not been refuted. With the means of conviction within their reach, they remain firmly fixed in their infidelity; and as long as they pursue this partial method of investigation, they must ever remain in the same darkness.

A third class, who wish to be considered as taking reason for their guide, are under the dominion of vicious passions; ambition, avarice, lust, or revenge. Men of this character, however strong their intellect, or extensive their erudition, can never reason impartially on any subject which interferes with the gratification of their predominant desires; and as religion forbids, under severe penalties, all irregular passions and vicious indulgences, they pursue it with malignant hatred. As one well observes, " they are against religion because religion is against them." Such men never reason calmly on the subject, and they are incapable of receiving any benefit from the arguments of others. They never think of religion but with a feeling of enmity; they never speak of it but in the language of sneer or abuse. There is no object which this race of infidels have more at heart, than to root up every principle of religion from the minds of men, and to drive it from the earth, so that not one vestige of it may remain to give them torment. Voltaire may be considered as the leader of this band, and his humble imitators have been too numerous in every Christian country.

But there is still another class of men, more distinguished, as masters of reason, than those who have been mentioned. They are the cold, speculative, subtle skeptics, who involve themselves in a thick mist of metaphysics, attack first principles, and confound their readers with paradoxes. The number of those who belong to this class is perhaps not large, but they are formidable; for while the other enemies of the truth scarcely make a show of reason, these philosophers are experienced in all the intricacies of a refined logic; so that in their hands error is made to appear in the guise of truth. Should we yield ourselves to the sophistry of these men, they will persuade us to doubt, not only of the truth of revelation, but of our senses and of our very existence. If it be inquired how they contrive to spread such a colouring of skepticism over every subject, the answer is, by artfully assuming false principles as the premises of their reasoning; by reasoning sophistically on correct principles; by the dexterous use of ambiguous terms; by pushing their inquiries beyond the limits of human knowledge; and by calling in question the first principles of all knowledge. It is not easy to conjecture what their motive is; most probably it is vanity. They are ambitious of appearing more profound and acute than other men, and distinction is not so readily obtained in the common course, as by flying off in an eccentric orbit. It cannot be any

sincere regard for truth which influences them; for
upon their principles, truth and reason are equally
worthless. They pull down every thing, but build
up nothing. Truth has no greater enemies in the
world than this Pyrrhonic sect; and it is to be lamen-
ted that sometimes ingenious young men are caugh*
in the wiles of their sophistry, and are led so far into
the labyrinth of their errors, that they are never able
to extricate themselves; and all their fair prospects
of virtue and usefulness are obscured for ever.

Before I leave the consideration of the various
classes of persons who, while they profess to be
guided by reason, make an improper use of this
faculty, I ought to mention a set of men, distinguished for their learning and ingenuity, who profess to
receive the Christian revelation and glory in the
appellation of Rational Christians. They proceed
on the plausible and (if rightly understood) correct
principle of receiving nothing as true but what their
reason approves; but these very men, with all their
fair appearances of rationality, are chargeable with
as gross a dereliction of reason as can well be conceived; and, in regard to consistency, are more vul-
nerable than any of those already mentioned. While
they admit that God has made a revelation, they insist upon the right of bringing the truths revealed to
the test of human judgment and opinion, and reject
them as unreasonable if they do not accord with this
standard. But the declaration of God is the highest
reason which we can have for believing any thing.
To set up our opinion against the plain expression
of his will, is surely presumption of the highest kind
Perhaps, however, I do not represent the case with
perfect accuracy. Perhaps no man is chargeable
with such an inconsistency, as to admit a thing to be
contained in an undoubted revelation, and yet reject
it. The exact state of the matter is this. The Scriptures, it is admitted, contain a revelation from God;
but there are many things in the Bible, which if
taken in the most obvious sense, are inconsistent with
reason; and as nothing inconsistent with reason can

be from God, it is concluded that this cannot be the true sense of Scripture. Accordingly, their wits are so to work, and their learning laid under contribution, to invent and defend some other sense. Upon these principles, a man may believe just as much, or as little as he pleases of what the Bible contains; fo, it has been found, that no text is so stubborn as not to yield to some of the modes of treatment which have been adopted. This whole procedure is contrary to right reason. The plain course which reason directs us to pursue, is, after examining the evidences of revelation until we are satisfied, to come to the interpretation of the Scriptures with an unbiased mind, and in the exercise of a sound judgment, and with the aid of those helps and rules which reason and experience suggest, to obtain the sense of the several parts of the document; and although this sense may contradict our preconceived opinions, or clash with our inclinations, we ought implicitly to receive it; and not by a refined ingenuity, and laboured critical process, to extort a meaning that will suit our own notions. This is not to form our opinions by the word of God, but to cut down the sublime and mysterious doctrines of revelation to the measure of our narrow conceptions. In the creed of many, called Rational Christians, the divine system of heavenly truth is shorn of its glory, and comes forth little more than an improved theory of Natural Religion. There is no reason in this.

But what if the plain sense of Scripture be absolutely repugnant to the first principles of reason? Let that be demonstrated and the effect will be rather to overthrow the Scriptures, than to favour such a method of forming a theory from them. But no such thing can be demonstrated. The reasonings by which it has been attempted to prove that the doctrines commonly called orthodox are contrary to reason, and fallacious, and a similar mode of reasoning on truths of Natural Religion, will land us in Atheism.

Deistical writers have been fond of representing

faith and reason as irreconcilable. They have in sinuated and even asserted, that revelation canno' be received without a renunciation of reason; and have affected to regret that it should be subjected to the trial of a rational investigation, which they allege it can by no means bear. This was a favourite topic with Morgan, Bolingbroke, Voltaire, and Hume. The last mentioned author, in the close of his Essay on Miracles, used the following language: "Our most holy religion is founded on *Faith*, not on reason, and 'tis a sure method of exposing it, to put it to a test, which it is by no means fitted to endure." —And again: "Mere reason is insufficient to convince us of its [the Christian religion's] veracity, and whoever is moved by faith to assent to it, is conscious of a continual miracle in his own person, which subverts all the principles of his understanding."

On the insidious nature of this attack, I shall not stop to remark, except to observe, that it may be taken as a specimen not only of Hume's method of treating Christianity, but of that of the whole tribe of deistical writers, until very recently, when they have come out boldly. Under the mask of friendship, and with words of respect on their lips, they have aimed the most deadly thrusts at the vitals of Christianity. But in regard to the sentiment expressed in this extract, the friends of revelation utterly disclaim it, and hold it to be false and unfounded. The state of the controversy between Christians and deists did not authorize any such assertion. The defenders of the truth have ever been ready to meet their antagonists on the ground of impartial reason. They *have* met them at every point where they have chosen to make the assault; and I may safely say, that no deistical argument remains unrefuted, no infidel objection undetected and unexposed. As Mr. Hume wrote this immediately after finishing his argument against miracles, he may have felt a confidence that he had achieved what none before were able to effect. But his confidence was premature; the argument which he claims the honour of having discovered, (though this might be disputed on good ground) has been refuted, with a clearness of evidence sufficient to bring a conviction to any mind but that of a sophist and skeptic. We shall have further occasion, in the sequel, to consider the force of Mr. Hume's reasoning against miracles.

It may perhaps require some apology, that a subject which has been so fully and ably discussed in numerous volumes, should be attempted to be treated in a short essay. My only apology is that the poison of infidelity is imbibed by many, who never have access to the antidote. It is much to be regretted that some of the books which are almost sure to fall into the hands of literary youth, are deeply tinctured with skepticism. How many read Hume and Gibbon, who never have seen the answers of Campbell and Watson! Now if we can present even a brief outline of the evidences of Christianity to those who may not be disposed to read larger works, we may be contributing, in some small degree, to prevent the progress of one of the greatest evils to which men are liable.

CHAPTER II.

IT IS IMPOSSIBLE TO BANISH ALL RELIGION FROM THE WORLD, AND IF IT WERE POSSIBLE, IT WOULD BE THE GREATEST CALAMITY WHICH COULD BEFAL THE HUMAN RACE.

IT is not my object here to consider religion as it is a matter of duty, or a means of obtaining happiness in a future world; for both these would be equally disregarded by those men who aim at the subversion of all religion. What I shall attempt, at present, is to state and establish the fact, that man is so consti-tuted that he must have some sort of religion.

And the truth of this will be manifest from an inspection of the principles of human nature, and

2 *

from the history of the world. Man has naturally a
sense of moral obligation, a perception of the differ
ence between right and wrong, feelings of remorse
or approbation on the review of his conduct, fears
of future retribution when he has committed a crime,
and a propensity to pay religious homage to some
object visible or invisible. These are what have
been called his *religious feelings;* and from them he
has received the appellation of a *religious animal.*
And certainly there is nothing by which man is so
clearly distinguished from the creatures below him,
as this capacity for religion; for whatever indications
they give of sagacity in other matters, it is impossible to communicate to them any ideas of morality,
or any impressions of a religious nature. That these
feelings are natural, and not adventitious is manifest.
because they are found to exist in men of all ages,
of all countries, and in every different state of society. And hence, no nation ancient or modern, has
ever been found without some kind of religion. It
would be as difficult to find a whole nation without
religion, as to find one destitute of speech. Some
travellers, it is true, from superficial observation,
have reported that some savage tribes had no ideas
of religion, and no species of worship; but on more
accurate examination it has been ascertained that this
was a mistake. And from our present knowledge
of the nations of the earth, we are authorized to
assert that there is not one totally destitute of some
sense of religion and some form of worship. The
same thing was well known to all the wisest men of
antiquity. It is a fact from which both Plato and
Cicero have derived many important conclusions.
And these principles of our nature are so deeply
radicated that they never can be removed. Men
may be induced to abandon their old religion and to
adopt a new one; but they never can remain long
free from all religion. Take away one object of worship and they will soon attach themselves to another.
If unhappily they lose the knowledge of the true
God, they will set up gods of their own invention

or receive them from others.—The history of all nations bears such ample testimony to this fact that it cannot be denied. Now, this universality of religion evinces, in the clearest manner, that the principle is natural, that it is an essential thing in the constitution of man: just as the fact that men are always found living in society, proves that the social principle exists and is natural to man.

Atheistical men have indeed attempted to trace all religious feelings and all rites of worship to the craft of priests and policy of rulers; but this opinion is not only unsupported by historical testimony, but is most unreasonable in itself. For if there had not existed a predisposition to religion in the minds of men, such a design would never have been conceived; and if it had, all attempts to introduce into the minds of men ideas so foreign to their nature, must have been abortive.

At any rate, such an imposition could not have continued for so long a time, and could not have been extended to every tribe and nation in the world. If no sense of religion had existed in the minds of men, priests and politicians, however cunning, would have had no handle to take hold of, no foundation on which to build. Besides, it seems to be forgotten by the advocates of this hypothesis, that the existence of priests supposes the previous existence of religion.

They have moreover alleged that fear produced the gods. Be it so; it still confirms the position, that there is something in the nature of man which leads him to religion; and it is reasonable to conclude that a cause, which has operated uniformly heretofore, will continue to produce the same effects as long as the world stands. It is impossible, therefore, to banish all religion from the world.

To what degree atheists have succeeded in divesting themselves of all religious impression, I do not pretend to know. That some men have gone to a great length in counteracting the constitutional tendencies and extinguishing the feelings of nature, is undoubtedly true; but there have been sufficient indications to lead to the opinion that there is more of affectation than reality in the bravery of their profession. It is known that some of them have, above other men, been the slaves of superstitious fears; and that others, in times of extreme peril, as in a storm at sea, have for the moment renounced their atheism, and cried as earnestly for mercy as those around them. Now if these philosophers, with all their reasoning, are not able to erase all religious impressions from their minds, it is vain to attempt to banish all religion from the world.

But suppose the great work achieved, and that every vestige of religion were obliterated, what would be the result? Would men remain without any objects of religious homage? Would they never again be afraid of invisible powers? Would the feelings of remorse at no time urge them to perform some sort of penance, or attempt some kind of expiation? Would no impostors and false prophets arise to deceive the world again with their dreams, fancies, and pretended revelations? They must have made but superficial observations on human nature, who think that none of these things would ever occur.

If those persons, therefore, who oppose Christianity, hope by its suppression to get rid of all religion, they do greatly deceive themselves. This work being accomplished, they would soon have more to perform in endless progression. Instead of the pure, mild, benignant religion of Christ, they would soon find themselves surrounded by superstitions as foul and as false, as monstrous and as absurd, as any which the hotbed of paganism ever produced. Look into the heathen world, and see the abominations and miseries which inveterate superstition perpetuates in some of the fairest and most populous regions of the globe. Look at the savage tribes of Africa and America, and contemplate the cruel bondage of superstition to which the people are subjected. Evils as great would soon grow up among us, were it not for the salutary influence of Christianity. Our forefathers, before they became Christians, were in the same degraded and wretched situation. And shall we curse our posterity by bringing back those evils from which our fathers escaped? It is a truth which should be proclaimed every where on the house tops, that it is the BIBLE which has delivered us from the horrid dominion of superstition, and it is the BIBLE which must prevent its return. Philosophy has had no hand in working out this deliverance from the horrors of idolatry. With all her celebrated schools and sages, she never turned one individual from the worship of idols; and she would be equally powerless in preventing the return of superstition, if other barriers were removed.

But I proceed now to the second part of my pro position, which is, that if religion could be banished from the world, it would be the greatest calamity which could befal the human race.

It has formerly been a matter of discussion with the learned, whether the influence of superstition or atheism is most baneful to society. Plutarch, Bacon, Bayle, Warburton, and others, have handled this subject in a learned and ingenious manner, and arrived at very different conclusions. However doubt ful this question may have been considered in former times, I believe all reflecting men are now pretty well satisfied, that the question is put to rest for ever We have recently beheld the spectacle of a great nation casting off contemptuously the religion of their fathers, and plunging at once into the abyss of atheism. We have seen the experiment tried, to ascertain whether a populous nation could exist without the restraints of religion. Every circumstance was as favourable to the success of the experiment as it could be. Learning was in its highest state of advancement; philosophy boasted of an approximation to perfection; refinement and politeness had never been more complete among any people. But what was the result? It is written in characters of blood. It was as if a volcano had burst upon the world, and disgorged ts fiery flood over all Europe. Such a

scene of cruelty, cold-blooded malignity, beastly impurity, heaven daring impiety, and insatiable rapa-
ciousness, the world never witnessed before, and, I
trust in God, will never witness again.   The only
ray of hope which brightened the dismal prospect
was, that this horrible system contained in itself the
principles of its own speedy downfall.   Atheism has
no bond of union for its professors, no basis of mutual confidence.   It breeds suspicion, and consequently hatred in every breast; and it is actuated
by a selfishness which utterly disregards all the
bonds of nature, of gratitude, and of friendship.   To
an atheist fear becomes the ruling passion.   Conscious of his own want of virtue, honour, and hu-
manity, he naturally views his fellows in the same
light, and is ready to put them out of the way as
soon as they appear to become obstacles to the accomplishment of his plans.   Hence the bloody actors
in this tragedy, after glutting their revenge, by shedding the blood of innocent Christians and unoffending priests, turned their murderous weapons against
each other.   Not satisfied with inflicting death on
the objects of their suspicion or envy, they actually
feasted their eyes daily, with the streams of blood
which incessantly flowed from the guillotine.   Never
was the justice of heaven against impious and cruel
men more signally displayed, than in making these
miscreants the instruments of vengeance upon each
other.   The general state of morals in France, during the period in which Christianity was proscribed,
and atheism reigned, was such as almost exceeds
belief.   An eye-witness of the whole scene, and an
actor in some parts of it, has drawn the following sketch:—"Multiplied cases of suicide; prisons
crowded with innocent persons; permanent guillo-
tines; perjuries of all classes; parental authority set
at naught; debauchery encouraged by an allowance
to those called unmarried mothers: nearly six thousand divorces within the single city of Paris, within
a little more than two years after the law authorized

them;—in a word, whatever is most obscene in vice, and most dreadful in ferocity!"* If these be the genuine fruits of atheism, then let us rather have superstition in its most appalling form. Between atheism and superstition there is this great difference; the latter may authorize some crimes, the former opens the flood-gates to all. The one restrains partially, the other removes all restraint from vice. Every kind of religion presents some terrors to evil doers; atheism promises complete immunity, and stamps virtue itself with the character of folly.

But we must not suppose that the whole mass of the French people became atheists during this period. Far from it. A large majority viewed the whole scene with horror and detestation; but the atheistical philosophers had the power in their hands; and, though a small minority of the nation, were able to effect so much mischief. But from this example we may conjecture what must be the state of things, if the whole mass of people in a nation should become atheists, or be freed from all the restraints of conscience and religion. Such an event will never occur, but if it should, all must acknowledge that no greater calamity could be imagined. It would be a lively picture of hell upon earth; for what is there in the idea of hell more horrible than the absence of all restraint and all hope, and the uncontrolled dominion of the most malignant passions? But there would be one remarkable point of difference, for while atheists deny the God that made them, the inhabitants of hell BELIEVE AND TREMBLE

* Gregoire.

CHAPTER III.

IF CHRISTIANITY BE REJECTED, THERE IS NO OTHER RELIGION WHICH CAN
BE SUBSTITUTED IN ITS PLACE; AT LEAST NO OTHER WHICH WILL AT
ALL ANSWER THE PURPOSE FOR WHICH RELIGION IS DESIRABLE.

IT has been proved in the former section, that it is
necessary to have some religion. We are already in
possession of Christianity, which, by the confession of
deists themselves, answers many valuable purposes.
It behoves us, therefore, to consider well what we
are likely to obtain by the exchange, if we should
relinquish it. If any man can show us a better religion, and founded on better evidences, we ought to
give it up willingly; but if this cannot be done, then
surely it is not reasonable to part with a certain good,
without receiving an equivalent. This would be, as
if some persons sailing on the ocean in a vessel which
carried them prosperously, should determine to abandon it without knowing that there was any other to
receive them, merely because some of the passengers,
pretending to skill, suggested that it was leaky, and
would sooner or later founder.

Let the enemies of Christianity tell us plainly what
their aim is, and what they design to substitute in
the place of the Bible. This, however, they are unable to perform: and yet they would have us to consent to give up our dearest hopes without knowing
what we are to receive, or whether we are to receive
any thing to compensate for the loss.

This is a point of vital importance, and demands
our most serious attention. If it is really intended to
substitute some other religion in the place of Christianity, we ought certainly, before we make the exchange, to have the opportunity of examining its
claims, that we may know whether it will be likely
to answer the purposes for which religion is wanted.
To bring this subject fairly into view, let us take a

survey of the world, and inquire, what it has to propose for our selection, if we should renounce Christianity

There are only three things, in that event, among which we must choose. The first, to adopt some of the existing or some of the exploded systems of Paganism; the second, to accept the Koran instead of the Bible; and the third, to embrace Natural Religion or pure deism.

Few men have had the effrontery to propose a return to Paganism; yet even this has not been too extravagant for some whose names stand high as men of literature. The learned Gibbon has not, that I recollect, expressed his opinion on this subject explicitly; but it may be fairly inferred, from many things in his History of the Decline and Fall of the Roman empire, that he deeply regretted the subversion of the old Pagan systems, and that the progress of Christianity was far from affording him any pleasure.

But although he makes it sufficiently manifest that, could his wishes have governed past events, the old systems would never have been disturbed, and Christianity never have had a footing; yet we cannot say whether he would have given his vote to have the temples rebuilt and the Pagan rites restored. It is difficult to tell what he wished to accomplish by his opposition to Christianity; or whether he had any definite view, except to manifest his hatred to the gospel and its Author.

Taylor, the learned translator of Plato, openly avowed his predilection for the religion of the Athenian philosopher, and his wish that it might be revived; and speaks in contemptuous terms of Christianity, in comparison with Platonism; but he never could have supposed *that* to be a suitable religion for the bulk of men, which had not the least influence upon them while the philosoper lived. This, then, would be no substitute for Christianity; for under *its* benign influence, even THE POOR HAVE THE GOSPEL PREACHED UNTO THEM. But I have no doubt

3

that, if the truth could be ascertained, we should find
that this sublime genius derived some of his best
ideas directly or indirectly from the Scriptures; and
that if he had lived under the light of the gospel, he
would never have spoken of it as his translator has
done.

In the time of the revolution in France, after some
trial had been made of having no religion, D'Auber-
menial proposed a new religion, in imitation of the
ancient Persians. His plan was to have the Deity
represented by a perpetual fire and offerings made to
him of fruits, oil, and salt; and libations poured out
to the four elements. It was prescribed, that worship
should be celebrated daily in the temple, that every
ninth day should be a Sabbath, and that on certain
festivals all ages should unite in dances. A few
fanatics in Paris and elsewhere, actually adopted the
new religion, but they were unable to attract any
notice, and in a little time it sunk into merited oblivion.

It has been common enough to set up the Mohammedan religion in a sort of rival comparison with
Christianity, but I do not know that any have gone
so far as to prefer the Koran to the Bible, except
those few miserable apostates, who, after being long
" tossed about with every wind of doctrine," at
length threw themselves into the arms of the Arabian impostor. How far this religion can bear a com
parison with Christianity, will be seen in the sequel.

Deism, then, or Natural Religion, is the only hope
of the world, if the Christian Religion be rejected.
The first English deists extolled Natural Religion to
the skies, as a system which contained all that man
needed to know; and as being simple and intelligible
to the meanest capacity. But strange to tell, scarcely any two of them are agreed what Natural Religion is; and the same discordance has existed among
their successors. They are not agreed even in those
points which are most essential in religion, and most
necessary to be settled before any religious worship
can be instituted. They differ on such points as

these; wrether there is any intrinsic diference between right and wrong; whether God pays any regard to the affairs of men; whether the soul is immortal; whether prayer is proper and useful; and whether any external rites of worship are necessary.

Again, if deism be the true religion, why has piety never flourished among its professors? why have they not been the most zealous and consistent worshippers of God? Does not truth promote piety and will it not ever be the case that they who hold the truth will love God most ardently, and serve him most faithfully? But what is the fact in regard to this class of men? Have they ever been distinguished for their spirit of devotion; have they produced numerous instances of exemplary piety? It is so much the reverse, that even the asking such reasonable questions has the appearance of ridicule. And when people hear the word " pious deist," they have the same sort of feeling as when mention is made of an honest thief, or a sober drunkard.

There is no slander in making this statement, for deists do not affect to be pious. They have no love for devotion. If the truth were known, this is the very thing they wish to get rid of; and if they believed that professing themselves to be deists laid them under greater obligations to be devout, they would not be so zealous for the system. Believe me, the contest is not between one religion and another, it is between religion and irreligion. It is impossible that a man of truly pious temper should reject the Bible, even if he were unacquainted with its historical evidences. He would find it to be so congenial to his taste, and so salutary in its effects on his own spirit, that he would conclude that it must have derived its origin from heaven. But we find no such spirit in the writings of deists. There is not in them a tincture of piety; but they have more than a sprinkling of profane ridicule. When you turn to them from the Bible, you are sensible of as great a transition, as if you passed suddenly from a warm and

genial climate into the frigid zone. If deists expect
ever to conciliate regard for their religion they must
appear to be truly pious men, sincerely engaged in
the service of God; and this will have more effect
than all their arguments. But whenever this event
shall occur, they will be found no longer opposing
the Bible, but will esteem it as the best of books, and
will come to it for fuel to feed the flame of pure
devotion. An African prince, who was brought to
England and resided there some time, being asked
what he thought of the Bible, answered, that he
believed it to be from God, for he found all the
good people in favour of it, and all the bad people
against it!

The want of a spirit of piety and devotion, must
be reckoned the principal reason why the deists have
never been able to establish and keep up any religious worship among themselves. The thing has
been attempted at several different times and in different countries, but never with success.

It is said, that the first enterprise of this kind was
that of David Williams, an Englishman, who had
been a dissenting minister in Liverpool, but passing
over first to Socinianism, and then to deism, went to
London, where, being patronized by some persons
of influence, he opened a house for deistical worship,
and formed a liturgy, consisting principally of praise
to the Creator. Here he preached for a short time,
and collected some followers; but he complained
that most of his congregation went on to atheism.
After four years' trial, the scheme came to nothing.
There were neither funds nor congregation remaining, and the Priest of Nature, (as Williams styled
himself) through discouragement and ill health, abandoned the project.

Some feeble attempts of the same kind have been
made in the United States; but they are unworthy
of being particularly noticed.

Frederick II., the deistical king of Prussia, had
once formed the plan of a Pantheon in Berlin for the
worshippers of all sects and all religions, the chief

object of which was the subversion of Christianity; but the scheme was never carried into execution.

The most interesting experiment of this kind was that made by the Theophilanthropists in France, during the period of the revolution. After some trial had been made of atheism and irreligion, and when the want of public worship was felt by many reflecting persons, a society was formed for the worship of God, upon the pure principles of Natural Religion. Among the patrons of this society, were men beloved for their philanthropy, and distinguished for their learning, and some high in power.

La Revellière Lepaux, one of the directory of France, was a zealous patron of the new religion. By his influence, permission was obtained to make use of the churches for their worship. In the city of Paris alone, eighteen or twenty were assigned to them, among which was the cathedral church of Notre Dame.

Their creed was simple, consisting of two great articles, THE EXISTENCE OF GOD, AND THE IMMORTALITY OF THE SOUL. Their moral system also embraced two great principles, THE LOVE OF GOD, AND THE LOVE OF MAN;—which were indicated by the name Theophilanthropists. Their worship consisted of prayers and hymns of praise, which were comprehended in a manual prepared for a directory in worship. Lectures were delivered by the members, which, however, underwent the inspection of the society, before they were pronounced in public. To these were added some simple ceremonies, such as placing a basket of fruit and flowers on the altar. Music, vocal and instrumental, was used; for the latter, they availed themselves of the organs in the churches. Great efforts were made to have this worship generally introduced in all the principal towns in France; and the views of the society were even extended to foreign countries. Their manual was sent into all parts of the republic by the Minister of the interior, free of expense.

Never did a society enjoy greater advantages at

its commencement. Christianity had been rejected
with scorn; atheism had for a short time been tried,
but was found to be intolerable ; the government
was favourable to the project; men of learning and
influence patronized it, and churches ready built
were at the service of the new denomination. The
system of Natural Religion which was adopted was
the best that could have been selected, and considerable wisdom was discovered in the construction of
their liturgy. But with all these circumstances in
their favour, the society could not subsist. At first,
indeed, while the scene was novel, large audiences
attended, most of whom however were merely spectators; but in a short time, they dwindled away to
such a degree, that instead of occupying twenty
churches in Paris, they needed only four; and in
some of the provincial towns, where they began
under the most favourable auspices, they soon came
to nothing. Thus they went on declining until.
under the consular government, they were prohibited
the use of the churches any longer; upon which they
immediately expired without a struggle, and it is
believed that not a vestige of the society now remains.

It will be instructive and interesting to inquire
into the reasons of this want of success, in a society
enjoying so many advantages. Undoubtedly, the
chief reason was, the want of a truly devotional
spirit. This was observed from the beginning of
their meetings. There was nothing to interest the
feelings of the heart. Their orators might be men
of learning, and might produce good moral discourses,
but they were not men of piety, and not always men
of pure morals. Their hymns were said to be well
composed, and the music good; but the musicians
were hired from the stage. There was also a strange
defect of liberality in contributing to the funds of the
society. They found it impossible to raise, in some
of their societies, a sum which every Christian congregation, even the poorest of any sect, would have
collected in one day. It is a fact, that one of the

societies petitioned government to grant them relief from a debt which they had contracted in providing the apparatus of their worship, not amounting to more than fifty dollars, stating, that their annual income did not exceed twenty dollars. In the other towns their musicians deserted them, because they were not paid, and frequently no person could be found to deliver lectures.

Another difficulty arose which might have been foreseen. Some of the societies declared themselves independent, and would not agree to be governed by the manual which had been received, any further than they chose. They also remonstrated against the authority exercised by the lecturers in the affairs of the society, and declared that there was danger of their forming another hierarchy. There were also complaints against them addressed to the ministers by the agents of government in the provinces, on account of the influence which they might acquire in civil affairs.

The Theophilanthropists were moreover censured by those who had made great advances in the modern philosophy, for their illiberality. It was complained that there were many who could not receive their creed, and all such must necessarily be excluded from their society. This censure seems to have troubled them much, and in order to wipe off the stigma they appointed a fête, which they called the anniversary of the re-establishment of Natural Religion. To prove that their liberality had no bounds, they prepared five banners to be carried in procession. On the first was inscribed the word, RELIGION; on the second, MORALITY: and on the others, respectively, JEWS, CATHOLICS, PROTESTANTS. When the procession was over, the bearers of the several banners gave each other the kiss of peace; and that none might mistake the extent of their liberality, the banner inscribed MORALITY was borne by a professed atheist, universally known as such in Paris. They had also other festivals peculiar to themselves, and four in honour of the following persons; Socrates

St. Vincent de Paul, J. J. Rousseau, and Washing
ton;—a strange conjunction of names truly.*

I have been thus particular in giving an account
of this society, because the facts furnish the strongest
confirmation of my argument, and are in themselves
curious and instructive. After the failure of this
enterprise, deists will scarcely attempt again to in
stitute any form of public worship.

But among those philosophers who believe in the
perfectibility of human nature under the fostering
influence of increasing knowledge and good government, there is a vague theory of a kind of mental,
philosophical religion, which needs the aid of no
external forms. The primary articles of their creed
are, that religion is a thing entirely between God
and every man's conscience; that all our Creator
requires is the homage of the heart; that if we feel
reverence, gratitude, and submission towards him,
and act our part well in society, we have fulfilled
our duty; that we cannot know how we may be
disposed of hereafter, and ought not to be anxious
about the matter. Whether this is expected to be
the religion of philosophers only, or also of the unlearned and the great mass of labouring people, I am
unable to say. But I know that such a system as
this will, to a large majority of every community,
be equivalent to no religion at all. The great body
of the people must have something tangible, something visible, in their religion. They need the aid
of the senses, and of the social principle, to fix their
attention, to create an interest, and to excite the
feelings of devotion. The truth is, that if the heart
be affected with lively emotions of piety, it will be
pleasant, it will be useful, and it will be natural, to
give them expression. This will hold in regard to
philosophers and men of learning, as well as others.
Wherever a number of persons participate in the
same feelings, there is a strong inclination to hold
communion together; and if sentiments of genuine

* Histoire de la Theophilanthropie, par. M. Gregoire.—See Quar
terly Review for January, 1823.

piety exist in the bosoms of many, they will delight
to celebrate in unison the praises of that Being whom
they love and adore.   There is no reason why pious
emotions more than others should be smothered, and
the tendency to express them counteracted.   Such
indeed will never be the fact.   " Out of the abundance of the heart the mouth speaketh."   Piety, it is
true, consists essentially in the exercises of the heart;
but that religion which is merely mental, is suspicious; at best very feeble; is not likely to produce
any permanent effect on the character or comfort of
the person entertaining it; and cannot be useful to
others in the way of example.

In the year 1802, when Christianity, which had
been proscribed in France, was restored by an act
of government, a speech was delivered by one of
the counsellors of state which contains excellent
sentiments on the subject here treated.   One or two
extracts will not be unacceptable to the reader.
" Science can never be partaken of but by a small
number, but by religion one may be instructed without being learned.   The Natural Religion to which
one may rise by the effects of a cultivated reason, is
merely abstract and intellectual, and unfit for any
people.   It is revealed religion which points out al
the truths that are useful to men who have neither
time nor means for laborious disquisitions.   Who
then would wish to dry up that sacred spring of
knowledge which diffuses good maxims, brings them
before the eyes of every individual, and communicates to them that authoritative and popular dress,
without which they would be unknown to the multitude and almost to all men?   For want of a religious education for the last ten years, our children
are without any ideas of a divinity, without any
notion of what is just and unjust; hence arise barbarous manners, hence a people becomes ferocious.
One cannot but sigh over the lot which threatens the
present and future generations.   Alas! what have
we gained by deviating from the path pointed out
to us by our ancestors?   What have we gained by

substituting vain and abstract doctrines for the creed
which actuated the minds of Turenne, Fenelon, and
Pascal?" The unhappy condition of that generation who grew up after this time in France, in regard
to religion, is repeatedly noticed by Allison, in his
history of Europe.

I think enough has now been said to establish, beyond all reasonable doubt, our second proposition,
that if Christianity be rejected, there is no other religion which can be substituted in its place, or at
least, no other which can at all answer the purpose
for which religion is desirable.

It may also be observed, in conclusion, that the
facts which have been adduced, not only serve to
confirm this proposition, but furnish new and cogent
arguments in proof of the proposition maintained in
the preceding chapter.

CHAPTER IV.

REVELATION NECESSARY TO TEACH US HOW TO WORSHIP GOD ACCEPTABLY
—THE NATURE AND CERTAINTY OF A FUTURE STATE, AND ESPECIALLY
THE METHOD BY WHICH SINNERS MAY OBTAIN SALVATION.

IT would be superfluous here to repeat what was
said in the preceding chapter, respecting the need in
which man stood of a revelation when he first proceeded from the hands of his Creator. The object
which we have, at present, in view, is, to inquire,
whether man, in the condition in which we now find
him, and in which history informs us he has existed
for ages, does not stand in urgent need of more light
than he possesses; and whether there are not some
points of vital importance, concerning which he must
remain in the dark, unless the knowledge of the truth
is communicated to him by a revelation from God.
Let it be understood, however, in what sense it is

asserted, that a revelation is necessary. Of course, it is not meant that there is any natural necessity for such an event; nor is it intended that God is obliged by any necessity to grant a revelation. The necessity contended for relates altogether to the wants of man It is found, that in all times and under all circumstances, he needs information, which he cannot obtain from the unassisted exercise of his own reason; or at least not so satisfactorily, as from divine revelation.

For even if it were possible for a few philosophers of the highest order of intellect, by long and profound investigation, to discover all the truths absolutely necessary to be known; yet, for the bulk of mankind, it might be all important to have these same things made known by divine revelation, because the great majority of our race have neither leisure nor ability for such tedious and difficult researches. But the truth as made known by history is, that on those very points on which it is most needful that man should be instructed, the wise men of this world have been as much at a loss as the vulgar. They reasoned much, and speculated as far as human intellect could go, but instead of clearly ascertaining truth, they rested at last in mere conjecture, or deviated into gross error.

Again, if the light of nature were sufficient to shed some light on the great truths needful to be known by man; yet a clear well-attested communication from heaven, might be of the greatest utility, by speaking decisively and authoritatively, in regard to matters concerning which the conclusions of reason are feeble and uncertain. To affect the conscience and influence the heart, it is highly important that religious truth should be attended with certainty, and should be felt to possess the sanction of divine authority. What men discover by the slow deductions of reason is found to operate feebly on the conscience, compared with the persuasion that God speaks to us immediately by divine revelation. In reasoning about the most important truths men differ exceed ingly from one another: and this very circumstance spreads doubt and uncertainty over all their speculations. When we peruse the discourses of the wisest of the heathen sages, and observe what darkness surrounded them, we cannot but feel commiseration for the imbecility of the human intellect; and, indeed, the best of them were deeply convinced of the insufficiency of their own reason to guide them; and sometimes seemed to entertain a glimmering hope, that at some future period, and in some unknown way, divine instruction might be communicated to the erring children of men.

It is also more than probable that the clearest and most important ideas, which the heathen philosophers entertained, were not the discoveries of their own reason, or a light struck out from an observation of the works of nature, but rays of truth derived more remotely or more directly from divine revelation, as has been remarked in another part of this essay. The heathen sages attributed all their knowledge to tradition.

But after all, it is an undeniable fact, that reason, aided as it was by tradition, left men to grope in the dark, and to fall into the most degrading idolatry.— Indeed, though reason may teach that there is a God, and that he ought to be worshipped; yet of what kind his worship should be in order to be acceptable, she never has made known, nor is it within the reach of her ability. All the rites of worship invented by man are altogether unworthy of God: and, truly, it is in the nature of things impossible, that men should devise a form of acceptable worship, for no service of this kind which he has not himself appointed, can be pleasing in the sight of God. Now, if men have lost the knowledge of the original institutions of religion; or, if these have become altogether corrupt, there must be a new revelation, before man will be able to render an acceptable service to his Creator. There is good reason to believe that many of the heathen rites of worship are nothing but corruptions of divine institutions, which were given to

men by an early revelation. This seems especially
to be the fact, in relation to sacrifices, which constituted an essential part of the worship of almost all
ancient nations, and some vestiges of which have
come down by tradition among the most barbarous
tribes. Reason certainly never taught men that
shedding the blood and taking away the life of an
animal, could be an acceptable sacrifice to the Deity,
or that presenting it on an altar, and consuming it
wholly or partially by fire, could be a propitiation
for sin; and yet these mysterious ceremonies were
almost as universal as the gift of speech. And between the sacrifices of nations, remote from each
other, there has been remarked a wonderful similarity in the circumstances of their sacred offerings;
in the erection of altars; in the pouring out of the
blood; in dividing the animal into pieces; in com-
bining the offering of salt, wine, bread, and incense,
with the sacrifice of animals; in considering the
blood and death of the victim, as expiatory for sin;
in having an order of priesthood to officiate in these
sacred rites, who were solemnly consecrated to the
service, and considered more holy than other men;
and when only a small part of the animal sacrificed
was consumed by fire, in feasting on the remainder,
within the precincts of the temple or sacred enclosure. This analogy may be traced even in the
names, by which similar sacrifices were denominated
among different nations. These and many other
striking resemblances in the rites of ancient nations,
go to prove, incontestably, that they must have had
a common origin; and no account of this is half so
probable as that which ascribes sacrificial rites to an
original revelation. And hence we see the credibility
of the Mosaic history in regard to the origin of reli
gious worship.

But supposing that any heathen nation should now
be convinced of the absurdity of idolatry, and should
become sensible of their obligations to render some
kind of external homage to the great Creator, by

what means could they learn what sort of service would be acceptable? Reason could not teach them what rites should be observed. Without a revelation from God, they must for ever remain without a form of worship; or if they attempted to invent certain rites, all experience teaches that these human inventions will ever be marked by human weakness, and reason herself intimates, that no worship, not appointed by God, can be acceptable to him. It appears then, that even if man were not a sinner, he would need a divine revelation to teach him how to render an acceptable worship to his Creator.

Some infidel writers have pretended that it is a matter of indifference by what rites God is worshipped, and that he is equally pleased with the services of all nations, however different from each other in their mode of worship. This doctrine is utterly inconsistent with the dictates of sound reason. Upon this principle even human sacrifices, which have been so common in the world, would be justified. And the most impure and abominable rites would be sanctioned by the Deity. The whole worship of Pagan nations, both in ancient and modern times, is detestable ; and no one who has any just conceptions of the attributes of God, can persuade himself that he ever could be pleased with services so characterized by cruelty, impurity, and folly. Their worship is not directed to the true God, but to the false deities of their own invention. They sacrifice not to God but to devils. They have substituted for the august Creator, creatures of almost every kind and species. No man under the government of reason can look into any heathen temple without being shocked and confounded, with the degrading and abominable rites of idolatry. The more this subject is contemplated the more clearly will the necessity of divine revelation be felt, and the greater will appear to be its value to the human race. Who can read an account of the mythology and idolatry of the ancient Egyptians, or of the modern Hindoos, and not be deeply impressed with the necessity of something to dispel this horrible darkness, and break asunder these cruel bonds of superstition?

Another argument for the necessity of a divine revelation is, that without it man must remain ignorant of his origin and his end, and utterly unable to account for the circumstances by which he is surrounded. He finds himself here upon the earth, and feels that he is borne along the stream of time with the rest of his generation, towards a dark gulf before him, which he perceives he can by no means escape. But when he inquires respecting the origin of the human race, when he seeks a solution of the enigma of his sinful, suffering, and mortal existence, he finds no one among the living or the dead, from whom he can obtain the least satisfactory information. All the traditions and histories of men are full of fables; and if they contain some rays of truth, they are so mingled with error that no man can distinguish the one from the other. Leave out of view the history contained in the Bible, and all that we can learn from others casts not a solitary ray of light on the points under consideration. We have no means of tracing up our race to its origin, and the deist can give no rational account of the wickedness of men and of their sufferings and death. The darkness and uncertainty resting on these subjects have led many who rejected the authority of the Bible, to adopt most absurd and atheistical hypotheses respecting the origin of man. Some have professed to believe that the earth and its inhabitants have existed from all eternity; which is too absurd to require refutation. Others have amused themselves and their readers with the idea, that originally mankind were merely a species of monkey or baboon, and that by degrees they laid aside their brutal appearance and manners, and certain *inhuman* appendages, and having in process of time invented language and the arts most necessary to provide for the clothing and shelter of the body, gradually rose higher and higher in the scale of improvement, until they arrived at that pitch of refinement and civilization, which has been attained by the most polished nations. These, it is true, are rather atheistical than deistical hypotheses; but they serve to show how little light reason can shed on this subject, and how much we need a divine revelation. For the deist can form no theory which can satisfy our reasonable desires. He can give no good reason for the moral condition and mortality of our race. He may say, that it is the law of nature; but this is merely to declare the fact, not to account for it.

But we might, perhaps, be contented to remain ignorant of our origin, if we could know what is to be our destiny hereafter, and how far it is connected with our present character and conduct. Reason has exerted and exhausted all her resources to demonstrate a future existence, and to place the immortality of the soul on an immovable basis. But what has been the result of all these reasonings Why, a possibility, or, to say the most, a strong probability, that the soul survives the body. But this, of all others, is the point, on which we want certainty—absolute certainty. How painful to be involved in a cloud of doubt and suspense, when we look forward to futurity; and, especially, when descending into the grave, to have nothing to lay hold of but the conclusions and conjectures of our own feeble reason! That I do not depreciate the force of the arguments for the soul's immortality, will appear from the fact, that many of the heathen philosophers held that the soul died with the body; that of those who believed in a future existence, some were of opinion, that after the lapse of a thousand years or some longer period, it would come to an end; others— and these very numerous—believed in the doctrine of metempsychosis, or the transmigration of souls from the body of one animal to that of another, in perpetual succession; and more still had no other idea of immortality, than that the soul—which they thought was a particle of deity—would at death be refunded into the divine essence which was virtu

ally to deny its future existence, as to its distinct per-
sonality, or as possessing individuality and conscious
ness. Even such men as Socrates, Plato, and Cicero, had no clear, consistent, and satisfactory views
of this interesting subject; not because they neglected to exercise their cultivated and powerful intellects
upon it; for it was a subject, which more than all
others engaged their thoughts;—but because it was
surrounded by a darkness which unassisted reason
could not penetrate. O how glad would these sages
have been to possess one ray of that revelation
which our infidels foolishly despise! The earlier
deists generally admitted the doctrine of a future
state of retribution, and affected to believe that reason was sufficient to establish the doctrine; but their
successors in modern times, or at least a large majority of them, have either denied or called in question this fundamental doctrine. And if we should
weigh impartially all the arguments which have
ever been adduced in ancient or modern times to
establish this point, we should be obliged to confess
that we need further light. And from the very nature of the case, no one can give us an absolute
assurance of our future and immortal existence, but
God alone. It is an event which depends on his
will and nothing else. Arguments may be adduced
to prove that the soul is naturally immortal; but
they prove no more than this, that the causes which
effect the dissolution of the body, can have no tendency to destroy the existence and activity of the
soul. And what are called the moral arguments
only go to prove that if God exercises a moral government over his creatures here, there must be a
place for a just retribution hereafter. But we want,
on this point, more certainty. We want one to
come from the other world to tell us that there is a
future state. We want to hear the voice of God
testifying that there is not only a future state, but a
day of righteous judgment. Here every man can
judge for himself, whether he needs a revelation.

This argument for the necessity of a divine reve-

lation, will be corroborated by observing the state
of religion and morals among all heathen nations.
It has often been remarked, that the most certain
method of ascertaining what reason is capable of accomplishing is to see what she has actually done in
time past, especially, when enjoying all the advantages of high culture and extensive information.   In
physical science we may expect new discoveries by
the exercise of reason; and the science of morals
may in time to come be better understood; but if all
nations, the most civilized and learned as well as the
rude and barbarous, have utterly failed in forming
correct opinions on the most essential points of theology and ethics, and have all fallen into the most
absurd and degrading errors, and acquiesced in the
most abominable and impure rites of idolatry; then,
what can be more evident, than that they needed a
divine revelation?   Probably one reason why the
nations were left so long to walk in their own ways,
was, to convince us of our own imbecility, and to
prepare us to receive gratefully when offered, this
most comprehensive gift of God.

To do justice to this argument would require
volumes; but as the subject has been amply treated
by LELAND, and others, I will pass it over, only re-
marking, that the abominable rites of Pagan worship, and the shocking cruelties and impurities which
have ever been perpetrated under the sanction of
every heathen religion, make but a faint impression
on our minds, because we only hear the distant report of these things, and are often tempted to think
that the narrative of these horrible doings must be
too highly coloured; but the half, and far more than
the half, remains untold, and cannot be publicly told,
without outrageously offending against decency.   It
is an awful thought, that for so long a time so many
millions of our fellow creatures have been under the
cruel bondage of superstition, a slavery which affects
the mind, and is productive of more human misery
than all other causes.   As Paganism still exists, and
as its evils are unmitigated by the lapse of time, it is

an easy matter to compare the Christian with the heathen world. Cast your eye over the map of the earth, and say, where is found the densest darkness? Where does the light of truth shine? Is not the line of demarkation between light and darkness visible? And is it not as evident as any thing can be, that the Bible is a rich blessing to all who possess and read it? We might here also institute a comparison between those Christian nations which freely circulate the Scriptures, and those who lock them up in a dead language; but this we omit, and go on to remark, that he who is informed of the events which have occurred on missionary ground, in our own times, must have his eyes covered with thick scales of prejudice, if he does not acknowledge that the gospel is the richest benefit which can be conferred on Pagan nations. Either then, a vile imposture, a cunningly devised fable, has the power of reforming and civilizing the most degraded of the heathen tribes; or Christianity is a Divine Revelation, and is still accompanied by the power of God, making it effectual to the illumination, conversion, and salvation of the Gentiles. Let the deist take his choice between these two things. But here let me ask, whether if a company of deists had gone out to Africa or to the Society or Sandwich Islands, any such reformation would have been wrought? The reader will smile at the idea of a deist turning missionary to the heathen; but this very feeling demonstrates that deism is not to be the means of regenerating the world. If the deist were right he would be the only proper person to send on a mission to convert the idolatrous world. But all are ready to pronounce the very idea to be ludicrous. What! a missionary society of deists! Why, they have no confidence in their own principles, in this respect, and no zeal for propagating them in such a field, and with such sacrifices as the Christian willingly makes.

But why should I go to distant and heathen lands, to prove that a revelation is necessary, when we have proof enough before our eyes? In any of our populous cities we may draw a visible line between that part of the population who are under the light of evangelical truth, and those who place themselves out of the reach of all the direct rays of the gospel. Between these two extremes there is a large class not properly reckoned with either; but let us, without caring for exact accuracy in our computation, suppose, that one-third of the adult population are regular church-going people, who hear the leading truths of the gospel from Sabbath to Sabbath; and that another third seldom or never attend any place of public worship. Between these two classes of citizens we can institute a comparison. Exceptions you may have to make on both sides, but taking them in mass, is there any room to doubt whether religion is useful and necessary? From which of these classes are our prisons crowded with inmates? Suppose, first, that all those who never read the Bible, and frequent no place of worship, were removed from among us, would the state of society be meliorated or deteriorated? Or again, suppose that all the church-going people should be translated to another country, what would then be the condition of society? If I am not egregiously erroneous in my calculations, on the former supposition we should be able to dispense with most of our means of coercion and restraint, and would save the enormous expense of keeping up such an array of courts, police-officers, and prisons. On the latter supposition, all the wealth of the country would be insufficient to provide places of confinement and means of support for the guilty; or, to come nearer to the truth, our large towns would soon become as Sodom, or as a den of thieves, and soon the doom of Sodom would sink them never to rise again.

But does any one think that this is not a fair statement of the matter, as it seems to take for granted that there is no religion, nor can be any, without revelation? I would request the person who makes this objection, to tell me what kind of religion might

be expected if the Bible were banished fiom among
us?   Suppose that instead of the hundreds of gospel
preachers, whose voices are lifted up on the first day
of every week, to warn men of the danger of a sinful
course, and to point out to them the way of life, all
these pulpits should be filled with infidel lecturers,
male and female; what, in your consciences, do you
think would be the effect on morals and social hap
piness?   We all know that many sinners have been
converted by the faithful preaching of the gospel; do
you know, or have you heard of any transgressors
being turned from the error of their ways by attending on deistical lectures, or even on the theatre, that
boasted school of morality?   No doubt, some of my
readers have heard of conversions at these places of
fashionable resort, but not to righteousness, not to
God.   And as I have happened to mention the theatre, I will further add, that I am far more afraid of
the moral influence of this institution, than of that of
deistical and atheistical lectures; not because it pleads
for vice—this would not be tolerated—but because
it draws thousands within the enchanted circle of
temptation, and plunges thoughtless youth into the
vortex of sensual pleasure.

I admit that there may be much religion without
revelation; the whole heathen world is a proof of it.
Some men of the world, indeed, confound all religions and all the ministers of religion together, as if
they were all alike; whereas, true and false religion
are as dissimilar as light and darkness; and the only
effectual barrier to false religion, is to cultivate that
which is true.   Infidelity may serve to sweep away
one form of superstition, but after a time the tide will
turn, and enthusiasm or superstition will come in like
a flood; for, as we have shown, the people must have
some sort of religion, and if you banish that which
is true, rational, sober, and benevolent, you will soon
be visited with the most absurd and degrading systems of wild fanaticism; and these will, when the
fires of enthusiasm are extinguished, settle down, or
rathe grow up, into hideous forms of superstition

The pagan religions had some mixture o truth de
rived from early tradition; for they were all, as we
have seen, a corruption of the primitive worship of
fallen man.   But banish the Bible, and you will
have in its place either the dark horrors of atheism,
accompanied with crime, in her polluted and blood-
stained robe, or you will have the reign of superstition, chilling every generous emotion, degrading
every noble affection, and blighting all domestic bliss.

Sometimes, a splendid temple rests upon a few
solid pillars, and falls to ruin if they be removed.
Thus the peace, and order, and comfort of civil society depend much on two institutions, for both of
which we are indebted to revelation.   The first of
these is the SACRED INSTITUTION OF MARRIAGE: the
second is, the RELIGIOUS OBLIGATION OF AN OATH or
solemn affirmation, which is virtually the same thing.
Remove these, and the fabric of human happiness
totters at once to its very base.

But the argument on which I chiefly mean to
dwell, to evince the necessity of a revelation, is, that
without it we can never learn how sin can be forgiven or the sinner saved.   Admitting that reason
can direct us with sufficient clearness in regard to all
our moral duties; admitting that if a man performs his
duty, no more is required of him, and he may confide in the justice and goodness of God; admitting
that from this course no evil will ensue, and the suitable reward will not be wanting; admitting all this
for argument's sake—yea, more, that all men possess this knowledge: yet, I maintain, that in relation
to the state in which man actually is, it amounts to
nothing.   It is one thing to have a system of religion
which suits the case of an innocent being, and quite
another to find out a plan by which A SINNER can
obtain forgiveness.   A citizen may know full well
that if he obeys the laws of his country he will be
protected by all upright magistrates; but if he has
already violated the laws and incurred a formidal le
penalty, the knowledge mentioned does not reach
his se.   What he needs now is, to know how he

can obtain a pardon, and evade the vengeance of the violated law. In every such case, there is an absolute need of a declaration or revelation from the supreme power of the state, of a willingness to pardon on some certain condition. In no government can a pardon be a matter of course, or provided for by the law itself; for such a provision would be subversive of all government. It would be a complete nullification of the obligation and authority of the law. Here then the momentous question occurs, is man a sinner? Have all men transgressed the law of God? I am willing to wave the proof of this point, for the present, and to leave it to the decision of every man's conscience. Is there a man upon earth who is not conscious of having violated the law of his nature, both by omissions of duty and the actual commission of sin?

Assuming it then as a fact, that men are sinners, I ask, what does the light of nature teach respecting the forgiveness of sin? I shall endeavour to demonstrate, that reason sheds not a ray of light on this fundamental point, and, therefore, that Natural Religion, if known ever so perfectly and universally, could not bring us the relief which we need. The main argument for the position which I have laid down, is short and simple. It is the dictate of right reason, that God is just, and will render to every one according to his character and conduct; and that his law being wise and good must not be violated with impunity. Can the deist conceive of an objection to this principle? Certainly not. It must be considered a self-evident truth by every theist who believes in the moral government of God. The case is plain, therefore, and so far as the dictates of reason extend, the sinner has no prospect before him but to suffer the just punishment of his offences, whatever that may be.

To suppose that reason can inform us that God will pardon our sins, is to suppose that its dictates are contradictory; for, to pardon is the same as not to punish; but as we have just seen, the voice of reason is, that God is just, and will render to every man what he deserves. These two things are not compatible. Before I proceed further, I must put the reader on his guard against loose and illogical reasoning on a point so vital. I scarcely know a subject on which most men appear to satisfy themselves with more vague and fallacious arguments. Some of the more common of these it will be my object now to consider.

In the first place, it is alleged, and with much confidence asserted by many, that God is a Being of too much benevolence and kindness to inflict severe punishments on his erring creatures. This suggestion, for it has not the shape of an argument, seems to give honour to God, while it is very soothing to the mind of the sinner. But when it is examined, it will be found to be rather an insult than an honour; for it supposes that the Ruler of the universe, out of kindness to a rebellious creature, will cease to be just; that rather than punish offences as they deserve. he will dishonour his own law. What sort of compliment would it be to an upright judge among men. to say of him, that his benevolence and compassion would surely prevent his inflicting the penalties annexed to the laws? But if the Judge of all the earth does not act upon the principle of punishing all sin as it deserves, on what other principle does he act? By punishing it half as much as it deserves? But this might be a severe suffering, and therefore the conclusion to which this reasoning must lead, is, tha God's goodness will altogether and for ever prevent him from inflicting any punishment on sin, however atrocious it may be.

Many in our days, who are not called deists or atheists, but who are more dangerous because they mingle some Christian truth with their errors, greedily embrace and zealously inculcate this very opinion. But look at its consequences. The infinitely perfect God will treat alike the most malignant rebel and the most affectionate and obedient servant. He will, in his treatment of his creatures, manifest no n.ore displeasure at sin, than he does towards the most perfect virtue. If such benevolence as this existed, it would be no moral perfection, but a defect. But no; God's attributes are never at variance. There is no goodness in God which forbids or prevents the fullest exercise of justice. If ever he chooses to rescue sinners from the consequences of their sins, it will not be by sacrificing his justice, but by fully satisfying it. But this is an affair of which mere reason knows nothing. If the deist, however should insist that all moral goodness consists in benevolence, and nothing else, and therefore God will not punish any but for his own good, I answer that the good of the whole is to be preferred by a benevolent being to the happiness of an offending individual; and in all communities, the general good requires that transgressors should be intimidated and restrained by punishment; so that it must be proved that the good of the universe does not require the punishment of the guilty, before any such conclusion can be drawn from the benevolence of God.

It is manifest, therefore, that the suggestion which we have been considering, however pleasing to the mind in love with sin, and however plausible at first sight, will not bear examination, and instead of tending to the honour of God, takes from him all that is estimable in moral character. It allows him no other excellence than an indiscriminate benevolence to his creatures, without the least regard to their moral character. Such a being would not be an object of veneration and esteem to all holy intelligences. An infinitely good God may punish transgressors according to the demerit of their crimes, without any disparagement of his goodness; and an infinitely just and holy God must punish sin. "Shall not the Judge of all the earth do right?"

Another suggestion, supposed by many to be a dictate of reason, is, that all the punishments ever inflicted on men for their sin is the evil which arises out of it from the laws of nature, and the constitution of the human mind; and that there is no good ground

5

for any apprehension of any further or greater penalty. There is no proof adduced of the truth of this
position, nor does it admit of proof. Who can tell
what the judge of all may think it necessary to inflict
hereafter on sinners, for the manifestation of his
justice, the vindication of his law, and as a terror to
other offenders?   Indeed, as far as we can judge of
the facts, men do not suffer in this life, in any just
proportion to their crimes.   The wicked are often
prosperous; and when the conscience becomes cal-
lous, they experience but little remorse for their worst
crimes.   Transgressors who are only beginning their
career, experience the agonies of an accusing conscience in the keenest manner; while the veteran in
iniquity has long since ceased to be much troubled
with these "compunctious visitings." But, supposing it true, that all the punishment of sin is that
which naturally follows it, who can tell what all the
consequences are, or where they will end?   Crimes
do not always produce their bitterest fruit immediately.   We see the sins of the intemperate, the lewd,
and the dishonest, often overtaking them with then
saddest consequences, long after the acts were committed.   Sins committed in youth often produce a
miserable old age.   Look into the history of multitudes whose vices have consigned them to a prison
or a mad house, and you will find that the cause of
their wretchedness and disgrace may be traced back
to the sins of their youth, those very sins which many
are disposed to regard with so indulgent an eye.
And as these evils go on increasing until death, who
can assure the sinner that this fearful progression
will not continue beyond the grave?   As we are not
now arguing with atheists, we have a right to assume
as a truth the soul's future existence; and if it exists
in conscious activity, will it not carry with it the
moral character acquired in this world? Will not the
selfish, the proud, the malignant, be selfish, proud,
and malignant, when the clay tabernacle is dropped?
Can death transform a sordid and guilty creature into
ar angel? Will not the man who is wicked up to

the moment of dissolution, continue to be wicked after death? Will not he carry with him his memory, his conscience, and his craving desires? There is then but little comfort for the sinner in this suggestion, if true; for he may find springing out of his own corruption a worm which will never die, and which will gnaw his vitals with as agonizing a pain as any which he is capable of enduring. Be it so, that conscience is the only fire to be dreaded in another world—who can tell us how intense and intermina ble the pain which this principle of our nature is capable of inflicting on the sinner? The fear, remorse, and horrible perturbation which sometimes surround the death-bed of profligate sinners, afford a tremendous intimation of what they may expect in a future state. How great or how long the evil consequences of sin may be, our reason certainly cannot tell; as far as her dictates extend, we can see no end to this progression in vice and misery.

But I now come to the consideration of a much more specious opinion, on which deists, and others who agree with them in these matters, place great confidence. It is, that whatever the deserved pen alty of sin may be, reason teaches us that it can be set aside, or evaded, by a sincere and seasonable repentance. This principle has been assumed as a fundamental article in all the systems of sober deists. It is well known that Lord Herbert laid it down as one of the five positions on which he founded his system; and, therefore, as perfectly understood by all men. And as many who wish to be considered rational Christians adopt the same principle, it has gained very general possession of the public mind. And again, as pardon and repentance are closely connected, according to the doctrines of the Gospel, this truth of revelation is by many not distinguished from what is considered a dictate of reason; and hence it becomes a matter of real difficulty to separate truth from error on this point; and in attempting it, we must encounter a formidable front of prejudice. Before I proceed further, I must request the reader to separate the evangelical doc.rine of pardon, on repentance, from the deistical principle under consideration; for they stand on entirely different grounds, as will appear in the course of the discussion,

And here let it be carefully remarked, that before this doctrine of reason, as it is called, can become a practical principle, two things must be pre-supposed; first, that all men know what that repentance is which will insure our pardon; and next, that every sinner has ability to perform it. The reasonableness of these pre-requisites is self-evident. But great difficulty attends the theory, as it relates to these points. We would ask whether by that repentance which reason inculcates, any thing more is meant than sorrow or compunction for our sins ; or whether it includes a thorough reformation of life, and that not merely extending to external acts, but to the motives and affections of the heart. It is also reasonable to ask, whether any certain degree or continuance of sorrow is requisite ; and whether repentance will not cease to be available, if the sinner revert to his former ways of iniquity. Moreover, whether repentance, flowing simply from fear of punishment, is genuine ; and if not, what sort of principles it must have as its source. It is also needful and important to inquire, whether an inveterate, hardened sinner can repent of his sins, so as to hate and forsake them ; and surely no other re-entance is worth any thing. With a mind filled with error, his conscience seared, and his habits deeply radicated, what hope is there of his turning about and commencing a new life? From what principle could we anticipate such a change in a confirmed villain or debauchee? You might as reasonably expect the Ethiopian to change his skin, as that he who has been long accustomed to do evil should learn to do well. It will answer no purpose to say, that he can repent if he will, and if he will not, the blame is all his own; for we are inquiring whether reason can teach a method of salvation adapted to the condition of sinners, and it matters not whether the obstacle be in the will or in something else: if it uniformly prevents the desired effect, it is plain, that something else is needed. As to the blame being on his own head, it is admitted; but this is true in regard to every sin. In every act of transgression the sinner is culpable, otherwise it would be no sin; and if the only object be to fix the blame upon the culprit, this is sufficiently provided for without offering him pardon upon repentance, for life and happiness can be secured without repentance, if men will only obey the law of God perfectly. And there is no greater, nor other inability in the way of his doing this, than in the way of his exercising true penitence. There is manifestly a radical defect in the deistical theory on this very point. It makes no provision for bringing the sinner to repentance, but merely offers pardon in case he will do that to which his whole heart is averse. And does not fact accord with our sentiments? Where are the instances of deists repenting of their sins, and yet adhering to this system? There are indeed many glorious examples of infidels being brought to repentance and reformation by the Gospel; but I would challenge the world to produce an instance of any one being brought to repentance, and a thorough change of life, merely on the principles of deism. And if the principle is in practice utterly ineffectual, of what value is it? and why should it be magnified into a matter of so much importance as to be adduced as a proof that a revelation is not needed?

As, however, I wish to give a full and impartial discussion to this point, I will now, for the sake of argument, suppose, that the repentance which is necessary to pardon is understood by all men, and that all have ability to perform it. The opinion then, is, that all sinners by repentance may escape the punishment justly due to their sins; and this repentance they can bring into exercise at any time when it may be needed. If this be true, and a dictate of reason, then it must be confessed that a revelation is not ab solutely necessary; for what method of salvation can be simpler, easier, or more intelligible than this? But I deny that any such doctrine belongs to the system of Natural Religion, or is dictated by the light of reason. This opinion of the efficacy of repentance is borrowed from the Gospel, and has been tacked to deism, with which it has no coherence. It is altogether incompatible with the first great fundamental principle of natural religion; namely, that God being just will render to every one according to his moral character and conduct. Deists have ever been in the habit of borrowing from revelation, without giving credit for what they take, and perhaps, without knowing whence the sentiment is derived. Men, born and educated under the light of revelation, however they may come to reject the Bible and all the positive institutions of Christianity, cannot divest themselves of all those important moral principles which directly or indirectly they have derived from this source. The light of divine revelation is widely diffused in Christian countries, and has given complexion to all our laws, institutions, and systems of education; so that a man can no more escape entirely from its influence than from the effect of the light of the sun. Many truths which the deist pretends to have discovered by the light of reason, are nothing else than the reflected light of divine revelation; for how else can you account for it, that the theories and moral systems of our sober deists should be so much superior to the attainments of Socrates, Plato and Cicero? Their conduct resembles that of a man who should light his taper by means of the sun's rays, and then pretend that all the light around him he had struck out himself, or that it was produced by the feeble taper which he held in his hand.

But to return to the point under discussion. If a man, now that he is a sinner, can certainly know that the punishment of his sins may be evaded by a repentance completely in his own power, he could also know this before he sinned. Then, with the law written on his heart, and sanctioned with a penalty, he had the clear knowledge from reason, that commit whatever atrocious sins he might, and incur whatever punishment he might, he would at any and at every moment of his existence, have it in his power to escape all the punishment which he had merited, simply by the act of repentance.   This is a plain and fair statement of the case, and it is easy to see that it is completely subversive of the law of God as a binding rule, and leaves it fully in the power of the creature to do whatever he pleases.   He may deliberately determine that he will rebel against his Maker, till the last moment of life, and then disarm his vengeance by repentance.   The penalty of the law may be in itself tremendous, but it can deter no one from any course which he may be inclined to pursue, because he can at any moment remove himself from its operation.   What greater license could the most daring rebel wish than what is thus granted? This single principle admitted into the moral government of God would be a complete nullification of the divine authority.

These consequences of the doctrine under consideration are evident and inevitable, and demonstrate that it cannot be a principle of reason or natural religion.   But it may be thought by some, that the same objection will lie with all its force against the doctrine of the gospel, which promises a plenary pardon to every true penitent.   But the evangelical doctrine of repentance stands on entirely different grounds. That such an offer would be made, could be known by no creature before he sinned.   This doctrine does not in the least clash with the justice of God; for all the sins of the penitent, to which pardon is granted, are virtually and actually punished in the sinner's substitute.   Here is the grand point of difference between Christianity and all other systems.   The former maintains the glory and harmony of all the divine attributes; the latter obscure or would destroy one attribute, to make way for another.   The consequence is, that the way in which pardon is granted to the penitent, according to the gospel, has no tendency to relax our obligation to obedience, or to lessen our sense of the evil of sin; but the deistica principle of forgiveness, as we have seen, nullifies the law and authority of the Governor of the universe, and leaves it completely at the option of the creature, whether he will obey or transgress the law of God. The former is perfectly consistent with the justice of God, extending pardon to no sin for which satisfaction has not been made; while the latter is in direct repugnance to the clearest demands of justice

Another objection to the opinion that the punishment of sin is remitted upon repentance is, that this is contrary to experience and fact. We have seen that the deist is fond of considering the punishment of sin as being nothing else but its consequences, arising out of the laws of nature. Is it true, then, that the laws of nature change their course as soon as a sinner repents? Is it not a fact that the penitent thief in the jail, and the repentant debauchee in the hospital, are still suffering the consequences of their crimes long since committed? Repentance cannot bring back lost health, ruined reputation, dissipated fortune, and alienated friends. How then can the deist, on his own principles, pretend that the punishment of sin is removed by repentance? He may allege that the future punishment of sin will be remitted; but how does he know this? Reason can judge nothing in regard to the future, but by some analogy with what is observed to take place in this life; and all analogy is against the opinion, that the evil consequences of sin will be terminated by death.

Again, if pardon be granted only to the penitent, and the impenitent be punished according to the demerit of their crimes, then there is a state of sinning which renders it proper that sin should be punished rigidly, according to its desert. There can, therefore, be no argument drawn from the goodness and compassion of God against the condign punishment of sinners. But why is impenitence alone to be considered as exposing a sinner to the wrath of God? And why are the penitent alone exempt from the

penalty of the law?   The answer must be, either
that the sin of impenitence is so great as to deserve
this severe treatment, or the merit of repentance is
such as to atone for the greatest sins.   But supposing
that impenitence draws after it deeper guilt than all
other sins, that does not prove that this alone should
be punished; it only proves that it should be punished more.   If there be a plain principle in jurispru
dence, it is, that every sin should certainly be visited
with punishment, but exactly according to its nature.
There is no reason why a less sin should be suffered
to pass rather than a greater.   Strict justice says, let
every sin have its due retribution.   The greatness of
the sin of impenitence, therefore, cannot be a reason
why the impenitent alone are to be punished.   Nor
can this great difference in the treatment of sinners
be owing to the merit of repentance; for it would be
difficult to tell wherein its extraordinary merit consists.   It must either be in the obedience or the suffering involved in the exercise of repentance.   But
it cannot consist in the degree of obedience which it
contains; for if this were perfect, it could do no more
than answer the demands of the moral law for the
time being, but could have no effect on sins already
committed.   I think it a self-evident truth, that my
obedience this moment cannot atone or satisfy for
my disobedience the preceding moment; for I do no
more than my duty.   Then certainly the obedience
included in repentance cannot atone for all past sins,
however enormous, for it is imperfect, and moreover
has nothing in it which enhances its value above
other acts of obedience.   Neither can the suffering
involved in repentance atone for past sins; for these
pangs of compunction owe all their virtue to the
obedience with which they are connected, and without which they would not even be of a moral nature.
Unless some one should be of opinion, that these
penitential sorrows are to be considered as an equivalent for the penalty of the law: but this cannot be
correct, because an equivalent for the penalty of the
law would be an equal degree and duration of suffer

ing. If indeed a person of higher dignity and greater worth is permitted to suffer in the place of another, in proportion to the difference in dignity, the sufferings may be diminished. It is, however, always a matter in the breast of the Supreme Judge, whether to allow of such a substitution. I see nothing unreasonable in it. But in the case under inquiry, the same person who owes the suffering, if I may so speak, endures the sorrows of repentance; and how, I would ask, can the pious grief of a few hours or days be an equivalent for the punishment of the most heinous transgressions? Besides, the penitent sinner ever feels, and is ready to confess, that he deserves other punishment. No one who ever truly repented, entertained the idea that by this he had made a complete atonement for his sins. These stains are of too deep a dye to be washed out by a few penitential tears. Nothing can be more opposed to this opinion than the views and feelings involved in the exercises of true repentance. Every true penitent is deeply convinced, that he deserves heavier punishment than is involved in the sorrows which he now experiences.

There is, however, one ground for the opinion, that there is a reasonable connexion between repentance and forgiveness, perhaps more plausible than any other argument; it therefore merits a distinct consideration. It is, that all good men acknowledge that it is a virtue to forgive those who offend us, when they appear to be penitent; and Christians cannot deny that this is a part of moral duty, for it is repeatedly and emphatically enjoined in the New Testament, as a thing essential. What is here alleged we fully admit, and are willing to go further and say, that it is made the duty of Christians to forgive those who injure them, whether they repent or not; for they are required to " love their enemies, to do good to them that hate them, to bless them that curse them, and pray for them which despitefully use them." But this is entirely a distinct case, and resting on principles entirely different from the one under consideration. It is no part of the duty of

Christians to inflict condign punishment on those who sin, even if they have been injured by them. They are forbidden to seek revenge, or to render to the wicked according to their iniquities; not because there is any thing improper or inconsistent with moral goodness in punishing the guilty as they deserve; but because this is the peculiar prerogative of the Governor of the universe. In those very passages of Scripture where vengeance is forbidden to the creature, in express and emphatical language it is claimed for the Almighty. " Vengeance is mine, I will repay, saith the Lord; therefore, if thine enemy hunger, feed him, if he thirst, give him drink, for in so doing thou shalt heap coals of fire on his head." If this duty of forgiveness in the Christian proved any thing, it would prove more than is wished; it would follow, that God would certainly pardon not only the penitent, but all sinners, however obstinate in their rebellion. But this conclusion is altogether at variance with the opinion which we have had under discussion, and is not even held by the deist.

Another argument in favour of the doctrine that repentance is naturally connected with pardon, is derived from the practice of granting pardon in human governments. But here there is a mistake respecting the real state of the fact · for although it is true that in all human governments, it is found expedient to have a pardoning power lodged somewhere, yet no government ever yet professed to act on the principle of pardoning all offences on the condition of repentance; nor indeed is the extension of mercy to certain criminals, who have incurred the penalty of the law, at all connected with this principle. The reason why it is sometimes right to pardon offences against the state, is either because, in some particular case, the rigid execution of law would not be entirely just; or, because on account of the number of persons implicated, sound policy may dictate that only the most guilty should be held up as an example. It appears, then, that the weakness of human governments is the ground on which the penalty of the law is remitted; but no such reason can exist in the divine government. In the execution of human laws, no inquiry is ever instituted whether the crimina. be penitent; nay, though his repentance should be most evident, this never disarms the law of its penalty. The penitent thief or murderer is punished by our laws, as well as the obstinate and impenitent. If in a few cases rulers who possessed the power of granting pardon have acted on the principle, that criminals who discovered signs of penitence should be on that account pardoned, it only proves, that men entrusted with power may be misled; for undoubtedly this principle carried out would soon be subversive of all law. If the only end of punishment were the good of the culprit, then, indeed, such a course might be defended; but as long as the good of the community is the chief end of punishment, it never can be safe to offer pardon to all who profess repentance, or who for a time appear to be reformed.

I think it is manifest from the preceding discussion, that the idea of a certain connexion between repentance and pardon in the moral government of God, is not derived from the light of nature, but from the gospel; and therefore, if pardon is to be had in this way, it is only on the ground of the atonement of Christ, and not on account of any merit or efficacy in repentance to take away the guilt of sin.

If these views are correct, then is a divine revelation absolutely necessary to teach us that God is willing to receive the penitent into favour, and to show on what terms this is practicable.

Hence we may learn the deplorable situation of our whole race, and the infinite obligations which we are under to God for the gospel. All our well-grounded hopes of pardon and salvation we owe to the free mercy of God in Christ, and to the expiatory efficacy of the great atonement

CHAPTER V.

THERE IS NOTHING IMPROBABLE OR UNREASONABLE IN THE IDEA OF A
REVELATION FROM GOD, AND CONSEQUENTLY NOTHING IMPROBAB E CR
UNREASONABLE IN SUCH A MANIFEST DIVINE INTERPOSITION AS MAY
BE NECESSARY TO ESTABLISH A REVELATION.

THAT a revelation is possible, will not be called in
question by any who believe in the existence of a
God; nor can it be believed that there is any thing
in the notion of a revelation repugnant to the moral
attributes of the Supreme Being. It cannot be inconsistent with the wisdom, goodness or holiness of
God, to increase the knowledge of his intelligent
creatures. The whole end of a revelation is to make
men wiser, better, and happier; and what can be
conceived more accordant with our ideas of divine
perfection than this?

That man is capable of receiving benefit from a
revelation is a truth so evident, that it would be
folly to spend time in demonstrating it; for whatever may be thought of the sufficiency of Natural
Religion if it were fully understood and improved,
all must admit, that men generally, have not been
sufficiently enlightened on the subject of religion.
The history of the world in all ages proves the deplorable ignorance of the greater part of the human
race, even on those subjects which the advocates of
Natural Religion confess to be most important and
fundamental, as has been proved in the preceding
chapter.

It cannot be thought an unreasonable supposition,
that when God made the original progenitors of our
race, he should furnish them with such knowledge as
was absolutely necessary, not only for their comfort
but for their preservation. As they were without
experience, and had none upon earth from whom
they could derive instruction is it unreasonable to

suppose, that the beneficent Creator communicated to them such a stock of knowledge as was requisite for the common purposes of life? The theory of those who suppose that man was at first a dumb, irrational animal, very little different from those which now roam the forest, that from this state he emerged by his own exertions, that he invented articulate speech and all the arts of life, without ever receiving any aid or any revelation from his Creator, has already been sufficiently refuted.

If then man received at first such ideas as were necessary to his condition, this was a revelation; and if afterwards he should at any time need information on any subject connected with his happiness, why might not the benevolent Creator, who does not abandon the work of his hands, again vouchsafe to make a communication to him? Such an exigency, deists themselves being judges, did arise. Men almost universally fell into the practice of idolatry, and lost the knowledge of the true God. They betook themselves to the worship of the luminaries of heaven, dead men, beasts, and inanimate things. They invented superstitious rites, not only irrational, but cruel and abominable. These were transmitted from generation to generation; and the children became still more involved in ignorance than their parents. That the righteous Governor of the universe may leave men to follow their own inventions, and suffer by their own folly, is certain; for he has done so. But is it not consistent with his wisdom and goodness to use extraordinary means to rescue them from a state so degraded and wretched? Would not every sober deist admit, that some means of bringing them back to just ideas of Natural Religion would be desirable? If then the apostasy of man from his Maker should render some further revelation necessary, would it not be highly benevolent to communicate whatever knowledge his circumstances required? Why should it be thought unreasonable, that God should sometimes depart from his common mode of acting, to answer great and valuable ends?

What is there in the established course of nature so sacred or so immutable, that it must never on any occasion or for any purpose be changed? The only reason why the laws of nature are uniform, is, that this is for the benefit of man, but if his interest requires a departure from the regular course, what is there to render it unreasonable? The author of the universe has never bound himself to pursue one undeviating course, in the government of the world. The time may come when he may think proper to change the whole system. As he gave it a beginning, he may also give it an end. General uniformity is expedient, that men may know what to expect, and may have encouragement to use means to obtain necessary ends; but occasional and unfrequent deviations from this uniformity have no tendency to prevent the benefit arising from it. This is so evident a truth that I am almost ashamed to dwell so long upon it; but by the sophistry of infidels a strange darkness has been thrown over the subject, so that it seems to be thought that there would be something immoral, or unwise and inconsistent, in contravening the laws of nature.

Let it be remembered that the object here is not to prove that there must be a revelation; it is only to show that there would be nothing unreasonable in the thing; and further, that it would be a very desirable thing for man, and altogether consistent with the perfections of God, and the princip es on which he governs the world.

If God should determine to reveal his will to man, how could this be most conveniently effected? We can conceive of two ways. The first, by inspiring all who needed knowledge with the ideas which he wished to comn.unicate; the second, by inspiring a few persons, and directing them to make known to others the truths received. The first would seem to be the most effectual, but the last is more analogous to his other dispensations. Reason might have been given in perfection at once, and not left to the uncertainty of education and human improvement;

but such is not the fact. By slow degrees and much
culture this faculty attains its maturity, and when
neglected never acquires any high degree of strength.
In regard to the best mode of making a revelation,
however, we are totally incompetent to judge; but
of one thing we may be certain, that if God should
give a revelation to men, he would so attest it as to
enable all sincere inquirers to know that it derives its
origin from him; for otherwise it would be useless,
as there would be no evidence of its truth. Supposing a revelation to be given, what would be a
satisfactory attestation of its divine origin? It must
be some sign or evidence not capable of being counterfeited; something by which God should in some
way manifest himself. And how could this be
effected, but by the exertion of his power or the
manifestation of his infinite knowledge ; that is, by
miracles, or by prophecies, or by both? There is
then just as much probability that miracles will
exist, (for prophecy may be considered one kind of
miracle) as that a revelation will be given. The
conjunction of these two things is reasonable; if we
find the one, we may be sure the other exists also.

It is admitted that a revelation from God would
have internal evidence of its origin, but this does not
strike the attention at once. It requires time before
it can be perceived; but in the first establishment of
a revelation, there is need of some evidence which is
obvious to the senses and level to the capacities of
all. Just such an evidence are miracles. Moreover,
internal evidence requires, in order that it may be
perceived and appreciated, a certain favourable state
of the moral feelings, without which it is apt to be
overlooked, and produces no conviction ; whereas,
external evidence is not only level to every capacity,
but adapted to bring home conviction to every description of men, to the bad as well as the good.

Miracles, then, furnish the best proof for the estab
lishment of a revelation; they seem to be its proper
seal ; they are the manifest attestation of God. No
hing can be conceived which will more strikingly

indicate his power and presence, than a visible suspension of the laws of nature. He is invisible he must make himself known by his works, and a miracle is such a work as no other can perform. When, therefore, a person professes to have received a revelation from God, and when we behold the effects of Almighty power accompanying his words, all are sure that God is with him, and that he is a teacher sent from God; for otherwise he could never perform such wonderful works; or rather, to speak more correctly, God would never exert his power to confirm the pretensions of an impostor, or to attest doctrines which are not true.

CHAPTER VI.

MIRACLES ARE CAPABLE OF PROOF FROM TESTIMONY.

I do not know that any one has denied that a miracle would be credible if exhibited to our senses. A man might, indeed, be deceived by an illusion arising from some disorder in his senses; but if he were conscious of being in a sound state of body and mind, and should witness not only one, but a variety of miracles; not only a few times, but for years in succession; and if he should find that all around him had the same perceptions of these facts as himself, I need not say that it would be reasonable to credit his senses, for the constitution of his nature would leave him no choice: he would be under the necessity of believing what he saw with his eyes, heard with his ears, and handled with his hands. But are there facts which a man would credit on the evidence of his senses, which cannot possibly be rendered credible by the testimony of any number of witnesses? Then there might be facts, the knowledge of which could never be so communicated as to be worthy of

credit. According to this hypothesis, the const   on of our nature would require us to withhold our assent from what was true, and from what others knew to be true. If a thousand persons of the strictest veracity should testify that they had repeatedly witnessed a miracle, and if all circumstances should concur to corroborate their testimony, yet upon this principle would be unreasonable to credit them, even if they should consent to die in confirmation of what they declared to be the fact.   This is the ground taken by Mr. Hume, in his boasted argument against miracles. But it appears to me that every man, even before examination, must be convinced that it is false; for it is contrary to common sense and universal experience of the effect of testimony.   The true principle on this subject is, that any fact which would be believed on the evidence of the senses, may be reasonably believed on sufficient testimony.   There may be testimony of such a nature as to produce conviction as strong as any other conceivable evidence; and such testimony in favour of a miracle would establish it as firmly as if we had witnessed it ourselves. But though this is the conclusion of common sense and experience, the metaphysical argument of Mr. Hume has had the effect of perplexing and unsettling the minds of many: and as he boasts that " it will be useful to overthrow miracles as long as the world endures," it seems necessary to enter into an examination of his argument, that we may be able to expose its fallacy.   This has already been done in a convincing manner, by several men,* eminent for their learning and discrimination; and if their works were read by all who peruse Hume, I should think it unnecessary to add a single word on the subject. But it may not be without its use to present a refutation in a condensed form, for the sake of those who will not take the trouble to go through a minute and extended demonstration.

The argument of Mr. Hume will be best exhibited in his own words.   "A miracle," says he, " support-

---

* Dr. Campbell, Prof. Vince, Mr. Adam, Dr. Douglas.

ed by any human testimony, is more properly a subject of derision, than of argument. No testimony for any kind of miracle can ever possibly amount to a probability."—" We establish it as a maxim, that no human testimony can have such force as to prove a miracle, and make a just foundation for any system of religion."—" Our belief or assurance of any fact from the report of eye witnesses, is derived from no other principle than experience; that is, our observa tion of the veracity of human testimony, and of the usual conformity of facts to the reports of witnesses Now, if the fact attested partakes of the marvellous, if it is such as has seldom fallen under our own observation; here is a contest of two opposite experiences, of which the one destroys the other as far as its force goes. Further, if the fact affirmed by the witness, instead of being only marvellous is really miraculous; if, besides, the testimony considered apart, and in itself, amounts to an entire proof; in that case there is proof against proof, of which the strongest must prevail. A miracle is a violation of the laws of nature; and as a firm and unalterable experience has established these laws, the proof against a miracle, from the very nature of the fact, is as entire as any argument from experience can possibly be imagined. And if so, it is an undeniable consequence, that it cannot be surmounted by any proof whatever from testimony. A miracle, therefore, however attested, can never be rendered credible, even in the lowest degree."

Here we have the substance of Mr. Hume's argu ment, on which I propose to make some remarks, intended to show that its whole plausibility depends on the assumption of false principles, and the artful use of equivocal terms.

1. Some prejudice is created in the mind of the unsuspecting reader, by the definition of a miracle here given. It is called " a violation of the laws of nature," which carries with it an unfavourable idea, as though some obligation were violated and some injury done. But the simple truth is, that the laws

of nature are nothing else than the common operations of divine power in the government of the world,
which depend entirely for their existence and continuance on the divine will; and a miracle is nothing
else than the exertion of the same power in a way
different from that which is common; or it may be a
mere suspension of that power which is commonly
observed to operate in the world.

2. Mr. Hume's argument will apply to the evidence of the senses as well as to that derived from
testimony, and will prove (if it prove any thing) that
it would be impossible to believe in a miracle, if we
should witness it ever so often. "The very same
principle of experience," says he, "which gives us a
certain degree of assurance in the testimony of witnesses, gives us also, in this case, another degree of
assurance against the fact which they endeavour to
establish, from which contradiction there arises necessarily a counterpoise, and mutual destruction of
belief and authority." The very same counterpoise
and mutual destruction of belief must also occur between the assurance derived from the senses and that
derived from experience. The reason why testimony
cannot be believed in favour of a miracle, is not,
according to Mr. Hume, because it has no force, for
taken by itself it may be sufficient to produce assurance; but let this assurance be as strong as it may,
it cannot be stronger than that derived from universal experience. "In that case," says he, "there is
proof against proof." It is evident that, upon these
principles, the same *equilibrium* from contradictory
evidence must take place between experience and
the senses. If one evidence be stronger than another, "the stronger must prevail, but with a diminution of force in proportion to that of its antago-
nist." But in the case of the senses and a firm and
unalterable experience, the evidence is perfect on
both sides, so that the "counterpoise and mutual
destruction of belief" must occur. According to this
metaphysical balance of Mr. Hume, a miracle could
not be believed if we witnessed it ever so often; for

though there is a great weight of evidence on each side, yet as there is an equilibrium, neither can have any influence on our assent. Whether Mr. Hume would have objected to this conclusion does not appear; but it is manifest, that it logically follows from his argument, as much as in the case to which he has applied it. And here we see to what a pitch of skepticism his reasoning leads.

3. Mr. Hume makes an unnecessary distinction between that which is *marvellous* and that which is *miraculous;* for though there is a real difference, there is none as to his argument. The force of his reasoning does not relate to events as being *miraculous*, but as being opposite to universal experience. If the conclusion therefore be correct, it will equally prove, that no testimony is sufficient to establish a natural event which has not before been experienced. If ever so many witnesses should aver that they had seen meteoric stones fall from the clouds, or the galvanic fluid melt metals, yet if we have never experienced these things ourselves we must not believe them.

4. The *opposite* or *contrary* experience of Mr. Hume in regard to miracles, can mean nothing more than that such things have not been experienced. There is no other opposite experience conceivable in this case, unless a number of persons present at the same time should experience opposite impressions. The distinction which he artfully makes in relation to "the king of Siam, who refused to believe the first reports concerning the effects of frost," between that which is contrary to experience and that which is not conformable to experience, is without foundation. For a fact cannot be contrary to experience in any other way than by being not conformable to it. There neither is nor can be any experience against miracles, except this, that they have not occurred in our own experience or that of others. When the proposition of our author is expressed in language free from ambiguity, it will amount to this, that what has never been experienced can never be

believed on any testimony; than which nothing can easily be conceived more false. In what a situation must man have been at the beginning of the world, if he had adopted the principles of this skeptic!

5. Mr. Hume uses the word *experience* in a two-fold sense, changing from one to the other as best suits his purpose. Sometimes it means *personal* experience, and at other times, and more commonly, the experience of the whole world. Now if it be taken to mean our own individual experience, the argument will be that no fact which we ourselves have not witnessed can be established by testimony; which, if correct, would cut off at a stroke the greater part of human knowledge. Much the most numerous class of facts are those which we receive upon testimony of others, and many of these are entirely different from any thing that we have personally experienced. Many learned men never take the trouble to witness the most curious experiments in philosophy and chemistry; yet they are as well satisfied of their truth as if they had personal experience of it.

But though an argument founded on an opposition between testimony and experience, in order to be of any validity, must relate to *personal* experience; yet Mr. Hume commonly uses the term to signify the experience of all men in all ages. This extensive meaning of the term must be the one which he affixes to it in most places of his essay; because it is experience by which we know that the laws of nature are uniform and unalterable; and he has given an example which clearly determines the sense of the word. "That a dead man should come to life," says he, "has never been witnessed in any age or country." Now, according to this use of the word, what he calls an argument is a mere assumption of the point in dispute, what logicians call a *petitio principii*, a begging of the question. For, what is the question in debate? Is it not whether miracles have ever been experienced? And how does Mr. Hume undertake to prove that they never did exist?

By an argument intended to demonstrate that no testimony can establish them; the main principle of which argument is that all experience is against them. If miracles have ever occurred, they are not contrary to universal experience; for whatever has been witnessed at any time, by any person, makes part of universal experience. What sort of reasoning is it then to form an argument against the truth of miracles, founded on the assumption, that they never existed? If it be true, as he says, that it has never been witnessed in any age or country, that a dead man should come to life, then indeed it is useless to adduce testimony to prove that the dead have on some occasions been brought to life. If he had a right to take this for granted, where was the use of such a parade of reasoning on the subject of testimony? The very conclusion to which he wished to come is here assumed as the main principle in the argument. It is however as easy to deny as to affirm; and we do utterly deny the truth of this position; so that after all we are at issue precisely on the point where we commenced. Nothing is proved by the argument which promised so much, except the skill of the writer in sophistical reasoning.

6. Our author falls into another mistake in his reasoning. The object is to prove that testimony in favour of miracles can never produce conviction, because it is opposed by uniform and unalterable experience. But how do we know what this universal experience is? Is it not by testimony, except within the narrow circle of our own personal experience? Then it turns out that the testimony in favour of miracles is neutralized or overbalanced by other testimony. That is, to destroy the force of testimony he assumes a principle founded on testimony. It is admitted that when testimony is adduced to establish any facts, if other and stronger testimony can be brought against them, their credibility is destroyed. But if I bring testimony for a fact, and some one alleges that he can show that this testimony is unworthy of credit because he can bring witnesses to

prove that many persons in different countries and ages never saw any such thing; to such a person I would reply, that even if these witnesses declared the truth, it could not overthrow the positive testimony which I had adduced, as they did not contradict the facts asserted; and besides, it must be determined which witnesses are the most credible, yours or mine. Just so it is in the case of Mr. Hume's argument He sets up uniform experience against testimony, and gives a preponderance to the former, on the ground that witnesses are known sometimes to lie; but all that he knows of what has happened in other ages and countries, is by testimony; and they who give this testimony are as fallible as others; therefore, there existed no ground for preferring the evidence of experience to testimony. Besides, he is not in possession of testimony to establish a thousandth part of what has been experienced; and as far as it goes, it amounts to no more than *non-experience*, a mere negative thing which can never have any weight to overthrow the testimony of positive witnesses. In a court of justice, such a method of rebutting testimony would be rejected as totally inadmissible. If we had sufficient evidence of a fact of any kind, *that* testimony would not be invalidated, if it could be proved that no person in the world had ever witnessed the like before. This want of previous experience naturally creates a presumption against the fact, which requires some force of evidence to overcome: but in all cases, a sufficient number of witnesses, of undoubted intelligence and veracity, will be able to remove the presumption and produce conviction.

7. Mr. Hume lays it down as a principle, that our belief in testimony arises from "experience, that is, observation of the veracity of human testimony." But this is not correct. Our belief in testimony is as natural and constitutional as our belief in our senses. Children at first believe implicitly all that is told them, and it is from experience that they learn to distrust testimony. If our faith in testimony arose from experi-

ence, it would be impossible to acquire any knowledge from instruction. If children were to believe nothing that was told them until they had made observations on the veracity of human testimony, nothing would be believed; for they would never arrive at the maturity and judgment necessary to make observations on a subject so complicated.

But although Mr. Hume's object in wishing to establish this false principle was, to exalt the evidence of what he calls *experience* above testimony; yet, if we should concede it to him, it could answer him no purpose, since we have shown that this experience itself depends on testimony. Whatever use he can make of this principle therefore against testimony, can be turned against himself, since his knowledge of what the experience of the world is, can only be obtained by the report of witnesses, who, in different ages, have observed the course of nature.

8. Mr. Hume, on reflection, seems to have been convinced that his argument was unsound; for in a note appended to his Essay on Miracles, he makes a concession which entirely overthrows the whole. But mark the disingenuity (or shall I not rather call it the malignity?) which is manifested in this only evidence of his candour. He concedes that there may be miracles of such a kind as to admit of proof from human testimony, in direct contradiction to his reiterated maxim, and in complete repugnance to all his reasoning; but he makes the concession with the express reservation that it shall not be applied to the support of religion. He however not only makes this concession, but gives an example of such miracles, and of the testimony which he admits to be sufficient to establish it. "Suppose," says he, "all authors in all languages agree, that from the first of January, 1600, there was a total darkness all over the earth for eight days; suppose that the tradition of this event is still strong and lively among the people; that all travellers bring us accounts of the same tradition, &c.—IT IS EVIDENT THAT OUR PHILOSOPHERS OUGHT TO RECEIVE IT FOR CERTAIN." And

this is a part of the same Essay, in which it is said that "a miracle supported by any human testimony, is more properly a subject of derision than of argument." "No kind of testimony for any kind of miracle can possibly amount to a probability, much less to a proof!"

It might appear that after so complete a renunciation of the principle which at first he so strenuously asserted, we might have spared ourselves the pains of a formal refutation. But not so. The author is resolved that his concession shall be of no service whatever to religion. Hear his own words: "But should this miracle be ascribed to any new system of religion; men in all ages have been so imposed upon by ridiculous stories of that kind, that, this very circumstance would be full proof of a cheat and sufficient with all men of sense, not only to make them reject the fact, but even reject it, without further examination." I have heard of a maxim which I believe the Jesuits introduced, that what is false in theology may be true in philosophy; but I never could have expected that a philosopher, a logician, and a metaphysician too, would utter any thing so unreasonable and so marked with prejudice as the declaration just quoted. The fact is admitted to have such evidence, that even philosophers ought to receive it as certain; but not if it is ascribed to a new religion. On this subject no evidence is sufficient. It is perfectly unexceptionable in philosophy; but in religion a sensible man will reject it, whatever it may be, even without further examination. The circumstance of its being a miracle connected with religion is sufficient, in his opinion, to prove it a cheat, however complete the testimony. The world, it seems, has been so imposed on by ridiculous stories of this kind, that we must not even listen to any testimony in favour of religious miracles. This author would indeed reduce the advocates of religion to an awkward dilemma. They are called upon to produce evidence for their religion, but if they adduce it sensible men will not notice it; even if it is good every where else, it must go for nothing in religion. Upon these prin ciples, we might indeed give up the contest; but we are not willing to admit that this is sound logic, or good sense. The reason assigned for proscribing, in this summary way, all the testimony in favour of religion, will apply to other subjects. Men have been imposed on by ridiculous stories in philosophy, as well as in religion; but when evidence is pro- posed, shall we not even examine it, because there have been impositions? This is the very reason why we should examine with care, that we may distinguish between the true and the false.

If it were true, that miracles had often been ascrit- ed to new religions, it would not prove that there never were any true miracles, but rather the contra- ry; just as the abounding of counterfeit money is evidence that there is some genuine; for that which has no existence is not counterfeited. But the clam- our that has been raised by infidels about new reli- gions being commonly founded on miracles, or the pretence of miracles, has very little foundation in fact. Beside the Jewish and Christian religions, (which are indeed parts of the same,) it would, I believe, be difficult to designate any other, which claims such an origin.

After all that has been said of the false maxims of the Jesuits, I doubt whether any one could be selected so perfectly at war with reason, as this of the philosopher; nay, I think I may challenge all the enemies of revelation, to call from any Christian writer a sentence so surcharged with prejudice.

But, to do justice to Mr. Hume—though he seems to have closed the door against all discussion on our part—yet, in one of his general maxims, he leaves us one alternative. The maxim is this, " That no testimony is sufficient to establish a miracle, unless it be of such a kind, that its falsehood would be more miraculous than the fact." An ingenious writer* has undertaken to meet Mr. Hume on his own ground,

* Dr. Gleig.

and has endeavoured to prove, that the testimony of the apostles and early Christians, if the facts reported by them were not true, is a greater miracle than any which they have recorded. But the maxim, as stated by Mr. Hume, is not correct. With the change of a single word, perhaps it may be adopted, and will place the question on its proper ground. The change which I propose, is to substitute the word *improbable* for *miraculous.* And it will then read: *No testimony is sufficient to establish a miracle, unless the testimony be of such a kind, that its falsehood would be more improbable, than the fact which it endeavours to establish.* The ground of objection to the word *miraculous*, is, that it involves a false principle, which is, that facts are incredible in proportion as they are miraculous; which principle he in several places avows, and which is indeed a cardinal point in his system of evidence. But it is not true. There are many cases which might be proposed, in which, of two events, one of which must be true, that which is miraculous is more probable than the one which is merely natural. I will mention only one at present. Man was either immediately created by God, or he proceeded from some natural cause. Need I ask, which of these is more probable? and yet the first is miraculous; the second is not. The plain truth is, that in all cases, the fact which has most evidence is most probable, whether it be miraculous or natural. And when all evidence relating to a proposition is before the mind, THAT IS TRUE WHICH IS EASIEST TO BE BELIEVED, because it is easier to believe with evidence than against it. We are willing, therefore, that this maxim, as now stated, should be the ground of our decision, and we pledge ourselves to prove that the falsehood of the miracles of the gospel would be more improbable, and consequently more incredible, than the truth of the facts recorded in them. But this discussion will be reserved for another place.

To conclude ; since it has been shown that there is no antecedent presumption against miracles from the nature of God, or from the laws by which he governs the universe; since a miraculous fact is not more difficult to be accomplished by omnipotence than any other; since miracles are no further improbable, than as they are unusual; since they are the most suitable and decisive evidences which can be given of a revelation; since even by the concession of Mr Hume himself, there may be sufficient testimony fully to establish them; and since the many false pretences to miracles, and the general disposition to credit them, are rather proofs that they have existed than the contrary; we may safely conclude, that Mr. Hume's argument on this subject is sophistical and delusive; and that so far from being incredible, whatever may be their evidence, when brought to support religion, this is, of all others, the very case in which they are most reasonabe and credible.

In a recent popular, but anonymous publication, entitled, "Essays on the Pursuits of Truth, on the Progress of Knowledge, and the Fundamental Principles of all Evidence and Expectation, by the Author of Essays on the Formation and Publication of Opinions," the doctrine of Hume, on the subject of testimony, has been exhibited in a form somewhat new and imposing. And as this writer has acquired considerable celebrity in England, and his Essays have been published in Philadelphia, and recommended strongly to the public upon the authority of the *Westminster Review* it seems necessary to guard the public against the insidious design of the writer. The ingenious author, indeed, never brings the subject of divine revelation directly into view, in all that he has written; and I believe, the word "miracles" does not occur in either of the volumes which he has published. It is a fact, however, that in the last of his Essays he has revived, in substance, the famous argument of Hume on miracles; and has, with even more concealed sophistry than the celebrated infidel employed, endeavoured to prove that no testimony, however strong, is sufficient to establish any fact which involves a de-

7*

viation from the regular course of the laws of nature
That I may not be suspected of misrepresenting the
sentiments of this discriminating and popular writer
I will here insert an extract from the essay before
mentioned, which contains the substance of the whole
argument.

"'Testimony must be either oral or written. As
far as the mere physical circumstances are concerned,
we evidently commence our use of it by reasoning
from effects to causes. We infer, for example, that
the writing before us has been the work of some
human being, in doing which we of course assume
the uniformity of causation. If from the circumstances attending the testimony we infer that it is
entitled to be received as veracious; if, for instance,
we find that it has proceeded from a man of tried
integrity, and who acted under the influence of motives which render it unlikely that he should deceive,
our inference still proceeds on the assumption of the
same principle. I may have, in other cases, found
these circumstances to have been the precursors or
causes of true testimony; but how can I or any one
tell that they have operated in the same way in the
instance before me? The reply must evidently be,
that it is impossible to avoid assuming that the same
causes have invariably the same effects.

" In fact, if we examine any of the rules which
have been laid down for the reception of the testimony, or any of those marks which have been pointed
out as enabling us to judge of its credibility, we shall
find them all involving the uniformity of causation.
It is allowed on all hands, that the concurrence of a
number of witnesses in the same assertion, their reputation for veracity, the fact of the testimony being
against their own interest, the probability of detec
tion in any false statements, are all circumstances
enhancing the credibility of what they affirm. These
are considered as general principles on the subject
gathered from experience, and we apply them in-
stinctively to any new case which may be presented
to us, either in the course of our own observation, or

as having taken place at some former period. But it is obvious from what has just been said, that unless we assume a uniformity in the succession of causes and effects, we cannot transfer our experience from any one case to another. That certain circumstances have produced true testimony in one or a hundred instances, can be no reason why they should produce it in a different instance, unless we assume that the same causes have necessarily the same effects.

" It is clearly shown by this reasoning, that in the reception of testimony and the use of physical evidence we proceed on the same principle. But in the case of testimony there is a peculiarity not belonging to physical evidence. In the former we not only have certain effects from which it is our task to infer the causes, or certain causes from which to infer the effects; as when we judge the writing before us to have been the work of some human being, or the testimony to be true on account of the circumstances under which it was given; but the testimony itself consists of the assertion of facts, and the nature of the facts asserted often forms part of the grounds on which the veracity of the testimony is determined; it frequently happens, that while external circumstances tend to confirm the testimony, the nature and circumstances of the facts attested render it highly improbable that any such facts should have taken place, and these two sets of circumstances may be so exactly equivalent as to leave the mind in irremediable doubt. In the consideration of both, however, the same assumption is involved. We think the facts improbable, because we have found them rarely occurring under the circumstances stated; we think the testimony likely to be true, because we have generally found true testimony to proceed from witnesses acting under the influence of similar motives, and what we have found to happen in other cases we are irresistibly led to conclude must also happen in the case before us.

" The opposition of the circumstances of the evidence and the nature of the facts may be carried still further.   Assertions are frequently made which in themselves imply a breach of uniformity of causation. From such cases the conclusions already established remove all difficulty.   To weigh probabilities, to determine what credit is due to two sets of conflicting circumstances, neither of which as far as our knowledge extends, is irreconcilable to the usual course of nature, is often a nice and arduous task; but if the principles of this essay are correct, it is easy to see what reception ought to be given to assertions professedly implying a deviation from the uniform succession of causes and effects.

" Suppose, for instance, any person to affirm that he had exposed a cubic inch of ice to a temperature of two hundred degrees of Fahrenheit, and that at the expiration of an hour it had retained its solidity. Here is a sequence of events asserted which is entirely at variance with the admitted course of nature; and the slightest reflection is sufficient to show, that to believe the assertion would involve a logical absurdity.   The intrinsic discrepancy of the facts could never be overcome by any possible proofs of the truth of the testimony.

" For let us put the strongest case imaginable; let us suppose that the circumstance of the ice remaining unmelted, rests on the concurrent testimony of a great number of people, people too of reputation, science, and perspicacity, who had no motive for falsehood, who had discernment to perceive, and honesty to tell the real truth, and whose interests would essentially suffer from any departure from veracity.   Under such circumstances false testimony it may be alleged is impossible.

" Now mark the principle on which this representation proceeds.   Let us concede the positions, that what is attested by a great number of witnesses must inevitably be true,—that people of reputation and intelligence without any apparent motive for falsehood are invariably accurate in their testimony, and that they are above all, incapable of violating truth, when a want of veracity would be ruinous to their interests. Granting all this, I ask the objector, how he knows that these things are so; that men of this character and in these circumstances speak truth?' He will reply that he has invariably found them to act in this manner: but why, because you found them to act in this manner in a few or even in many cases, within your own experience or in the experience of ages, do you conclude that they have acted so in all cases and in the case before us? The only answer is, that it is impossible not to take for granted, that in precisely similar circumstances similar results will ensue, or that like causes have always like effects.

"Thus on the ground of unifomrity of causation, he would be maintaining the competency of testimony to prove a fact which implies a deviation from that uniformity."

It will abbreviate the answer to this specious argument, to acknowledge, that the general principle which this author takes so much pains to establish, and on which he builds his reasoning, is freely admitted to be not only correct, but self-evident. That the same causes uniformly produce the same effects, is a truth so obvious, and so generally admitted, that it was unnecessary for the ingenious author of this essay, to spend so much time in rendering it evident. And I am willing to admit its certainty to be as undoubted in moral, as in physical subjects. But while I freely admit, that the same causes will uniformly be followed by the same effects, I do by no means accede to the proposition, which our author seems to consider as of the same import; namely, that the course of nature, or the laws of nature, never have been interrupted, or suspended: and the whole appearance of force and plausibility which the argument of this writer possesses, arises from the artful confounding of these distinct propositions. I agree, that no testimony can be strong enough to induce a rational man to believe that the same causes will not be attended with the same effects; for this would be to assent to an evident absurdity. But it is an entirely different thing

to believe that the laws of nature have sometimes
been suspended; for in this case, we suppose that
an extraordinary cause has intervened. To believe
that a divine power has interposed to change the
course of nature, is surely not the same thing, as to
believe that the same cause which commonly pro
duced one effect, is now attneded by another entirely
different. The natural causes, it is true, remain the
same, but the general proposition stated above, is
not true, if confined only to these. If there exist
supernatural causes, or a power superior to the laws
of nature—and this our author does not profess to
deny—then the laws of nature, or mere natural
causes may remain the same; and yet, by the operation of these supernatural causes, effects entirely
diverse from those that would be the sequence of
natural causes, may take place. And the author
himself seems in one place to have been aware of
this distinction, and to admonish the reader of its
existence; and yet, through the whole of the argument he proceeds, as if the two propositions were
identical. He ought, however, to have recollected,
that while no man in his senses disbelieves the first
proposition, much the greater number of men have
believed, that in some cases the laws of nature have
been suspended; not, that they thought that the
same causes did not, in these instances, produce the
same effects, but that other causes of greater potency
than natural causes, were put into operation.

When our author, therefore, infers from the uniformity of causation, that no testimony is sufficient
to be the foundation of a rational belief, that there
has been a deviation from the common course of
nature, he applies a correct principle to a case to
which it evidently does not belong. Because the
same cause must produce the same effects, does it
follow, that when another and superior cause ope-
rates, the same effects must be produced? This
would be in direct repugnance to his own maxim
Then, before this principle of the uniformity of causes
and effects can be applied it must be demonstrated.

.hat in the case under consideration, no other causes operate, but such as are usual and natural, and whenever he shall be able to establish this, there will be no further contest respecting the matter.

That I do not misrepresent the argument of the author will appear satisfactorily, by considering the cases which he had adduced. " Suppose, for instance," says he, "any person to affirm, that he had exposed a cubic inch of ice to a temperature of two hundred degrees of Fahrenheit, and that at the expiration of an hour, it had retained its solidity. Here is a sequence of events asserted, which is entirely at variance with the admitted course of nature; and the slightest reflection is sufficient to show, that to believe the assertion, would involve a logical absurdity. The intrinsic discrepancy of the facts could never be overcome by any possible proofs of the truth of testimony."

In another page, he says, " If a number of men were to swear, that they had seen the mercury of the barometer remain at the height of thirty inches, when placed in the exhausted receiver of an air-pump, their testimony would be instantly rejected. The universal conclusion would be, that such an event was impossible." What is here confidently asserted, would only be true upon the supposition, that no causes but such as were natural operated in the cases adduced; but on the hypothesis of the operation of a supernatural cause, there would neither be absurdity nor impossibility in either of the facts. What! could not He, who established these laws and gave to heat and air, respectively, their peculiar power and qualities, suspend their usual operation? Could not He cause the ice to remain unmelted in any temperature; and the mercury to remain suspended, without the pressure of the atmosphere? But the sophistical nature of the argument used, is most evident. The principle is, that similar causes must have similar effects. Very good—what then? Why, if ice remain unmelted at two hundred degrees of Fahrenheit, then this principle would be violated

I answer, not at all, provided another cause is in operation, of such potency as to counteract the usual effects of caloric; or to counteract the gravity of the quicksilver, in vacuo. And it will not do to allege, that God, who established these laws, will not contravene them, on any occasion; for this would be an entire change of the ground of the argument, and a relinquishment of the principle on which the reasoning of our author is founded. Besides, it would be a mere begging of the question in dispute.

Now, in both the cases adduced by this writer, to illustrate and confirm his argument, on which he pronounces so confidently, that the judgment of men would universally reject any testimony, I beg leave to be of a different opinion, and will appeal to the common sense of all reflecting men, whether, on the supposition, that a dozen men, of perspicacity and undoubted integrity, should solemnly affirm that they had seen a cubic inch of ice remain an hour unmelted at two hundred degrees of Fahrenheit, whether they could refuse their assent, even if they knew of no good reason why the laws of nature should be suspended? But if they knew that an important purpose in the divine government could be answered by such a miracle, much less testimony would be sufficient to produce unwavering conviction of the truth of the extraordinary fact. And while they assent to such facts, on sufficient testimony, they are guilty of no absurdity, and violate no rule of common sense. It is true, that the credibility of the event reported, may be reduced to this question—whether it is more probable, that the laws of nature should, for a good end, be suspended, or that twelve men of tried veracity, should agree to assert a falsehood, without any motive to induce them to do so? And here our ingenious author revives the metaphysical balance of Mr. Hume; and after admitting that the evidence from testimony may be so strong that nothing is wanting to give it force, yet the maxim that the same causes may have the same effects, is also a truth so certain, that no evidence can countervail it.

We have, therefore, according to this statement, the equipoise of evidence, which we have already considered, in Mr. Hume's argument. The rational mind, in such circumstances, must remain neutral; it can neither believe nor disbelieve; for the evidence for the one exactly counterbalances that for the other. But after stating this hypothesis, our author finds that the evidence from testimony never can be so convincing, as that which we have for the uniformity of causation. His words are—"If the rejection and the admission of the testimony equally implied a deviation from the uniform terms of causes and effects, there could be no reason for rejecting or admitting it." "But the rejection of the testimony is not in this predicament. The causes of testimony, or in other words, those considerations which operate on the minds of the witness, cannot always be ascertained; and as we are uncertain as to the causes in operation, we cannot be certain of the effect; we cannot be sure that the circumstances of the witness are such as have given rise to true testimony, and consequently we cannot be sure that the testimony is true."

On this whole subject I have several remarks to make. First, this method of destroying the equipoise of evidence granted by Mr. Hume, and conceded by our author, is not altogether fair; because it does not admit what is obviously true, that in regard to some kinds of testimony, the evidence is so certain, that we might as soon doubt our own existence as the truth of the facts attested. Now, this being the case, there was no propriety in representing all testimony as being involved in some degree of uncertainty.

Again, what is here said of testimony will apply just as fully to what we ourselves witness, and for the truth of which we have the testimony of our own senses. I mean, that if the argument of our author is at all valid, it will prove, that if we saw the ice remain unmelted in the heat, and beheld it ever so often, and found that thousands around us received the same impression, we must not credit our own senses, nor believe what we saw with our own eyes, because, however certain this kind of evidence may be, it cannot be more certain than the principle, that the same causes will uniformly produce the same effects.   Therefore, although we should, under all manner of circumstances, see such events, they could not be believed; for to believe them would be a logical absurdity.   And thus would these men, by their metaphysics, reason us out of the evidence of our very eye-sight.   I know, indeed, that neither Hume, nor the author whose reasoning we are now considering, has pushed the argument to this its just consequence; but I would defy any man to show, that it is not as applicable to the evidence of the senses as to that derived from testimony.   Now, as the kind of evidence which will invariably command assent, is not learned by metaphysical reasoning, but by experience, I would leave the matter to be decided by every man of impartial judgment, for himself. Every man knows whether or not he would believe his own eyes, if he should see ice remain unmelted in two hundred degrees of temperature, according to Fahrenheit: or whether he would say, "it seems to be so, but it cannot be true, because it contradicts a self-evident principle, that the same causes must always be followed by the same effects."   To which a man of plain, unsophisticated common sense would reply, "I must believe my own senses; if doing so contradicts a thousand abstract principles, I care not —'seeing is believing.'"   And the same may be said in regard to testimony.   Suppose a thousand persons entirely disinterested to aver, that they had seen ice remain unmelted in a very high temperature, we could not but believe them, account for the fact as we might.   But we have already proved, that believing in such an event violates no maxim, but only supposes that some extraordinary power or cause is in operation; and when it is understood, that this deviation from the laws of nature is intended to confirm the declarations of some person who claims to be a messenger of God, there is not only no absurdity in the thing, but all presumption against the probability of such supernatural interposition is removed, as has been shown in the argument on that subject.

It might also be demonstrated, that upon the principles of this author, it would be absurd, upon any evidence, to believe not only in a fact which involved a real deviation from the laws of nature, but in any one which was entirely different from all our own experience of the laws of nature. For if it would be absurd to believe, on the testimony of thousands of unconnected witnesses, that ice did not melt in a certain case when placed in the fire; then it was altogether rational for the king of Siam, and all others in similar circumstances, to disbelieve the fact that water had been known to become as hard as a stone, so that men and animals could walk upon it. Persons so situated never could know that such an effect existed, but by testimony; yet as this testimony contradicted all their own experience about the laws of nature, in relation to water, they ought rather to reject the testimony, however strong, than to credit a fact which seemed to involve a deviation from " the sequence of cause and effect," to use the language of this author. And thus we should be reduced to the necessity of rejecting all facts not consonant to our own personal experience; for to receive them on the ground of testimony, would be to violate the principle that causation is uniform.

But the zeal of our author to establish his favourite point, has led him, not only to assert that a deviation from the regular succession of the laws of nature was incredible on the ground of testimony, but that it is, in the nature of things, impossible. In this assertion he certainly may lay claim to originality; for I believe no one before him, not even Hume, has gone so far in bold affirmation. His words are— " An event is impossible which contradicts our experience, or which implies that the same causes have produced different effects, or the same effects been preceded by different causes. Thus, when we pronounce that it was impossible for a piece of ice to remain in the midst of burning coals without being dissolved, our conclusion involves a complete knowledge of this particular effect of fire on ice."

And he is so confident that this is the true import of the word *impossible*, that he says, " If I am not greatly deceived, the acutest reasoner, the closest thinker, the most subtle analyser of words, will find himself unable to produce any other meaning of the term impossible, than that which is here assigned to it." But he seems to have felt that he had gone too far in this dogmatical, and I must say, irrational assertion; for in a note he himself gives another, and one of the true meanings of the word impossible. But as confident assertion, accompanied by no proof nor reason, is sufficiently answered by a confident denial, I would take the liberty of saying, therefore, that if I am not greatly mistaken, no accurate philologist will admit that this is the true meaning of the word impossible. And certainly, men of plain common sense never can be persuaded, that it is impossible for the succession of events according to the laws of nature, to be changed. It is true, when we confine our ideas to the mere powers and qualities of nature, we do assert that their effects will be uniform, and that it is impossible that the same causes should produce different effects; but when we extend our views to the Great First Cause, it is not only absurd, but impious, to assert that he cannot suspend or alter the laws of nature. Nothing is impossible to him which does not imply a contradiction, or is not repugnant to his attributes.

The conclusion which is rational on this subject, is, that all things are possible to God, and whatever is possible may be believed on sufficient testimony. which testimony, however, must be strong, in proportion to the improbability of the event to be confirmed.

CHAPTER VII.

THE MIRACLES OF THE GOSPEL ARE CREDIBLE

HAVING shown, in the preceding chapter, that miracles may be so attested as to be credible, I come now to examine the evidence by which the miraculous facts recorded in the New Testament are established. This is the main point in our inquiry; for after all that has been said, it must be admitted that unless the Christian religion is attended with sufficient evidence, we cannot believe in it, even if we would.

Before entering directly on this discussion it may be useful to premise a few things respecting the nature and force of testimony, which, it is presumed, will be admitted by all who have attended to the subject. This species of evidence admits of all conceivable degrees, from the weakest probability to the fullest assurance; for while, on this ground, we yield to some reports the most hesitating assent, we are as certainly persuaded of others as of those things which we perceive by our senses, or have demonstrated by mathematical reasoning.

The exact force of testimony cannot be calculated by rule nor estimated by reason, but is known only from experience. Many things are believed on testimony with the most unwavering confidence, when we are utterly unable to explain the precise ground on which our conviction rests. The sources of our information have been so numerous, and the same facts presented to us in so many forms, that it is impossible to attribute to each its influence in gaining our assent. If we were asked on what particular testimony we believe there is such a place as Rome, or why we believe that such a person as Bonaparte lately figured in Europe, we could only answer, in the general, that multiplied testimonies of these facts

had reached us so that all possibility of doubting was
excluded. The same assurance, and resting on the
same grounds, is experienced in relation to facts
which occurred in ages long past. Who can bring
himself to doubt whether such persons as Julius
Cæsar, Paul, Mohammed, Columbus, or Luther ever
existed?

When we have obtained evidence to a certain
amount, nothing is gained by the admission of more
The mind becomes, as it were, saturated, and no increase of conviction is produced by multiplying witnesses. One sound demonstration of a theorem in
mathematics is as good as a hundred. A few upright witnesses who agree and are uncontradicted by
other evidence, are as satisfactory as any conceivable
number. On a trial for murder, if there were a
thousand witnesses who could attest the fact, a judicious court would not deem it necessary to examine
more than half a dozen, or at most a dozen, if there
were a perfect agreement in their testimony. Experience only can inform us what degree of evidence
will produce complete conviction; but we may judge
from former experience what will be the effect of the
same evidence in future, and from the effect on our
own minds, what it will be on the minds of others.

Testimony, not of the strongest kind, may be
so corroborated by circumstances, and especially by
the existing consequences of the facts reported, that
it may be rendered credible and even irresistible.
Should an historian of doubtful credit assert that an
eclipse of the sun occurred on a certain day and was
visible in a certain place; if we possessed no other
evidence of the fact, it might be considered doubtful
whether the testimony was true or false; but if by
astronomical calculation it should be found, that
there must have been an eclipse of the sun at that
time, and visible at that place, the veracity of the
witness would be confirmed beyond all possibility of
doubt. Or should we find it recorded by an anonymous author, that an earthquake at a certain time
nad overthrown a certain city; without further evi-

dence, w should yield but a feeble assen to the statement; but if on personal observation or by the report of respectable travellers, it was ascertained, that the ruins of an ancient city existed in that place, we should consider the truth of the history as sufficiently established.

The evidences of the Christian religion may be sufficient, and yet not so strong as inevitably to produce conviction. Our conduct in the pursuit and reception of truth may be intended by our Creator to be an important part of the probation to which we are subjected; and therefore the evidence of revelation is not so great as to be irresistible, but is of such a kind, that the sincere and diligent inquirer will be in no danger of fatal mistake; while men of pride and prejudice, who prefer darkness to light, will be almost sure to err.*

It is natural for all men to speak the truth; falsehood requires an effort. Wicked men lie only when they have some sinister end in view. Combinations to deceive are never formed, but with a view to accomplish some object desirable to those concerned. No set of men will be at the trouble of forging and propagating a falsehood, which promises them no profit or gratification. Much less will they engage in such an enterprise, with the view of bringing evil on themselves, or when they foresee that it can be productive of nothing but pain and reproach.

Between truth and falsehood there is so great a difference, that it is extremely difficult for the latter so effectually to assume the garb and exhibit the aspect of the former as, upon a strict scrutiny, not to be detected. No imposture can stand the test of rigid inquiry. The style and manner of truth are entirely different from those of falsehood. The one pursues a direct course, is candid, unaffected, and honest; the other is evasive, cunning, tortuous, and inconsistent; and is often betrayed by the efforts made to avoid detection.

When both sides of a question are pressed with

* See Pascal's Thoughts.

difficulties, reason teaches us to choose that whit b, is attended with the fewest. Objectors to Christianity often forget to notice the difficulties of their own hypothesis. Every question has two sides; if we reject the affirmative, we of necessity receive the negative with all the consequences which may burden it. If we reject the evidence of Christianity and deny that miracles ever existed, we are bound to account for the existence of the Christian Church, and for the conduct of the first preachers and primitive believers, on other principles. And whoever seriously undertakes this will impose on himself a difficult task. Gibbon has put forth his strength on this subject with very small success. His account of the origin of Christianity is very unsatisfactory and totally defective in historical evidence.*

If the evidence on both sides of an important question appear to be pretty equally balanced, it is the dictate of wisdom to lean to the safe side. In this question, undoubtedly, the safe side is that of religion; for if we should be mistaken here, we shall suffer no loss and obtain some good by our error; but a mistake on the other side must prove fatal.

When a proposition has been established by proper and sufficient evidence, our faith ought not to be shaken by every objection which we may not be able to solve. To admit this, would be to plunge into skepticism on all subjects, for what truth is there to which some objection may not be raised that no man can fully answer? Even the clearest truths in science are not exempt from objections of this sort. It must be so, as long as our minds are so limited and the extent of human knowledge so narrow. That man judges incorrectly who supposes that when he has found out some objection to Christianity which cannot be satisfactorily answered, he has gained a victory. There are indeed objections which relate to the essence of propositions, which, if sustained, do overthrow the evidence; but there are other nume-

---

* Decline and Fall of the Roman Empire, c. xv. and xvi.

rous objections which leave the substantial evidence undisturbed. Concerning these I speak when I say that objections, though not admitting of an answer, should not be permitted to unsettle our faith.

Let us now proceed to the examination of the testimony for the miracles recorded in the gospel. In this discussion we shall take it for granted, that such a person as Jesus Christ lived in Judea about the time mentioned by the evangelists, that he inculcated a pure and sublime morality, lived a virtuous and unblamable life, and was put to death by Pontius Pilate at the instigation of the Jewish rulers; that his apostles went forth into various countries preaching to the people, and declaring that this crucified Jesus was a person sent from God for the salvation of the world, and that many were induced to connect themselves with the Christian church. These facts not being of a miraculous nature, and it being necessary to suppose some such events, deists have commonly been disposed to admit them. But Volney and some others have pretended that such a person as Jesus Christ never existed, that this is the name of one of the celestial luminaries, and that the gospel history is an allegory. Such visionary theories do not deserve a serious answer: they are subversive of all historical truth, and have not a shadow of evidence. They may be well left to sink by the weight of their own extravagance. Volney, however, has received a learned answer from a gentleman* who has met him on his own ground, and being as much attached to astronomical allegories as the Frenchman, has vanquished him with his own weapons.

In the examination of written testimony, the first thing requisite is to prove the authenticity of the document in which it is recorded. The evidence on which we depend for the truth of the miracles performed by Jesus Christ and by his apostles, is contained in the New Testament. Here we have four distinct narratives of the life, miracles, death, resurrection, and ascension of Jesus of Nazareth; and also

* Mr. Roberts.

a history of the acts and sufferings of the apostles in preaching the gospel and laying the foundation of the first Christian churches, after the resurrection and ascension of their Master. We have also in this collection of writings a number of epistles addressed to the church in general, to particular churches, and to individuals. These, with a book of prophecy, compose the volume called the New Testament.

These books are certainly not of recent origin; for there are extant copies of the New Testament in the original Greek, which are, at the least, twelve hundred years old. And before the time when these manuscripts were penned, we have in other books numerous testimonies to the existence of the Christian Scriptures. They are not only mentioned but quoted, expounded and harmonized, so that if every copy of the New Testament had been lost, a large portion of it might be recovered by means of the numerous quotations in the early Christian writers. Besides, there are extant versions of the New Testament into several languages made at a very early period. By these means we are able to trace these writings up to the time in which the apostles lived.

There is also ample proof, not only from Christian but heathen authors, that a society calling themselves Christians existed as early as the reign of Nero who was contemporary with the apostles. It is evident, from the necessity of the case, that some such accounts as those contained in the gospels must have been received as true from the first existence of the Christian church. Unless it had been preached and believed that Christ was a divine Teacher and performed extraordinary works in attestation of his mission, how is it possible that such a society could have been formed? To suppose such a thing would be to conceive of a superstructure without a foundation. The resurrection of Christ from the dead must have been an article of the faith of Christians, from their very origin; for it is the corner stone of the whole edifice. Take the belief of this away and the Christian system has no existence. There are also some external institutions peculiar to Christianity, which we must suppose to be coeval with the formation of the society, for they are the badges of the Christian profession, and constitute a part of their worship. I refer to baptism and the eucharist. To suppose that in some way Christianity first existed, and afterwards received these articles of faith and these institutions of worship, is too improbable to be admitted by any impartial man. It would be to suppose that a religious society existed without any principles, or that they rejected their original principles and adopted new ones; and that they who imposed these upon them, had the address to persuade them, that they had always belonged to their system;—than which it is not easy to conceive any thing more improbable. Let us for a moment attempt to imagine, that previously to the publication of the gospels, the Christian church had among them no report of the miracles, and no account of the institutions, recorded in these books. When they opened them, they would read that their society was founded on the belief of the resurrection of Jesus, and that baptism and the eucharist were instituted by him before he left the world, and had existed among them ever since. Nothing can be more evident than that the substance of what is contained in the gospels, was believed and practised by Christians from the commencement of the society.

As these books have come down to us under the names of certain apostles and disciples of Jesus Christ, so they were ascribed to the same persons from the earliest mention of them. It is by the ancient Fathers spoken of as a fact universally believed among Christians, and contradicted by nobody. And we must not suppose that in the first ages of Christianity there was little care or discrimination exercised, in ascertaining the true authors and genuine character of the books in circulation. The very reverse is the fact. The most diligent inquiries were instituted into matters of this kind. Other books were published in the name of the apostles, professing to give an account of Jesus Christ, which were not genuine. The distinction between the books of the New Testament and all others of every class, was as clearly marked in the earliest ages as it has ever been since. The writings of the apostles were held in great veneration, were received by the churches all over the world, as the rule of their faith and directory of their lives, and publicly read at their meetings for the instruction of the people. When any controversy arose they were appealed to as an authoritative standard. As soon as published, they were so widely scattered and so carefully guarded, that no persons had it in their power to make any alteration in them.

The style and dialect in which these books are written furnishes an evidence of their authenticity, of a peculiar kind. It does not indeed ascertain the persons of the writers, but proves that they must have been exactly in the circumstances of those to whom these books have been uniformly ascribed. The words are Greek but the idiom is in Hebrew, or rather Syro-Chaldaic, the vernacular tongue of Judea in the time of Christ and his apostles. This is a peculiarity which none could counterfeit, and which demonstrates that the New Testament was not composed by men of a different country and age from those in which the apostles lived.

In the New Testament there are numerous references to rivers, mountains, seas, cities, and countries, which none but a person well acquainted with the geography of Judea and the neighbouring countries could have made, without falling into innumerable errors. There is moreover incidental mention of persons and facts known from other authorities to have existed, and frequent allusions to manners and customs peculiar to the Jews.

From all these considerations, it ought to be admitted without dispute, that these are indeed the writings of the apostles, and of those particular persons to whom they are ascribed. It would not however estroy their credibility even if other persons had written them, since they were certainly composed in that age and were received by the whole body of Christians. But what imaginable reason is there for doubting the genuineness of these books? What persons were so likely to write books to guide the faith of the church as the apostles? If *they* did not write them who would? And why would they give the credit of them to others? But their universal reception without opposition or contradiction should silence every cavil. The persons who lived at this time knew the apostles, and were deeply interested in the subject, and they are the proper judges of this question. They have decided it unanimously, as it relates to the historical books of the New Testament. From them the testimony has come down, through all succeeding ages, without chasm. Even heathen writers and heretics are witnesses that the gospels were written by the persons whose names they bear.*

In other cases we usually possess no other evidence of the genuineness of the most valued writings of antiquity, except the opinion of contemporaries handed down by uncontradicted tradition. How soon would Homer be deprived of his glory, if such evidence was insisted on as is required for the genuineness of the New Testament? Certainly, as it respects evidences of genuineness, no books of antiquity stand upon a level with the books of the New Testament. The works of the Greek and Latin historians and poets have no such evidence of being the writings of the persons whose names they bear, as the writings of Matthew, Mark, Luke, and John. For we have the testimony, not merely of individuals, but of numerous societies, widely scattered over the world. We have internal evidence of a kind which cannot be counterfeited. We have, in short, every species of evidence of which the case admits. It may therefore be considered as an established fact, that the books of the New Testament are the genuine productions of the apostles, and consequently contain

* See Lardner's Heathen Testimonies.

their testimony to the miracles of Jesus Christ. and
also to those miracles which in his name they per
formed after his ascension.

It is also certain that the books of the New Testament have not undergone any material change since
they were written; for there is a general agreement
in all copies, in all the versions, and in all the quotations.   There are, it is true, small discrepancies,
which have occurred through the ignorance or carelessness of transcribers, but not more than might
naturally be expected.   There is no ancient book
which has come down to us so entire as the Scriptures, and which is accompanied by so many means
of correcting an erroneous reading where it has occurred.   This representation may appear surprising
to those who have heard of the vast multitude of
various readings which learned critics have collected
from a collation of the manuscripts; but it ought to
be understood by all who have ever heard of these
discrepancies, that not one in a thousand is of the
least consequence; that a great majority of them are
merely differences in orthography, in the collocation
of words, or in the use of words perfectly synony-
mous, by which the sense is not in the least affected.
A cursory reader would find as little difference in the
various manuscripts of the New Testament, as in the
different printed editions of the English version.

Having established the authenticity of the record
which contains the testimony, we shall next proceed
to consider its credibility.

I. Many of the facts related in the gospel are
undoubtedly of a miraculous nature.   It is declared
that Jesus Christ, in several instances, raised the
dead.   In one case the person had been dead four
days, so that the body began to be offensive to the
smell.   In every case, this miracle was wrought in
stantly and without any other means than speaking
a word.   It is declared that he healed multitudes of
the most inveterate and incurable diseases; that he
gave sight to the blind, hearing to the deaf, speech
to the dumb, and active limbs to the withered and

the maimed; that he delivered those who were furious and unmanageable by reason of the possession of demons; that on different occasions he fed thousands of people with a few loaves and fishes until they were satisfied, and that the fragments which were gathered up were much greater in quantity than the original materials; that he walked upon the sea and with a word allayed the raging storm and produced a great calm. And finally, it is repeatedly and solemnly declared by all the witnesses, that Jesus Christ after being crucified and after having continued in the sepulchre three days, rose from the dead, and after showing himself frequently to his disciples, ascended to heaven in their presence.

That all these were real miracles, none can for a moment doubt. It is true, we do not know all the powers of nature; but we do know, as certainly as we know any thing, that such works as these could not be performed but by the immediate power of God. The same remark may be extended to the miracles wrought by the apostles in the name of the Lord Jesus, and especially to that stupendous miracle on the day of Pentecost, when the Holy Ghost descended on the apostles in visible form, and conferred on them the gift of tongues and other extraordinary endowments. All must admit, that if these events ever occurred, then there have existed undoubted miracles.

II. The miracles of Jesus were performed, for the most part, in an open and public manner, in the presence of multitudes of witnesses, under the inspection of learned and malignant enemies, in a great variety of circumstances, and for several years in succession. There was here no room for trick, sleight of hand, illusion of the senses, or any thing else which could impose on the spectators. This circumstance is important, because it proves to a certainty, that the apostles themselves could not be deluded and deceived in the testimony which they have given. To suppose that they could think that they saw such miracles every day for years, and yet be deceived, would be nearly as extravagant a supposition, as that we were deceived in all that we ever experienced in our whole lives.

III The character of the miracles recorded in the gospels ought to be carefully observed. They were all worthy of the majesty, justice, and benevolence of the Son of God. They are characterized by dignity, propriety, and kindness. Most of them indeed were acts of tender compassion to the afflicted. Although so many miracles were performed, in so great a variety of circumstances, yet there is nothing ludicrous, puerile, or vindictive in any of them. Christ never exerted his power to gratify the curiosity of any, or to supply his own daily wants. He made no ostentatious display of his wonderful power, and never used it to acquire wealth and influence. While he fed hungry multitudes by a miracle, he submitted to hunger and want himself; while he could command all nature, he remained in poverty, not having so much as a home of any kind, to which he could retire to find repose. Although he was rejected and ill-treated by the Jews, he never refused to relieve any who sincerely sought his aid. His life, in consequence of the multitudes who flocked to him, was fatiguing, and on many accounts unpleasant, but he never grew weary in doing good.

Let any man compare the narrative of the miracles of Christ, contained in the genuine gospels, with those fictitious accounts which may be found in the apocryphal and spurious gospels still extant, and he will be struck with the remarkable contrast between them. The same result will be the consequence of a comparison of the miracles of Christ with those ascribed to Mohammed by his followers, or those contained in the legends of the church of Rome. I know not how any impartial man can read attentively the account of the miracles recorded in the gospels, and not be convinced, from the very nature and circumstances of the facts reported, that they were real.

IV. There are no signs of fraud or imposture to

be discovered in the record itself. There is, on the contrary, every indication of truth, honesty, and good intention in the writers. Although they differ from each other in style and manner so much that it is evident the same person did not compose the four gospels; yet there is a character of style which belongs to the whole of them, and which is without a parallel among any writers but the penmen of the sacred Scriptures. It is an apparent exemption from the passions and frailties of human nature. The most stupendous miracles are related without one exclamation of wonder from the historian, and without the least appearance of a desire to excite the wonder of the reader.

The character of Christ is drawn in no other way than by simply telling what he did and said. There is no portraying of character in the way of general description, or by using strong epithets to set him forth. There is perhaps no such thing in the gospel as an expression of admiration of any discourse or action, on the part of the evangelists. If they relate such things, they are the words of others which they faithfully set down. When they describe the sufferings of Christ, they never fall, as men usually do, into pathetic declamation. They are never carried away from their simple course by the power of sympathy. The facts are related as though the writer felt nothing but the strong purpose of declaring the truth, without giving any colouring whatever to the facts. Neither do they indulge themselves in those vehement expressions of indignation against the enemies of Christ, which we should naturally have expected. They never give utterance to a harsh expression against any one. They relate the treachery of Judas with the same unaffected simplicity as if they had no feelings relative to his base conduct.

But there is something which exhibits the true character of the writers in a light still stronger. It is the manner in which they speak of themselves. Few men can write much concerning themselves without betraying the strength of self-love. Weak

9*

men, when they speak on this topic, are commonly disgusting: and even when persons seem willing to let the truth be known, there is usually an effort to seek compensation in something for every sacrifice which they make of reputation.   But we may challenge any one to designate any instance in which the least indication of this moral weakness has been given by the evangelists.   They speak of themselves and their companions, with the same candour which characterizes their narrative in regard to others. They describe in the most artless manner, the lowness of their origin, the meanness of their occupation, the grossness of their ignorance, the inveteracy of their prejudices, their childish contentions for superiority, their cowardice in the hour of danger, the fatal apostacy of one, and the temporary delinquency of another of their number.   If any person supposes that it is an easy thing to write as the evangelists have done, he must have attended very little to the subject.   It cannot be imitated even now when the model is fully before us.   That these unlearned men should be able to write books at all with propriety, is wonderful.   Few fishermen or mechanics, confined all their lives to laborious occupations and untutored in the art of composition, could produce, without committing great faults, a narrative of their own lives.   But that men of such an education should possess such self-command and self-denial, as is manifest in these compositions, cannot be accounted for on common principles.

That, however, which deserves our special atten tion, is the absence of all appearance of ill-design.   I should like to ask a candid infidel to point out in the gospel, some fact or speech, which in the remotest degree tends to prove that the writers had a bad end in view.   I need not say that he could find nothing of the kind.   Then upon his hypothesis, we have this extraordinary fact, that four books, written by impostors who have imposed on the world a series of falsehoods, do in no part of them betray the least appearance of ill design or sinister purpose.   Certainly no otner books written by deceivers possess tｈe same characteristics.

We havｅ some instances of men of learning and piety manifesting uncommon candouｉ, in the accounts which they have left of their own eｉrors, prejudices, and faults; but in all of them you perceive the semblance, if not reality, of human frailty. These works, however, are very valuable. Some eminent infidels also have come forward before the world, with CONFESSIONS and narratives of their lives, and even of their secret crimes. None has made himself more conspicuous in this way than J. J. Rousseau, who professes to exhibit to the world a full confession of his faults, during a period of many years. And to do him justice, he has exposed to view moral turpitude enough to make, if it were possible, a demon blush. But this infatuated man gloried in his shame, and declared it to be his purpose, when called before the tribunal of heaven, to appear with his book in hand and present it to his judge as his confession and apology. Through the transparent covering of affectation, we may observe the most disgusting pride and arrogance. While common sense and decency are outraged by a needless confession of deeds which ought not to be once named, he is so far from exhibiting any thing of the character of a true penitent, that he rather appears as ｈe shameless apologist of vice. By his unreserved ｄisclosures he aspired to a new sort of reputation and glory. Perhaps there is not, in any language, a composition more strongly marked with pride and presumption. His confessions were manifestly made in a confidence of the corruption of mankind, from whom he expecｔed much applause for his candour, and small censure for his vices; but as he has appealed to another tribunal, we may be permitted to doubt whether he will there find as much applause, and as slight condemnation, as he affected to expect. Between such impious confessions as these, and the simple, humble, and sober statements of the evangelists, there can be no comparison.

There is only one thing in the style of the apostles, which I wish to bring into view. In all the detailed narratives which they have given of Jesus Christ, no allusion is ever made to his personal appearance. We are as much unacquainted with his stature, his aspect, his complexion, his gait and manner, as if the gospel had never been written. There is profound wisdom in this silence; yet I doubt whether any writers, following merely the impulse of their own feelings, would have avoided every allusion to this subject.

V. There is no just ground of objection to the testimony on account of the paucity of the witnesses. In regard to most facts handed down to us by authentic history, it is seldom that we have more than two or three historians testifying the same things; and in many cases we receive the testimony of one as sufficient, if all the circumstances of the fact corroborate his narrative. But here we have four distinct and independent witnesses. who were perfectly acquainted with the fact which they relate. Two of these, Matthew and John, were of the number of the twelve who accompanied Jesus wherever he went, and saw from day to day the works which he performed. Mark and Luke might also have been eye-witnesses. Many think that they were of the number of the seventy disciples sent out by Christ to preach; but even if they were not, they may have been his followers, and often present in Jerusalem and other places where he performed his miracles. It is not necessary, however, to resort to either of these suppositions. They were contemporaries, early disciples, constant companions of the apostles, and travelled much among the churches. Mark was at first the companion of Paul and Barnabas, and afterwards attached himself to Peter, from whose preaching, according to the universal tradition of the early Fathers, he composed his gospel. Luke was chosen by the churches in Asia to accompany Paul in his labours, and was almost constantly with him until his first imprisonment at Rome; at which time his history of he life and labours of that apostle terminates.

Besides these four evangelists, who have professedly written an account of the miracles of Jesus Christ, we have the incidental testimony of those apostles who wrote the epistles, especially of Paul. It is true, Paul was not one of the twelve apostles who accompanied Christ on earth, but he became an apostle under circumstances which rendered his testimony as strong as that of any other witness. He informs us that he was met by Jesus near to Damascus, when he was " breathing out threatening and slaughter" against the disciples of Christ; that he appeared to him in the midst of a resplendent light, and spoke to him. From that moment he became his devoted follower, and the most laborious and successful preacher of the gospel. He abandoned the most flattering worldly prospects which any young man in the Jewish nation could have. He possessed genius, learning, an unblemished character for religion and morality; was in high favour with the chief men of his nation, and seems to have been more zealous than any other individual to extirpate Christianity. How can it be accounted for, that he should suddenly become a Christian, unless he did indeed see the risen Jesus? Instead of bright worldly prospects which he had before, he was now subjected to persecution and contempt wherever he went. The catalogue of only a part of his sufferings, which he gives in one of his epistles, is enough to appal the stoutest heart; yet he never repented of his becoming a Christian, but continued to devote all his energies to the promotion of the gospel as long as he lived This change, in a person of Paul's character and prospects, will never be accounted for upon the supposition of imposture or enthusiasm.* Here, then, we can produce what deists often demand, the testimony of an enemy; not of one who was unconvinced by the evidence of Christianity, which would

---

* See Lord Lyttleton's Conversion of Paul.

ne an inconsistent testimony and liable to great ob
jections; but of one whose mind had been long in
flamed with zeal against Christianity; and yet by the
force of evidence was converted to be a zealous disciple, and retained all his life a deep and unwavering
conviction of the truth of the gospel.* This man,
although he has not written a gospel, has given
repeated testimonies to the truth of the leading facts
which are now in question. He is especially one of
the best witnesses on the subject of the resurrection
of Christ; for he not only saw and conversed with
Jesus after his ascension, but has informed us of some
circumstances of great importance not mentioned by
any of the evangelists. He asserts that Christ was
seen by five hundred persons at one time, most of
whom were still living when he wrote. If there had
been any falsehood in this declaration, how soon
must it have been detected! His letters, no doubt,
were immediately transcribed and conveyed to every
part of the church; and how easy would it have been
to prove the falsehood of such a declaration, if it had
not been a fact! But almost every page of Paul's
writings recognises as true the resurrection of Jesus
Christ. It is constantly assumed as a truth most
assuredly believed by all Christians. It is the great
motive to exertion and source of consolation, in all
his epistles. And when he would convince certain
heretics of the absurdity of denying the resurrection
of the body, he reduces them to this conclusion, that
" if the dead rise not, then is Christ not risen," which
would be at once to subvert the Christian religion.
His appeal to the common assured belief of Christians
is remarkably strong and pertinent to our purpose:
" If," says he, " Christ be not risen, then is our preaching vain, and your faith is also vain. Yea, and we

* There is a remarkable testimony to the extraordinary character
and works of Jesus Christ, in Josephus, which has been rejected as
spurious by modern critics; not for want of external evidence, for it
is found in all the oldest and best manuscripts, but principally because it is conceived that Josephus, being a Jew and a Pharisee,
never could have given such a testimony in favour of one in whom
he did not believe.

are found false witnesses of God; because we have testified of God that he raised up Christ, whom he raised not up, if so be that the dead rise not." Would any man in his senses have written thus, if the resurrection of Christ had not been a fundamental article of faith among Christians, or if he had not been fully persuaded of its truth? Had Paul been an impostor, would he have dared to appeal to five hundred persons, most of whom were living, for the truth of what he knew to be false? How easy and how certain must have been the detection of an imposture thus conducted!

The same is evident from the epistles of the other apostles, and from the Apocalypse.

Now, when we can clearly ascertain what any persons believed in relation to a fact, we have virtually their testimony to that fact; because, when they come forward and give testimony explicitly, they do no more than express the conviction of their own minds. Certainly, then, if we can, by any means, ascertain what the primitive Christians believed in regard to the resurrection of Christ and other miraculous facts, we are in possession of all the testimony which they could give.* This is an important point as it relates to the number of witnesses. Now, that all Christians, from the beginning, did believe in the facts recorded in the gospels and epistles of the apostles, we have the strongest possible evidence. It is proved incontestably from the fact of their becoming Christians; for how could they be Christians without faith in Christianity? unless any one will be so extravagant as to believe, that not only the apostles, but all their converts, were wilful deceivers. It is proved also from the manner in which Christians are addressed by the apostles in all their epistles. Suppose, for a moment, that the Corinthian Church had no belief in the resurrection of Christ, when they received the above mentioned epistle from Paul, would they not have considered him perfectly insane? But the universal reception of the gospels

* See Dr. Channing's Dudleian Lecture.

and epistles, by all Christian churches throughout
the world, is the best possible evidence that they
believed what they contained. These books were
adopted as the creed and guide of all Christians.
It is manifest, therefore, that we are in possession of
the testimony of the whole primitive church, to the
truth of the miracles recorded in the gospels. Suppose a document had come down to us, containing a
profession of the belief of every person who embraced
the Christian religion, and a solemn attestation to
the facts on which Christianity is founded, would
any man object that the witnesses were too few?
The fact is, that we have substantially this whole
body of testimony. I do not perceive, that its force
would have been sensibly greater had it been transmitted to us with all the formalities just mentioned.
There is, therefore, no defect in the number of witnesses. If every one of the twelve apostles had
written a gospel, and a hundred other persons had
done the same, the evidence would not be essentially
improved. We should have no more, after all, than
the testimony of the whole primitive church, which,
as has been proved, we possess already.

VI. The credibility of the testimony is not im-
paired by any want of agreement among the witnesses. In their attestation to the leading facts and
to the doctrines and character of Christ, they are perfectly harmonious. The selection of facts by the
several evangelists is different, and the same fact is
sometimes related more circumstantially by one than
another; but there is no inconsistency between them.
In their general character and prominent features,
there is a beautiful harmony in the gospels. There
is no difference which can effect, in the judgment of
the impartial, the credibility of the testimony which
they contain. If all the evangelists had recorded
precisely the same facts, and all the circumstances in
the same order, the gospels, would appear to have
been written in concert, which would weaken their
testimony. But it is almost demonstrable, from internal evidence, that the evangelists, with the excep-

tion of John, never had seen each other's productions before they wrote. Their agreement therefore ought to have the effect of witnesses examined apart from each other; and their discrepancies serve to prove that there could be no concerted scheme to deceive; for in that case every appearance of this kind would have been carefully removed.

I am aware, that on the ground of supposed contradictions or irreconcilable discrepancies, the most formidable attacks have been made on Christianity. It is entirely incompatible with the narrow limits of this essay to enter into a consideration of the various methods which have been adopted for harmonizing the gospels, and removing the difficulties which arise from their variations. I can only make a few general observations, with the view of leading the reader to the proper principles of solution.

It ought to be kept in mind, that the gospels were written almost two thousand years ago, in a language not now spoken, and in a remote country, whose manners and customs were very different from ours. In all such cases, there will be obscurities and difficulties, arising entirely from the imperfection of our knowledge.

The gospels do not purport to be regular histories of events, arranged in exact, chronological order, but a selection of important facts out of a much greater number left unnoticed. The time when, or the place where, these facts occurred, is of no consequence to the end contemplated by the evangelists. In their narratives, therefore, they have sometimes pursued the order of time; in other cases, the arrangement has been suggested by the subject previously treated, or by some other circumstance.

In recording a miracle, the number of persons benefited is not of much consequence; the miracle is the same, whether sight be restored to one person or two: or whether demons be expelled from one or many. If one historian, intent on recording the extraordinary fact, selects the case of one person, which might in some respects be more remarkable, and

10

another mentions two. there is no contradiction. Ii they professed to give an accurate account of the number healed, there would be ground for this objection; but this was no part of the design of the evangelists.

If a writer, in order to exhibit the skill of an oculist, should mention a remarkable instance of sight being restored to a person who had been long blind, it could not be fairly inferred from the narrative that no person received the same benefit at that time; an'ı if another person should give a distinct account of all the cases, there would be no contradiction between these witnesses. All the difference is, that one selects a prominent fact out of many; the other descends to all particulars.

There is no source of difficulty more usual than the confounding of things which are distinct. The narratives of events truly distinct may have so striking a similarity, that the cursory reader will be apt to confound them. It has been remarked that if the two miracles of feeding the multitude had been mentioned by two different evangelists, each giving an account of one case, it would have been supposed by many that they were accounts of the same occurrence, and that the evangelists did not agree in their testimony; but in this case, both these miracles are distinctly related by the same evangelist, and distinctly referred to by Christ in his conversation with his disciples. This confounding of distinct things is never more commonly done, than when a fact was attended with a great number of circumstances and occurrences, rapidly succeeding each other, and the historian mentions only a few out of many. This remark is fully verified with respect to Christ's resurrection. The narrative of all the evangelists is very concise. Few particulars are mentioned; and yet from the nature of the case, there must have been an extraordinary degree of agitation among the disciples; a great running from one part of Jerusalem to another, to tell the news; and a frequent passing to and from the sepulchre. It is not wonderful, therefore, that, as each evangelist mentions only a few of the accompanying occurrences, there should seem, at first view, to be some discrepancy in their accounts. Companies of women are mentioned by each, and it is hastily taken for granted that they were all the same; and the obje.tor proceeds on the supposition, that these women all arrived at the sepulchre at the same time, and that they continued together. He forgets to take into view, that the persons who might agree to meet at the sepulchre, probably lodged at very different distances from the place, and allows nothing for the agitation and distraction produced by the reports and visions of this interesting morning. But on this, as on several other subjects, we are indebted to the enemies of revelation for being the occasion of bringing forward able men, who have shed so much light on this part of the gospel history, that even the appearance of discrepancy is entirely removed.*

The genealogy of Jesus Christ, as given by Matthew and Luke, has furnished to modern infidels much occasion of cavil; but it ought to be sufficient to silence these objectors that the early enemies of Christianity made no objections on this ground. If one of these is the genealogy of Joseph and the other of Mary, there will be no discrepancy between them. Why it was proper to give the descent of Joseph the husband of Mary, it is not now necessary to inquire. But on this whole subject I would remark, that we are very little acquainted with the plan on which genealogical tables were constructed. It seems to have been a very intricate business, and it is not surprising that we should be at a loss to elucidate every difficulty. Again, it is highly probable that these lists were taken from some genealogical tables of the tribe and family of the persons to whom they refer. Every family must have had access to such tables, on account of their inheritance. Public tables of acknowledged authority would be far better for

---

* See West on the Resurrection; Townson; Macknight; Ditton Sherlock, &c.

the purpose which the evangelists had in view than new ones, even though these should have been more full and accurate. These genealogies had no other object than to prove that Jesus of Nazareth was a lineal descendant of David and Abraham; which purpose is completely answered by them: and there are no difficulties which may not be accounted for by our ignorance of the subject.

Finally, it may be admitted that some slight inaccuracies have crept into the copies of the New Testament, through the carelessness of transcribers. It is impossible for men to write the whole of a book without making some mistakes; and if there be some small discrepancies in the gospels with respect to names and numbers, they ought to be attributed to this cause.

VII. The witnesses of the miracles of Christ could have had no conceivable motive for propagating an imposture. That they were not themselves deceived is manifest from the nature of the facts, and from the full opportunity which they had of examining them. It is evident, therefore, that if the miracles recorded by them never existed, they were wilful impostors. They must have wickedly combined to impose upon the world. But what motives could have influenced them to pursue such a course we cannot imagine; or how men of low condition and small education should have ever conceived it possible to deceive the world in such a case is equally inconceivable. These men had worldly interests which it was natural for them to regard: but every thing of this kind was fully relinquished. They engaged in an enterprise not only dangerous, but attended with certain and immediate ruin to all their worldly interests. They exposed themselves to the indignation of all authority, and to the outrageous fury of the multitude. They must have foreseen, that they would bring down upon themselves the vengeance of the civil and ecclesiastical powers, and that every species of suffering awaited them. Their leader was crucified, and what could they expect from declaring that he was alive.

ar.d had performed wonderful miracles? If they could have entertained ar y hopes of exemption from evils so apparent, expe1 ence must soon have convinced them that they had engaged not only in a wicked, but most unprofitable undertaking. It was not long after they began their testimony, before they were obliged to endure unrelenting persecution from Jews and Gentiles. Could they have been influenced by a regard to fame? What renown could they expect from proclaiming a crucified man to be their master, and the ground of all their hope and confidence? If this was their object, why did they give all the glory to another who was dead? But the fact is that instead of fame they met with infamy. No name was ever more derided and hated than that of *Christian.* They were vilified as the most contemptible miscreants that ever lived, as the refuse and offscouring of all things, as the pests and disturbers of society, and the enemies of the gods. They were pursued as outlaws, and punished for no other reason but because they acknowledged themselves to be Christians. Would men persevere in propagating an imposture for such fame as this? It cannot be supposed that they expected their compensation in another world; for the supposition is that they were wilful impostors, who were every day asserting, in the most solemn manner, what they knew to be false. It would be just as reasonable to suppose that the murderer or highway robber is influenced in the commission of his atrocious crimes, by the hope of a future reward.

The only alternative is to suppose that they were fanatics, as it is known that men under the government of enthusiasm contemn all the common considerations which usually influence human conduct, and often act in a way totally unaccountable. This representation of enthusiasm is just, but it will not answer the purpose for which it is adduced. Enthusiasts are always strongly persuaded of the truth of the religion which they wish to propagate; but these men, upon the hypothesis under consideration, knew that all

which they said was false.   Enthusiasm and impos
ture are irreconcilable.   It is true that what begins in
enthusiasm may end in imposture; but in this case
the imposture must have been the beginning, as well
as the end, of the whole business.   There was no
room for enthusiasm; all was imposture, if the facts
reported were not true.   But the best evidence that
the evangelists were not fanatics, is derived from
their writings.   These are at the greatest remove
from the ravings or reveries of enthusiasm.   They
are the most simple, grave, and dispassionate narra
tives that ever were written.   The writers are actuated by no phrensy; they give no indication of a
heated imagination; they speak uniformly the lan
guage of "truth and soberness."

VIII. But if we could persuade ourselves, that the
apostles might have been actuated by some unknown
and inconceivable motive, to forge the whole account
of Christ's miracles, and were impelled by some unaccountable phrensy to persevere through all difficulties and sufferings to propagate lies; can we believe
that they could have found followers in the very
country, and in the very city, where the miracles
were stated to have been performed?

When these accounts of stupendous and numerous miracles were published in Jerusalem, where the
apostles began their testimony, what would the people think?   Would they not say, " These men bring
strange things to our ears.   They tell us of wonders
wrought among us, of which we have never before
heard.   And they would not only have us to believe
their incredible story, but forsake all that we have,
abandon our friends, and relinquish the religion of
our forefathers, received from God: and not only so,
but bring upon ourselves and families the vengeance
of those that rule over us, and the hatred and reproach
of all men."   Is it possible to believe that one sane
person would have received their report?

Besides, the priests and rulers who had put Jesus
to death, were deeply interested to prevent the circulation of such a story; it implicated them in a hor-

rid crime. Would they not have exerted themselves
to lay open the forgery, and would there have been
the least difficulty in accomplishing the object, if the
testimony of these witnesses had been false? The
places of many of the miracles are recorded, and the
names of the persons healed or raised from the dead,
are mentioned. It was only one or two miles to the
dwelling of Lazarus; how easy would it have been
to prove that the story of his resurrection was a falsehood, had it not been a fact! Jerusalem, and indeed
the temple itself, were the scenes of many of the miracles ascribed to Christ. As he spent much time in
that city, it is presumable that not a person residing
there could have been totally ignorant of facts which
must have occupied the attention and excited the
curiosity of the public. An imposture like this could
never be successful in such circumstances. The presence of an interested, inimical, and powerful body
of men, would soon have put down every attempt at
an imposition so gross and groundless. If the apostles had pretended that at some remote period, or in
some remote country, a man had performed miracles,
they might have persuaded some weak and credulous persons; but they appealed to the people to
whom they preached, as the witnesses of what they
related. No more than a few weeks had elapsed
after the death of Jesus, before this testimony was
published in Jerusalem: and notwithstanding all the
opposition of those in authority, it was received, and
multitudes willingly offered themselves as the disciples of him whom they had recently crucified.

IX. The last particular which I shall mention, to
set the testimony of the witnesses to the miracles of
the gospel in its true light, is that there is no counter
testimony. These witnesses have never been con-
fronted and contradicted by others. Whatever force
or probability their declarations are entitled to, from
the circumstances of the case and from the evidences
which we possess of their integrity and intelligence,
suffers no deduction on account of other persons
giving a different testimony.

The Jewish priests and rulers did indeed cause a story to be circulated relative to the dead body of Christ, contrary to the testimony of the apostles which has been handed down to us by the evangelists. They hired the soldiers to report that Christ's disciples had come by night and stolen the body while they slept, a story too absurd and inconsistent to require a moment's refutation. But as the body was gone out of their possession, they could not perhaps have invented any thing more plausible. It proved nothing, however, except that the body was removed while the soldiers slept, and for aught they could testify, might have risen from the dead, according to the testimony of the apostles.

Deists sometimes demand the testimony of the enemies as well as the friends of Christianity. To which I would reply, that the silence of enemies is all that can reasonably be expected from them. That they should come forward voluntarily with testimony in favour of a religion which, through prejudice or worldly policy, they opposed, could not reasonably be expected. Since they would have contradicted these facts if it had been in their power, their not doing so furnishes the strongest negative evidence which we can possess. And no other evidence than that which is negative or merely incidental, ought to be expected from the enemies of the gospel; unless, like Paul, they were convinced by the evidence exhibited to them. But no denial of the reality of the miracles of Christ has reached us from any quarter. As far as we have any accounts, there is no reason to think that they were ever denied by his most implacable enemies; they said that he performed his works by help of Beelzebub. The first heathen writers against Christianity did not dare to deny Christ's miracles. Neither Celsus, Porphyry, Hierocles, nor Julian, pretend that these facts were entirely false, for they attempted to account for them. The Jewish rabbies, in the Talmud, acknowledge these miracles, and pretend that they we e wrought by magic, or by the power of the venerab e name of JEHOVAH, called *tetragrammaton*, which they ridiculously pretended that Jesus stole out of the temple, and by which they say he performed his wonderful works.

From what has been said, I trust it is sufficiently manifest that we have such testimony for the miracles of the New Testament, as will render them credible in the view of all impartial persons. We have shown that the miracles recorded are *real* miracles; that they were performed in an open and public manner; that the witnesses could not possibly have been deceived themselves; that enemies had every opportunity and motive for disproving the facts, if they had not been true; that there is every evidence of sincerity and honesty in the evangelists; that the epistles of the apostles furnish strong collateral proof of the same facts; that all Christians from the beginning must have believed in these miracles, and they must therefore be considered competent witnesses; that none of the witnesses could have any motive to deceive; that they never could have succeeded in imposing such a fraud on the world, even if they could have attempted it; that it would have been the easiest thing in the world for the Jewish rulers to have silenced such reports if they had been false; that the commencement of preaching at Jerusalem, and the success of Christianity there, cannot be accounted for on any other supposition than the truth of the miracles; that the conduct of the apostles in going to the most enlightened countries and cities, and their success in those places, can never be reconciled with the idea that they were ignorant impostors; and finally, that no contrary evidence exists, but that even the early enemies of Christianity have been obliged to admit that such miracles were performed.

When all these things are fairly and fully considered, is it not more probable that miracles were performed, than that such a body of testimony, so corroborated by circumstances, and by effects, reaching to our own times, should be false?

If all this testimony is false, we may call in ques

tion all historical testimony whatever; for what facts have ever been so fully attested?

But why should this testimony be rejected? No reason has ever been assigned, except that the facts were miraculous: but we have shown that it is not unreasonable to expect miracles in such a case, and that miracles are capable of satisfactory proof from testimony. It is, therefore, a just conclusion, that THE MIRACLES OF THE GOSPEL ARE CREDIBLE.

CHAPTER VIII.

THE RAPID AND EXTENSIVE PROGRESS OF THE GOSPEL, BY INSTRUMENTS SO FEW AND FEEBLE, IS A PROOF OF DIVINE INTERPOSITION.

THE success of the gospel, under the circumstances of its first publication, is one of the most wonderful events recorded in history; and it is a fact beyond all dispute. In a little time, thousands of persons embraced the Christian religion in Jerusalem, and in other parts of Judea. In heathen countries its success was still more astonishing. Churches were planted in all the principal cities of the Roman Empire, before half a century had elapsed from the resurrection of Christ. The fires of persecution raged; thousands and tens of thousands of unoffending Christians were put to death, in a cruel manner; yet this cause seemed to prosper the more, so that it became a proverb, that "the blood of the martyrs was the seed of the Church." And it went on increasing and prevailing, until in less than three centuries, it became the religion of the empire.

That the Christian religion did actually prevail and was widely extended within a short period after its first publication, is matter of undoubted history. The testimony confirming this fact is not derived merely from the authority of Christian writers however nu merous, but also from that of the most respectable heathen historians. TACITUS, SUETONIUS, and PLINY have all borne witness to the fact, that Christianity was extensively prevalent in their day; and as such impartial witnesses who did not believe in Christianity but held it in abhorrence, is of great weight in establishing this fact, and it may not be easily accessible to the reader, a translation of their words is here subjoined.

TACITUS lived during the first century of the Christian era; and his high character as an historian is known to all. After describing the destructive fire which desolated Rome, he proceeds thus: "But neither by human aid, nor by the costly largesses by which he attempted to propitiate the gods, was the prince able to remove from himself the infamy which had attached to him in the opinion of all, for having ordered the conflagration. To suppress this rumour, therefore, Nero caused others to be accused, on whom he inflicted exquisite torments, who were already hated by the people for their crimes, and were vulgarly denominated CHRISTIANS. This name they derived from CHRIST their leader, who in the reign of TIBERIUS was put to death as a criminal, while PONTIUS PILATE was procurator. This destructive superstition, repressed for a while, again broke out, and spread not only through Judea where it originated, but reached this city also, into which flow all things that are vile and abominable, and where they are encouraged. At first, they only were seized who confessed that they belonged to this sect, and afterwards, a vast multitude, by the information of those who were condemned, not so much for the crime of burning the city, as for hatred of the human race. These, clothed in the skins of wild beasts, were exposed to derision, and were either torn to pieces by dogs, or were affixed to crosses: or when the daylight was past, were set on fire, that they might serve instead of lamps for the night."

SUETONIUS also lived in the first century, but his life extended into the second. His character as a well informed and correct historian is also high. His testimony is as follows: "He [Claudius] banished the Jews from Rome who were continually raising disturbances, Christ (Chrestus) being their leader." And in the life of Nero, he says, "The Christians were punished, a sort of men of a new and magical religion." But the fact which we wish to establish is, perhaps, more fully confirmed by the testimony of PLINY THE YOUNGER, than by any other Roman writer. It is contained in a letter addressed by this distinguished philosopher to the emperor TRAJAN, in the beginning of the second century. " Pliny, to the emperor Trajan, wisheth health, &c. It is my custom, Sir, to refer all things to you of which I entertain any doubt; for who can better direct me in my hesitation or instruct my ignorance? I was never before present at any of the trials of the Christians; so that I am ignorant both of the matter to be inquired into, and of the nature of the punishment which should be inflicted, and to what length the investigation is to be extended. I have, moreover, been in great uncertainty whether any difference ought to be made on account of age, between the young and tender, and the robust; and also whether any place should be allowed for repentance and pardon; or whether those who have once been Christians should be punished, although they have now ceased to be such, and whether punishment should be inflicted merely on account of the name, where no crimes are charged, or whether crimes connected with the name are the proper object of punishment. This, however, is the method which I have pursued in regard to those who were brought before me as Christians. I interrogated them whether they were Christians ; and upon their confessing that they were, I put the question to them a second, and a third time, threatening them with capital punishment; and when they persisted in their confession, I ordered them to be led away to execution; for whatever might be the nature f their crime, I could not doubt that perverseness and inflexible obstinacy deserve to be punished

There were others, addicted to the same insanity, whom, because they were Roman citizens, I have noted down to be sent to the city. In a short space, the crime diffusing itself, as is common, a great variety of cases have fallen under my cognizance An anonymous libel was exhibited to me, containing the names of many persons who denied that they were Christians or ever had been: and as an evidence of their sincerity, they joined me in an address to the gods, and to your image, which I had ordered to be brought along with the images of the gods for this very purpose. Moreover, they sacrificed with wine and frankincense, and blasphemed the name of Christ : none of which things can those who are really Christians be constrained to do. Therefore I judged it proper to dismiss them. Others, named by the informer, at first confessed themselves to be Christians, and afterwards denied it ; and some asserted that although they had been Christians, they had ceased to be such for more than three years, and some as much as twenty years. All these worshipped your image and the statues of the gods, and execrated Christ. But they affirmed that this was the sum of their fault or error, that they were accustomed, on a stated day, to meet together before day, to sing a hymn to Christ in concert, as to a God, and to bind themselves by a solemn oath not to commit any wickedness—but on the contrary, to abstain from theft, robbery, and adultery—also, never to violate their promise, nor deny a pledge committed to them. These things being performed, it was their custom to separate ; and to meet again at a promiscuous, innocent meal; which, however, they had omitted, from the time of the publication of my edict, by which, according to your orders, I forbad assemblies of this sort. On receiving this account, I judged it to be more necessary to examine by torture, two females, who were called deaconesses. But I discovered nothing except a depraved and immoderate superstition. Whereupon, suspending further judicial proceedings, I have recourse to you for advice; for it has appeared to me that the subject is highly deserving of conside ration, especially on account of the great number of persons whose lives are put into jeopardy. Many persons of all ages, sexes, and conditions are accused, and many more will be in the same situation; for the contagion of this superstition has not merely pervaded the cities, but also all villages and country places; yet it seems to me that it might be restrained and corrected. It is a matter of fact, that the temples which were almost deserted begin again to be frequented; and the sacred solemnities which had been long intermitted are again attended; and victims for the altars are now readily sold, which, a while ago, were almost without purchasers. Whence it is easy to conjecture what a multitude of men might be reclaimed, if only the door to repentance was left open.''

To which the emperor replied as follows:—" Trajan to Pliny—Health and happiness.

" You have taken the right method, my Pliny, in dealing with those who have been brought before you as Christians; for it is impossible to establish any universal rule which will apply to all cases. They should not be sought after; but when they are brought before you and convicted, they must be punished. Nevertheless, if any one deny that he is a Christian, and confirm his assertion by his conduct; that is, by worshipping our gods, although he may be suspected of having been one in time past, let him obtain pardon on repentance. But in no case permit a libel against any one to be received, unless it be signed by the person who presents it, for that would be a dangerous precedent, and in no wise suitable to the present age.''

Other heathen testimonies might be adduced, and which may be seen in " Lardner's heathen testimonies;'' but for the sake of brevity they are omitted. And the testimonies of the two Christian fathers— IRENÆUS and TERTULITAN, who both lived at the close of the second, and beginning of the third century, will be sufficient to show, beyond all controversy, how extensively the Christian religion prevailed in their day.

Irenæus, speaking of the uniformity of the faith of Christians, says, " Neither do those churches which are established among the Germans believe or teach otherwise; nor do those among the *Hiberii* or the *Celts;* nor those in the *East*, nor those in *Egypt*, nor those in Libya. nor those established in the central parts of the world."*

The language of Tertullian is still more to our purpose, and nothing further will be needed in the way of testimony, to show the extent of Christianity in less than one century after the death of the last of the apostles. " In whom," says he, " but the Christ now come, have all nations believed? for in whom do all other nations (but yours, the Jews) confide? Parthians, Medes, Elamites, and the dwellers in Mesopotamia, Armenia, Phrygia, Cappadocia, and the inhabitants of Pontus, Asia, and Pamphylia; the dwellers in Egypt, and inhabitants of Africa beyond Cyrene; Romans and strangers; and in Jerusalem, both Jews and proselytes;—so that the various tribes of the Getuli, and the numerous hordes of the Mauri; all the Spanish clans and different nations of Gauls, and the provinces of the Britons inaccessible to the Romans, but subdued by Christ—and of the Samaritans and Dacians, and Germans, and Scythians: and many unexplored nations, and countries, and islands unknown to us, and which we cannot enumerate—in all which places the name of the CHRIST who has come, now reigns; for who could reign over all these but Christ, the Son of God?"†

There is another testimony of this father, in his APOLOGY, which was written a little before the close of the second century; and seems to have been addressed to the Proconsul of Africa, and to the other præfects of that province, of which he was an inhabitant. He there speaks in the following manner:— " If we Christians were disposed to array ourselves

* Iren. Adv. Hær. 1. 1, c. X.
† Tertullian Contra Jadæos. cap. 7.

as open r secret enemies of our opposers, a sufficier
force of numbers is not wanting to us. Many of the
Moors and Marcomanni, as well as other tribes more
remote, even to the very ends of the earth, and
throughout the world, are with us. We are but of
yesterday, and yet we have filled all your places·
your cities, your islands, your castles, your towns
your council houses, your very camps, your tribes
your palace, your senate, your forum. We have left
you nothing but your temples. If we should break
away from you and should remove into some other
country, the mere loss of so many citizens would
overwhelm your government; and would itself be
an effectual punishment. Doubtless you would be
frightened at your own solitude. The silence and
stupor which you would witness, would cause the
world over which you reign to appear as dead.
Your enemies would then be more than your citizens
who should remain."* It will be unnecessary to
adduce more testimonies, for the fact is undisputed·
and in a short time the majority of the empire were
professedly Christians.

Learned infidels have in vain attempted to assigr
an adequate cause for this event on natural principles. Gibbon exerted all his ingenuity to account for
the progress and establishment of Christianity; but
though he, has freely indulged conjecture, and disregarded the testimony of Christians, his efforts have
been unavailing. The account which he has given
is entirely unsatisfactory. Upon the deistical hypothesis, it is a grand revolution without any adequate
cause. That a few unlearned and simple men, most-
ly fishermen of Galilee, without power or patronage,
and employing no other weapons but persuasion,
should have been successful in changing the religion
of the world, must forever remain an unaccountable
thing, unless we admit the reality of miracles and
supernatural aid.

The argument from the rapid and exter sive pro

---

* Tertull Apologeticus.

gress of the gospel may be estimated, if we consider the following circumstances.

1. The insufficiency of the instruments to accomplish such a work without supernatural aid. They had neither the learning nor address to make such an impression on the minds of men, as was requisite to bring about such a revolution. It would have been impracticable for a few unlettered Jews to acquire the languages of all the nations, among whom the gospel spread in so short a time. They must have had the gift of tongues, or this conquest could never have been achieved. Besides, it ought to be remembered, that Jews were held in great contempt by all the surrounding nations. A few persons of this nation, exhibiting a very mean appearance, as must have been the case, would have called forth nothing but derision and contempt, in any of the large cities of the empire. It is more unlikely that they could have been able to make many converts, than that a few poor Jewish mechanics should now proselyte to Judaism vast multitudes in all the principal cities of Europe and America.*

2. The places in which the gospel was first preached and had greatest success, furnish proof that it could not have been propagated merely by human means. These were not obscure corners, remote from the lights of science, but the most populous and polished cities, where every species of the learning of the age was concentrated, and whither men of learning resorted. Damascus, Antioch, Ephesus, Corinth, Philippi and Rome furnished the theatre for the first preachers of the gospel. It is believed, that there was no conspicuous city in the central part of the Roman empire, in which the Christian church was not planted before the death of the apostles. And it ought to be remembered, that this did not occur in a dark age, but in what is acknowledged by all to be the most enlightened age of antiquity: it was the period which immediately succeeded the AUGUSTAM

* See Dr S. S. Smith's Lectures on the Evidences of Christianity

AGE, so much and so deservedly celebrated for its classical authors. If the gospel had been an imposture, its propagators would never have gone to such places in the first instance; or, if they had, they could not have escaped detection.

3. The obstacles to be overcome were great, and insurmountable by human effort. The people were all attached to the respective superstitions in which they had been educated, and which were all adapted to retain their hold on corrupt minds. How difficult it is to obtain even a hearing from the people in such circumstances, is manifest from the experience of all missionaries in modern times. Philosophers, priests, and rulers, were combined against them. All that learning, eloquence, prejudice, interest, and power, could oppose to them, stood in their way.

Not only were priests, philosophers, and rulers combined against them, but the prejudices of the multitude in favour of the corrupt religion in which they had been educated, inspired them with a furious zeal in opposition to all attempts to convert them from their errors. In the Acts of the Apostles, we have many instances recorded of the blind fury of the people leading them to acts of outrage and violence towards the first preachers of the gospel, both among Jews and Gentiles. In one of these tumults, Stephen was martyred; and in another, which took place in the temple, Paul had like to have been torn to pieces by the violence of the people. And at Ephesus, we know what a tumult was excited by Demetrius the silversmith; and at several other places. But it appears that only a few of these tumults which extended to personal violence, are recorded in the ACTS, for Paul in his second epistle to the Corinthians writes thus:—" Of the Jews five times received I forty stripes save one. Three times was I beaten with rods—once was I stoned." And it is probable that all the apostles and primitive preachers experienced similar treatment; and had they not been divinely supported and aided, they would never have been able to withstand such infuriated opposition;

much less could they have brought over thousands
and tens of thousands to subject themselves to the
yoke of Christ, and expose themselves to the same
ignominy and persecution to which they were continually exposed themselves.

4. The terms of discipleship which the apostles
proposed, and the doctrines which they preached,
were not adapted to allure and flatter the people,
but must have been very repulsive to the minds of
men. Impostors, when they attempt to propagate
a new religion, always endeavour to adapt their doctrines and precepts to the tastes of the people whom
they aim to proselyte. But the author of Christianity
and his apostles pursued no such man-pleasing course.
Their first requisition was that men should deny
themselves, and take up their cross. Their hearers
were commanded to repent and forsake all their sins,
however profitable, pleasant, or inveterate. They
were peremptorily required to forsake all their worldly possessions, and even their nearest and dearest
friends, for the sake of the gospel. And this was not
all; they were explicitly told, that they must hold
themselves ready to sacrifice life itself when they
could not preserve it without disobeying Christ. And
no prospect of ease or honour in this world was held
out to them, but they were assured. that persecution
awaited them as long as they lived, and that through
much tribulation they must pass; and that their only
reward was spiritual peace, and eternal life in the
world to come. Would any impostors have been so
stupid as to propose such terms, or if they could have
been so foolish, can any one believe that they would
have been successful in converting the world to embrace their system? Nothing more is necessary to
prove that the Christian religion was divine, than to
contemplate the terms of discipleship, and then consider the multitude of converts of all ages, ranks, and
countries. And the prospect of persecution and death,
held up to the first disciples by Christ and his apostles, was fully realized, and yet the success of Christianity was irresistible. Many Christians were cut off

by persecution, but still Christianity made progress, and was extended in all directions. Because Christianity increased and flourished under bloody persecutions, many persons have adopted it as a maxim, that persecution has a tendency to promote any cause; than which it is difficult to conceive of any thing more contrary to common sense and experience. In most cases, by cutting off the leaders of a party, however furious their fanaticism, the cause will decline and soon become extinct. The increase of Christianity, under ten bloody persecutions, can only be accounted for, by supposing that God by his grace persuaded men to embrace the truth, and inspired them with more than heroic fortitude in suffering for the sake of their religion. Many of the primitive Christians attested the truth by martyrdom. They sealed their testimony with their blood. To this argument it is sometimes answered, that men may suffer martyrdom for a false as well as a true religion, and that, in fact, men have been willing to die for opinions in direct opposition to each other. While this is admitted, it does not affect the argument now adduced. All that dying for an opinion can prove (and of this it is the best possible evidence,) is the sincerity of the witnesses. But in the case before us the sincerity of the witnesses proves the facts in question; for we have seen that they could not themselves have been deceived. Every martyr had the opportunity of knowing the truth of the facts on which Christianity was founded; and by suffering death in attestation of them, he has given the most impressive testimony that can be conceived.*

The sufferings of the primitive Christians for their religion were exceedingly great, and are attested by heathen as well as Christian writers. It is a circumstance of great importance n this argument, that they could at once have escaped all their torments by renouncing Christianity. To bring them to this was the sole object of their persecutors; and uniformly it was put to their choice, to offer sacrifice or incense

* See Addison's Evidences

to the heathen gods, or be tormented. One word would have been sufficient to deliver them; one easy action would have restored them to worldly comforts and honours. But they steadfastly adhered to their profession. Some indeed were overcome by the cruelty of their persecutors; but was it ever heard that any of them confessed that there was any fraud or imposture among them? So far from it, they whose courage had failed them in the trying hour, were commonly deep penitents on account of their weakness, all the rest of their days. Let it be remembered, that no person suffered for Christianity through necessity. Every martyr made a voluntary sacrifice of himself, to maintain the truth and to preserve a good conscience.

5. There is yet another light in which these sufferings of the primitive Christians ought to be viewed. It is the temper with which they endured every kind of torment. Here again is a problem for the deist to solve. Persons of all ages, of all conditions of life, and of both sexes, exhibited under protracted and cruel torments, a fortitude, a patience, a meekness, a spirit of charity and forgiveness, a cheerfulness, yea often a triumphant joy, of which there are no examples to be found in the history of the world. They rejoiced when they were arrested; cheerfully bade adieu to their nearest and dearest relatives; gladly embraced the stake; welcomed the wild beasts let loose to devour them; smiled on the horrible apparatus by which their sinews were to be stretched, and their bones dislocated and broken; uttered no complaints; gave no indication of pain when their bodies were enveloped in flames; and when condemned to die, begged of their friends to interpose no obstacle to their felicity (for such they esteemed martyrdom,) not even by prayers for their deliverance.* What more than human fortitude was this? By what spirit were these despised and persecuted people sustained? What natural principles in the human constitution can satisfactorily account for such

* See the Epistles of Ignatius and Polycarp.

s iperiority to pain and death? Could attachment to
a.1 impostor inspire them with such feelings? No;
it was the promised presence of the risen JESUS which
upheld them, and filled them with assurance and
joy. It was the PARACLETE, promised by their
Lord, who poured into their hearts a peace and joy
so complete, that they were scarcely sensible of the
wounds inflicted on their bodies. Proud and obsti
nate men may perhaps suffer for what they are
secretly convinced is not true; but that multitudes,
of all conditions, should joyfully suffer for what they
know to be an imposture, is imposssible. Tender
women and venerable old men were among the most
conspicuous of the martyrs of JESUS. " They loved
not their lives unto the death," and have given their
testimony and sealed it with their blood. They are
now clothed in white robes, and bear palms in their
hands, and sing the song of MOSES and the LAMB.
Blessed martyrs! they have rested from their labours
and their works have followed them!

CHAPTER IX.

PROPHECIES RESPECTING THE JEWISH NATION WHICH HAVE BEEN RE
MARKABLY FULFILLED.

THE Bible contains predictions of events which no
human sagacity could have foreseen, and these predictions have been exactly and remarkably accomplished.

The subject of prophecy is so extensive, and the
difficulty of presenting, with brevity, the argument
which it furnishes so great, that if I had not detcr-
mined to give a general outline of the evidences of
revelation, I should have omitted this topic as one to
which justice cannot be done in so short an essay.

But I would not be understood as intimating, that

the evidence from prophecy is of an inferior kind.
So far from believing this to be the fact, I am persuaded that whoever will take the pains to examine
the subject thoroughly, will find that this source of
evidence for the truth of revelation is exceeded by
no other in the firmness of conviction which it is calculated to produce. Prophecy possesses, as a proof
of divine revelation, some advantages which are
peculiar. For the proof of miracles we must have
recourse to ancient testimony; but the fulfilling of
prophecy may fall under our own observation, or
may be conveyed to us by living witnesses. The
evidence of miracles cannot, in any case, become
stronger than it was at first; but that of prophecy
is continually increasing, and will go on increasing,
until the whole scheme of predictions is fulfilled.
The mere publication of a prediction furnishes no
decisive evidence that it is a revelation from God;
it is the accomplishment which completes the proof.
As prophecies have been fulfilled in every age, and
are still in a course of being fulfilled; and as some
most remarkable predictions remain to be accomplished, it is plain, from the nature of the case, that
this proof will continue to increase in strength.

It deserves to be well weighed, that any one prediction which has been fulfilled, is of itself a complete evidence of divine revelation; or to speak more
properly, is itself a revelation. For certainly no one
but God himself can foretell distant future events,
which depend entirely on the purpose of Him " who
worketh all things after the counsel of his own will. '

If, then, we can adduce one prophecy, the accomplishment of which cannot be doubted, we have
established the principle that a revelation has been
given; and if in one instance, and to one person, the
probability is strong that he is not the only person
who has been favoured with such a communication.

The remark which is frequently made, that most
prophecies are obscure, and the meaning very uncertain, will not affect the evidence arising from such as
are perspicuous, and of which the accomplishment is

exact. There are good reasons why these future events should sometimes be wrapped up in the covering of strong figures and symbolical language; so that often the prophet himself, probably, did not understand the meaning of the prediction which he uttered. It was not intended that they should be capable of being clearly interpreted, until the key was furnished by the completion. If these observations are just, the study of the prophecies will become more and more interesting every day, and they will shed more and more light on the truth of the Scriptures.

What I shall attempt, at present, and all that is compatible with the narrow limits of this discourse, will be, to exhibit a few remarkable predictions, and refer to the events in which they have been fulfilled. They who wish for further satisfaction, will find it in the perusal of Bishop Newton's excellent Dissertations on the Prophecies, to which I acknowledge myself indebted for a considerable part of what is contained in this chapter, and to Keith on the Prophecies.

The first prophecies which I shall produce, are those of Moses respecting the Jews. They are recorded, principally, in the twenty-sixth chapter of Leviticus and in the twenty-eighth chapter of Deuteronomy; of which the following predictions deserve our attention.

1. "The Lord shall bring a nation against thee from afar, from the end of the earth, as swift as the eagle flieth; a nation whose tongue thou shalt not understand." This prophecy had an accomplishment in the invasion of Judea by the Chaldeans and by the Romans, but more especially the latter. Jeremiah, when predicting the invasion of the Chaldeans, uses nearly the same language as Moses. "Lo, I will bring a nation upon you from afar, O house of Israel, saith the Lord; it is an ancient nation, a nation whose language thou knowest not."* And again, 'Our persecutors are swifter than the eagles of the

* Jer. x. 15.

heaven."[*] But with still greater propriety may it be said that the Romans were a nation "from afar;" the rapidity of whose conquests resembled the eagle's flight; the standard of whose armies was an eagle; and whose language was unknown to the Jews.

The enemies of the Jews are always characterized as "a nation of fierce countenance, who shall not regard the person of the old, nor show favour to the young"—an exact description of the Chaldeans. It is said, 2 Chron. xxxvi. 17, that God brought upon the Jews "the king of the Chaldees, who slew their young men with the sword in the house of their sanctuary, and had no compassion upon young man or maiden, old man, nor him that stooped for age." Such also were the Romans. Josephus informs us, that when Vespasian came to Gadara, "he slew all, man by man, the Romans showing mercy to no age." The like was done at Gamala.

2. It was predicted, also, that their cities should be besieged and taken. "And he shall besiege thee in all thy gates until thy high and fenced walls come down, wherein thou trustedst." This was fulfilled when Shalmaneser, king of Assyria, came against Samaria, and besieged it,[†] when Sennacherib came up against all the fenced cities of Judah, and when Nebuchadnezzar took Jerusalem, burned the temple, and broke down the walls of Jerusalem round about.[‡] The Jews had great confidence in the strength of the fortifications of Jerusalem. And Tacitus, as well as Josephus, describes it as a very strong place; yet it was often besieged and taken before its final destruction by Titus.

In their sieges they were to suffer much by famine, "in the straitness wherewith their enemies should distress them." Accordingly, at Samaria, during the siege there was a great famine, "so that an ass's head was sold for four score pieces of silver."[§] And when Jerusalem was besieged by Nebuchadnezzar, "the famine prevailed in the city, and there was no

---

[*] Lam. iv. 19.
[†] 2 Kings xviii. 9, 10.
[‡] 2 Kings xxv. 10.
[§] 2 Kings vi. 6.

bread for the people of the land."[*]   And in the siege of the same city by the Romans, there was a most distressing famine.[†]

It was foretold that in these famines women should eat their own children.   " Ye shall eat," says Moses, " the flesh of your sons and of your daughters." And again, " thou shalt eat the fruit of thine own body."[‡]   " The tender and the delicate woman among you, who would not venture to set the sole of her foot upon the ground, for delicateness and tenderness—she shall eat her children for want of all things, secretly in the siege and straitness, wherewith thine enemies shall distress thee in thy gates."   This extraordinary prediction was fulfilled six hundred years after it was spoken, in the siege of Samaria, by the king of Syria; when two women agreed together to give up their children to be eaten; and one of them was eaten accordingly.[§]   It was fulfilled again nine hundred years after Moses, in the siege of Jerusalem, by the Chaldeans.   " The hands of the pitiful women," says Jeremiah, " have sodden their own children."[‖]   And again, fifteen hundred years after the time of Moses, when Jerusalem was besieged by the Romans, Josephus informs us of a noble woman killing and eating her own sucking child; and when she had eaten half, she secreted the other part for another meal.

3. Great numbers of the Jews were to be destroyed.   "And ye shall be left few in number, whereas ye were as the stars of heaven for multitude."   In the siege of Jerusalem by Titus, it is computed that eleven hundred thousand persons perished by famine, pestilence, and sword.   Perhaps, since the creation of the world, so many persons never perished in any one siege as this.   The occasion of so great a multitude of people being found at Jerusalem, was, that the siege commenced about the celebration of the passover; and the people throughout the adjacent

---

* 2 Kings xxv. 3.   § 2 Kings vi. 28, 29.
† Josephus de Jud. Bello.   ‖ Lam. iv. 10.
‡ Jer. xxvi. 29. Deut. xxvii 23.

country took refuge in Jerusalem, at the approach of the Roman army.

Moses also predicted that the Jews should be carried back to Egypt, and sold as slaves for a very low price, and described the method of their conveyance thither: "and the Lord shall bring thee into Egypt again with ships, where you shall be sold unto your enemies for bondmen and bondwomen, and no man shall buy you." Josephus informs us that when the city was taken, the captives who were above seventeen years of age, were sent to the works in Egypt; but so little care was taken of these captives, that eleven thousand of them perished for want. There is every probability, though the historian does not mention the fact, that they were conveyed to Egypt in ships, as the Romans had then a fleet in the Mediterranean. The market was so overstocked that there were no purchasers, and they were sold for the merest trifle.

4. It is moreover predicted, in this wonderful prophecy of Moses, that the Jews should be extirpated from their own land, and dispersed among all nations. "And ye shall be plucked from off the land whither thou goest to possess it. And the Lord shall scatter thee among all people, from one end of the earth even unto the other." How remarkably has this been fulfilled. The ten tribes were first carried away from their own land by the king of Assyria; next, the two other tribes were carried captive to Babylon; and, finally, when the Romans took away "their place and nation," their dispersion was complete.

5. The Emperor Adrian, by a public edict, forbade the Jews, on pain of death, to set foot in Jerusalem: or even to approach the country around it. In the time of Tertullian and Jerome, they were prohibited from entering Judea. And from that day to this, the number of Jews in the holy land has been very small. They are still exiles from their own land, and are found scattered through almost every country on the globe.

It was foretold that, notwithstanding their disper

sion, they should not be totally destroyed, but should still exist a distinct people. " And yet for all that, when they be in the land of their enemies, I will not cast them away, neither will I abhor them, to destroy them utterly, and to break my covenant with them." " What a marvellous thing is this," says Bishop Newton, " that after so many wars, battles, and sieges; after so many rebellions, massacres, and persecutions; after so many years of captivity, slavery, and misery; they are not " destroyed utterly," and though scattered among all people, yet subsist a distinct people by themselves! Where is any thing like this to be found in all the histories, and in all the nations under the sun?"

The prophecy goes on to declare, that they should be every where in an uneasy condition; and should not rest long in any one place. " And among these nations shalt thou find no ease, neither shall the sole of thy foot have rest." How exactly has this been verified in the case of this unhappy people, even to this day! There is scarcely a country in Europe from which they have not been banished, at one time or another. To say nothing of many previous scenes of bloodshed and banishment, of the most shocking kind, through which great multitudes of this devoted people passed in Germany, France, and Spain, in the thirteenth and fourteenth centuries; eight hundred thousand Jews, are said by the Spanish historian, to have been banished from Spain, by Ferdinand and Isabella. And how often, when tolerated by government they have suffered by the tumults of the people, it is impossible to enumerate.

The prophet declares that "they should be oppress ed and crushed alway; that their sons and their daughters should be given to another people; that they should be mad for the sight of their eyes, which they should see." Nothing has been more common in all countries where the Jews have resided, than to fine, fleece, and oppress them, at will; and in Spain and Portugal their children have been taken from them by order of the government, to be educa ted in the Popish religion. The instances in which their oppressions have driven them to madness and desperation, are too numerous to be stated in detail.

6. Finally, it is foretold by Moses, "That they should become an astonishment, a proverb, and a by-word, among all nations; and that their plagues, should be wonderful," even great plagues, and of long continuance. In every country the Jews are hated and despised. They have been literally "a proverb and a by-word." Mohammedans, Heathens, and Christians, however they may differ in other things, have been agreed in vilifying, abusing, and persecuting the Jews. Surely the judgments visited on this peculiar people, have been wonderful and of long continuance. For nearly eighteen hundred years, they have been in this miserable state of banishment, dispersion, and persecution.

The prophecy of Isaiah respecting the restoration of the Jews to their land after seventy years captivity, is very remarkable. Cyrus is designated by name, not only as the conqueror of Babylon, but as the restorer of Israel and rebuilder of Jerusalem. "That saith of Cyrus, he is my shepherd, and shall perform all my pleasure; even saying to Jerusalem, thou shalt be built; and to the temple thy foundations shall be laid."* We are informed by Josephus, that when Cyrus had got possession of Babylon, the predictions concerning himself were made known to him, and that he was struck with admiration at the manifest divinity of the writing. This will account for the kindness of this prince to the children of Israel, and the opportunity which he gave them to return to their own land, and the facilities which he granted for the restoration of the temple. Indeed, it is certain from what is said in Ezra, that, by some means, Cyrus knew that God had appointed him to rebuild the temple for there it is written, "That the Lord stirred up the spirit of Cyrus, king of Persia, that he made a proclamation throughout all his kingdom, and put it also in writing, saying, Thus saith Cyrus

* Isa. xliv. 28.

12*

the king of Persia, the Lord God of heaven hath given me all the kingdoms of the earth AND HE HATH CHARGED ME TO BUILD A HOUSE IN JERUSALEM WHICH IS IN JUDAH."

He then gave liberty and encouragement to the people of God to engage in this pious enterprise, and to receive pecuniary aid from all who were disposed to co-operate in this good work. And, as the sacred vessels of the temple had been brought to Babylon by Nebuchadnezzar, these Cyrus brought forth and delivered to the proper officer, to be brought up from Babylon to Jerusalem.

" What nation," says the distinguished writer already quoted, " hath subsisted as a distinct people in their own country, so long as these have done in their dispersion, into all countries? And what a standing miracle is this exhibited to the view and observation of the whole world!" " Here are instances of prophecies delivered above three thousand years ago, and yet, as we see, fulfilling in the world, at this very time; and what stronger proof can we desire of the divine legation of Moses? How these instances may affect others, I know not, but for myself I must acknowledge, they not only convince, but amaze and astonish me beyond expression."

CHAPTER X.

PROPHECIES RELATING TO NINEVEH, BABYLON, TYRE, &C.

THE walls of Nineveh, the capital of Assyria, are said to have been a hundred feet in height, sixty miles in compass, and defended by fifteen hundred towers, each two hundred feet high. Diodorus Siculus relates, that the king of Assyria after the complete discomfiture of his army, confided in an old prophecy

that Nineveh would not be taken unless the river should become the enemy of the city; that after an ineffectual siege of two years, the river, swollen with long continued and tempestuous torrents, inundated part of the city, and threw down the wall for the space of twenty furlongs; and that the king, deeming that the prediction was accomplished, despaired of his safety, and erected an immense funeral pile, on which he heaped his wealth, and with which himself, his household, and palace were consumed.*
The book of Nahum was avowedly prophetic of the destruction of Nineveh; and it is there foretold, "that the gates of the river shall be opened, and the palace shall be dissolved—Nineveh of old, like a pool of water—with an overflowing flood he will make an utter end of the place thereof." The other predictions of the prophet are as literally described by the historian. He relates, that the king of Assyria, elated with his former victories, and ignorant of the revolt of the Bactrians, had abandoned himself to scandalous inaction; had appointed a time of festivity; and supplied his soldiers with abundance of wine; and that the general of the enemy apprized by deserters, of their negligence and drunkenness attacked the Assyrian army while abandoned to revelling, destroyed a great part of them, and drove the rest into the city. The words of the prophet were hereby verified. "While they were folden together as thorns, and while they are drunken as drunkards, they shall be devoured as stubble fully dry." Much spoil was promised to the enemy, "Take the spoil of silver, take the spoil of gold; for there is no end of the store and glory, out of all the pleasant furniture." Accordingly the historian affirms, that many talents of gold and silver preserved from the fire, were carried to Ecbatana. The prophet declares, that the city was not only to be destroyed by an overflowing flood, but the fire was also to devour it; which exactly agrees with the account of the historian The utter and perpetual destruction of the city was

* Diod. Sic. Lib. ii. p. 32, 33.

distinctly predicted, "The Lord will make an utter
end of the place thereof. Affliction shall not rise up
the second time, she is empty, void and waste. The
Lord will stretch out his hand against the north and
destroy Assyria, and will make Nineveh a desolation
and dry like a wilderness. How is she become a
desolation, a place for beasts to lie down in." In the
second century, Lucian, who was born on the banks
of the Euphrates, testified, that Nineveh was utterly
perished—that there was no vestige of it remain
ing—and that none could tell where it was once
situated. A late traveller who has visited that country, testifies, "that neither bricks, stones, nor other
materials of building," are now to be seen; but the
ground is, in many places, grown over with grass,
and such elevations are observable, as resemble the
mounds left by the intrenchments and fortifications
of ancient Roman camps; and *the appearances* of
other mounds and ruins less marked than even these
extending for ten miles and widely spread, and seeming to be the wreck of former buildings, show that
Nineveh is left without any monument of royalty,
without any token whatever of its splendour or
wealth; that it is indeed a desolation, "empty, void,
and waste;" its very ruins perished, and less than
the wreck of what it was. "Such an utter ruin," says
Bishop Newton, "has been made of it: and such is
the truth of the divine predictions."

BABYLON.

The prophecies respecting the taking of Babylon,
its utter destruction, and the complete desolation
which should reign where this proud city once stood,
have been remarkably fulfilled. Our limits will only
admit of the selection of a few particulars out of
many; but for more minute and extended information on this interesting subject, the reader is referred
to the works of Bishop Newton, and the Rev. Alexander Keith, on Prophecy, where he will meet with
full satisfaction, and to which we acknowledge our

selves indebted for the substance of wh. is here introduced.

The very nations by whom Babylon was to be taken and destroyed, are predicted by name by the prophet Jeremiah. "Go up, O Elam, (this was the ancient name of Persia,) besiege, O Media. The Lord hath raised up the spirit of the kings of the Medes; for his device is against Babylon to destroy it."*

And Isaiah says, " Babylon is fallen, is fallen; and all the graven images of her gods he hath broken unto the ground."† Thus saith the Lord " that saith unto the deep, Be dry; and I will dry up thy rivers: that saith of Cyrus, he is my shepherd, and shall perform all my pleasure. And I will loose the loins of kings, to open before him the two-leaved gates— and the gates shall not be shut."‡ " Thus saith the Lord to *Cyrus* his anointed, to subdue nations before him." This prediction of Isaiah, in which Cyrus is named, must have been uttered at least two hundred years before he was born, and when the Persians were an obscure and inconsiderable nation.

A confederacy having been formed between the Medes and Persians, and Cyrus having in person taken the command of the Persians, and having disciplined them with consummate skill, and inspired them with heroic courage, joined his uncle Cyaxares, (by Daniel called Darius the Mede,) and their united forces having conquered the Armènians, the Hyrcanians, the Lydians, the Cappadocians, and other allies of the king of Babylon; and having so treated all these conquered nations as to conciliate their friendship, and add their forces to their own, they marched towards the city of Babylon.

Although Cyrus commenced his military career with a small army of Persians, yet by conquest and wise policy, his army had become exceedingly numerous before he reached the famous city. But what could be done by courage or military skill against a city so defended on every side? This consummate

* Jer li.   Isa. xxi. 9.   † Isa. xliv. 27, 28.

general, as soon as he had arrived on the ground with his army, made it his first business, in company with some of his chief officers, to ride entirely round the walls, and to ascertain whether there was any weak point where an assault might successfully be made. But he found every part fully secured, so that there seemed no possibility of taking the city but by a long siege. He therefore sat down before it, and dug a trench entirely around the walls, and towers were erected, and every other preparation made for a regular siege. Thus, in the prophecy, it is said, "They camped against it round about. They put themselves in array against Babylon around about. They set themselves in array against Babylon, every man put in array."

Another important circumstance distinctly noticed in the prophecy, is, the cowardice of the Babylonians. Formerly, her armies were a terror to the whole earth, and nothing could withstand their fierce courage. But now, faint-heartedness had come over them. " The mighty men of Babylon have forborne to fight. They have remained in their holds. Their might hath failed, they became as women."* Their timidity was manifest in their shutting themselves up; and all the challenges of their enemies could not provoke them to come out and meet them in the open field. Xenophon relates, that Cyrus challenged the king of Babylon to decide the contest by single combat, which he declined. The people within the walls, though very numerous, made no sallies from their gates; nor did they use any efforts to disperse or annoy the besiegers. Literally, " they remained in their hold, and the hands of the king of Babylon waxed feeble."

Cyrus, as we have said, found every thing secure against assault; for what could battering rams, or other engines of war accomplish against walls which were thirty, or, as some assert, fifty feet in thickness? He was, therefore, not a little perplexed until the thought occurred, that an entrance might possibly

* Jeremiah i.

be obtained by turning out of its channel the river
Euphrates, which flowed through the city.   This
hazardous enterprise as a last resort was determined
on, and the work was commenced, but the design
was carefully concealed from the besieged; for, as
Herodotus observes, if they had had the least intimation of the device, or if they had discovered the
Persians while passing through, they could not only
have prevented its execution, but have destroyed the
whole army of Cyrus while pent up within the channel of the river.   All that was necessary to prevent
the Persians from entering was, to close the gates
which gave entrance to the city through the embank-
ment built upon both sides of the river.   To guard
against the danger of discovery, Cyrus selected for
the execution of this important but dangerous enterprise, the season of a great Babylonish festival, on
which occasion he knew the whole population gave
themselves up to revelling and drunkenness.   The
river was a full quarter of a mile wide, and twelve
feet deep, but there was an artificial lake in the
neighbourhood, prepared to receive the surplus waters, when it overflowed its banks, or when for any
other reason it was desirable to diminish the waters
of the river.   The entrance of this canal was en-
.arged, and the great trench dug round the walls by
the army of Cyrus, was so connected with the river
above the town, that this also was capable of con
taining a large body of water.   Moreover, the country was exceedingly low and flat; so that the water,
if it could once be diverted from its usual channel,
would readily spread itself in all directions.   The
scheme succeeded to their most sanguine expectation.   The channel of the river was left nearly dry
by the subsiding of the water, and the army of Cyrus
entered by night.   One detachment was placed where
the river entered the city, and another where it left
it; and the Persian army entered so silently, and
the inhabitants were so completely drowned in their
drunken revels, that no alarm was sounded, and no
care had been taken t close the gates leading to the

river, no danger being apprehended on that side
So completely were the Babylonians surprised, that
Cyrus had reached the royal palace before a messenger arrived to tell the king that the city was taken.
The noise of the invading army, at first, was not distinguished from the mad tumult of the rioters. Even
the guards stationed around the palace were found
intoxicated, and slain; when the Persians rushed
into the splendid hall, where Belshazzar and his
thousand lords, and wives, and concubines, had been
drinking out of the sacred vessels of the Lord's house,
which had been impiously brought forth on this occasion. But their profane mirth had already been
arrested before the arrival of the victorious Persians,
by the appearance of a hand, writing certain words
in a strange character on the wall. This had produced the utmost consternation in all the assembly,
although none could decipher the writing, until Daniel
was brought in, who quickly denounced the fatal
destiny of the monarch, and the overthrow of his
kingdom; "And in that night was Belshazzar, the
king of the Chaldeans, slain."

How exactly the events, described above, were
predicted, will be at once seen by the following quotations from the prophets.

"I will dry up thy sea, and make thy springs dry
—that saith to the deep, Be dry, I WILL DRY UP THY
RIVERS."

"And one post did run to meet another, and one
messenger to meet another, to show the king of
Babylon that his city is taken at the end, and that
the passages are shut."

"But a snare was laid for Babylon. It was taken,
and it was not aware. How is the praise of the
whole earth surprised! For thou hast trusted in thy
wickedness, and in thy wisdom, and thy knowledge
it hath perverted thee; therefore shall evil come upon
thee, and thou shalt not know whence it ariseth; and
mischief shall come upon thee, and thou shalt not be
able to put it off—none shall save thee."

"In their heat I will make their feasts, and I will

make them drunken, that they may rejoice, and sleep a perpetual sleep, and not wake, saith the Lord. I will make drunken her princes and her wise men, her captains and her rulers, and her mighty men, and they shall sleep a perpetual sleep."

" The gates (*i. e.* those from the river to the city) were not shut. The loins of kings were loosed to open before Cyrus the two-leaved gates."*

The king hearing a noise and tumult without, sent some to see whence it arose: but no sooner were the gates of the palace opened, than the Persians rushed in. " The king of Babylon heard the report of them. Anguish took hold of him." He and all about him perished. God had " numbered his kingdom and finished it." It was " divided and given to the Medes and Persians."

The multitude of soldiers who now entered the city, and the slaughter of the citizens in the streets, are exactly foretold. " I will fill thee with men as with caterpillars. Her young men shall fall in the streets, and all her men of war shall be cut off in that day."

The number of the Persian army, which was reviewed immediately after the capture of the city, is said by Herodotus to have amounted to one hundred and twenty thousand horse, six thousand chariots of war, and six hundred thousand infantry.

Cyrus issued a proclamation that the people should remain in their houses, with strict orders to slay every person who should be found in " the streets."

Cyrus now became master of all the hidden treasures of Babylon. " The treasures of darkness and hidden riches of secret places being given into his hand;" that he might know " that the Lord, which had called him by his name, was the God of Israel."

From the time of the first capture of this famous city by Cyrus, her glory began to fade. God had predicted her downfall, and his word never fails. After its first conquest it was, according to Herodotus. reduced from an imperial to a tributary city;

* Jeremiah li.

13

which seems to be foretold by the prophet, when he says—"Come down and sit in the dust, O virgin daughter of Babylon—sit on the ground, there is no throne, O daughter of the Chaldeans."

The next step towards the downfall of this famous city was after the rebellion against Darius. When he captured the city, he ordered the height of the walls to be reduced, and all the gates to be destroyed. To which the prophet alludes, in express terms:— "The wall of Babylon shall fall—her walls shall be thrown down."

Xerxes, after his return from his unfortunate Grecian expedition, entered the city and rifled its most valuable and sacred treasures, laid up in the temple of Belus. This the prophet Jeremiah had foretold. "I will punish Bel in Babylon, and I will bring out of his mouth that which he has swallowed up. I will do judgment on the graven images of Babylon."

No efforts made by the conquerors of Babylon to restore her glory, or even to prevent her decay, were at all successful. Cyrus made Babylon his usual place of residence, but his successors preferred other cities: and when Alexander conquered Babylon, it was fully his purpose to restore Babylon to her pristine glory; but the counsel of Jehovah was adverse. The prophet had long before signified that all such attempts would prove ineffectual. "Take balm for her pain, if so be that she may be healed. We would have healed Babylon, but she is not healed." The proximate cause of the rapid decline of Babylon was twofold; first, the turning of the river inundated the surrounding country and filled it with stagnant pools; secondly, the building of another city in the neighbourhood, drew off multitudes of inhabitants, who transferred their residence and wealth from the old to the new city. Babylon also was oppressed with some of the most cruel tyrants that ever ruled over any city. One of these, named Humerus, who lived about one hundred and thirty years before Christ, reduced many of the inhabitants to slavery on the slightest pretexts, burned the forum and some of the temples, and banished many of the people into Media. In foresight of such scenes, the prophet says, " They shall remove, they shall depart both man and beast."

The cruelty of the conquerors of Babylon is strongly portrayed by the inspired pen. " They are cruel both in anger and fierce wrath, to lay the land desolate." This has been in an eminent degree verified, in the Persians and Medes, the Macedonians, the Parthians, the Syrians, the Romans, and the Saracens; all of whom, in their turn, by their cruel anger and fierce wrath, assisted to render desolate this once " golden city," and these once beautiful and feitle regions.

" A sword is upon the Chaldeans. A sound of battle is in the land and great destruction. I will kindle a fire in his cities, and it shall burn all round about him. And Chaldea shall be a spoil, all that spoil her shall be satisfied, saith the Lord. A sword is upon her treasures, and they shall be robbed. O thou that dwellest upon many waters, abundant in treasures, thine end is come."

The prophet's description of the utter desolation of Babylon could scarcely have been more vivid and exact if he had been present to view the scene. " I will punish the land of the Chaldeans, and will make it perpetual desolations; cut off the sower from Babylon and him that handleth the sickle in time of harvest. A drought is upon her waters, and they shall be dried up. Behold the hindermost of the nations, a dry land and a desert. Her cities are a desolation, a dry land and a wilderness; a land where no man dwelleth; neither doth the son of man pass by there. I will send unto Babylon fanners that will fan her, and empty her land. The land shall tremble and sorrow; for every purpose of the Lord shall be performed against Babylon, to make the land of Babylon a desolation without an inhabitant."[*]

The decline of this famous city was gradual but

* Jeremiah li.

constant. In the second century of the Christian era nothing remained but the walls, and in the fourth century, these were repaired to serve as an enclosure or park for wild beasts, and Babylon became a hunting ground for the kings of Persia. Under the Saracens the desolation became complete, and for many ages past the following prediction has been literally fulfilled. " No man dwelleth there, and no son of man passeth by. Neither shall the Arabian pitch his tent there; neither shall the shepherds make their folds there." The only remains of the former city are heaps of ruins and mounds of half decayed bricks; in exact conformity with the prediction of Jeremiah. " Babylon shall become heaps. Cast her up as heaps. Let nothing of her be left. Babylon is fallen—is cut down to the ground. Her foundations are fallen. It shall never be inhabited from generation to generation."

The following are statements made by recent travellers. "Our path," says Mignan, "lay through the great mass of ruined heaps on the site of ' shrunken Babylon.' And I am perfectly incapable of conveying an adequate idea of the dreary lonely nakedness, that appeared before us." Porter remarks, " that a silence profound as the grave, reigns throughout the ruins. Babylon is now a silent scene, a sublime solitude." According to Rauwolf, even as early as the sixteenth century, there was not within the limits of ancient Babylon a single human habitation. " The eye," says he, " wanders over a barren desert, in which the ruins are nearly the only indication, that it ever has been inhabited." "It is impossible," says Keppel, " to behold the scene, and not be reminded how exactly the predictions of Isaiah and Jeremiah have been fulfilled." As the wild Arabs inhabit the wilderness, and often visit this region it may seem strange and improbable that they should never pitch their tents on the ruinous site of Babylon; but Mignan informs us that nothing will induce them to remain all night near the principal mound, as they have a superstitious belief that evil spirits dwell there. He informs us, that he was accompanied by six Arabs, well armed, and accustomed to the desert, but no inducement could have prevailed on them to remain on the ground after night.

The place is also full of "doleful creatures" and of stagnant pools. Among the ruins, travellers inform us, there are many dens of wild beasts. " In most of the cavities," says Rich, "are numerous owls and bats." On the very mound supposed to have been produced by the ruins of the temple of Belus, Porter saw three large lions. The hyena and the jackal have also their residence here. Who can fail to see, in these circumstances, the exact fulfilment of that prediction—"Wild beasts of the desert shall be there, and their houses shall be full of doleful creatures, and owls shall dwell there, and satyrs shall dance there." The western bank of the Euphrates has now disappeared, and the river having no barrier freely overflows the adjacent land, so that on this side a large part of the ruins of Babylon are inundated; and for a great distance, even after the river has subsided, the whole country is one continued swamp, which is entirely inaccessible to the traveller. To this the prophet seems to have alluded, when he says, "The sea is come upon Babylon. She is covered with the multitude of the waves thereof." But that which at first view appears to be incompatible with this description is nevertheless true. Babylon is described by the prophets as "a dry land, a wilderness, and a desert." But the fact is, that while on one side of the river, the site is inundated, on the other, it is exceedingly dry, and a mere arid desert.

As far as the light of history reaches, among all the structures ever reared by the hands of men, the temple of Belus seems to have been the most elevated. This temple was probably built on the foundation of the tower of Babel, and according to the lowest computation, was higher than the greatest of the Egyptian pyramids. The highest mound now among the ruins is supposed, by discerning travellers, to be on the site of this famous temple. This ruin

13*

covers more ground than the temple did when stand
ing. "It has." says Mignan, "the appearance of a
hill surmounted with a castle." This hill is called
by the Arabs *Birs Nimrud.* Of this vast ruin, Sir
Robert Ker Porter has given a very particular and
interesting account. "On the summit of the hill are
immense fragments of brick-work, of no determinate
figures, tumbled together, and converted into vitrified
masses." Some of these huge fragments measure
twelve feet in height by twenty-four in circumference; these fragments have been entirely preserved
while every thing else is crumbled to dust, because
they have been exposed to the action of the fiercest
fire; they are completely molten.

The high gates of the temple of Belus, which were
standing in the time of Herodotus, have been burnt
with fire. "Bel boweth down. Bel is confounded.
The hand of the Lord has been stretched upon it—
it has been rolled down from the rocks—and has
been made a burnt mountain." The noble palaces
of Babylon, the larger of which was surrounded by
three walls of great extent, have entirely disappeared. Although the strength of the walls seemed to
promise durability, and almost to bid defiance to time;
yet now, of these palaces, the most splendid perhaps
that the world ever saw, nothing but the mere vestiges of the walls which surround them, remain. The
circumference of this ruin is about half a mile, and
its height one hundred and forty feet; but it is a
mass of confusion, the receptacle of wild beasts, and
full of doleful creatures. Wild beasts cry in the desolate houses, "and dragons in the pleasant palaces."
"Venomous reptiles," says Mignan, "are very numerous throughout the ruins." "On pacing over the
loose stones," says the same writer, "and fragments
of brick-work, which lay scattered through the immense fabric, and surveying the sublimity of the
ruins, I naturally recurred to the time when these
walls stood proudly in their original splendour; when
the halls were the scenes of festive magnificence, and
when they resounded to the voices of those whom

death has long since swept from the earth. This very pile was once the seat of luxury and vice, now abandoned to decay, and exhibiting a melancholy instance of the retribution of heaven. It stands alone. The solitary habitation of the goat-herd marks not the forsaken site." " Thy pomp is brought down to the grave, and the noise of the viols; the worms are spread under thee, and the worms cover thee."

In this wonderful city there was nothing more wonderful than the height and thickness of the walls. They were so broad that six chariots abreast could be drawn on them, and their original height is said to have been three hundred and fifty feet; or at the lowest computation of the length of the cubit, three hundred feet. Darius, it is true, lowered these walls; but still they were elevated above the height of most walls. Where are they now? Not a vestige of them any where remains. Two travellers, Buckingham and Frederick, have both made diligent search to find some traces of the wall of Babylon. The latter says: " Neither of the wall or of the ditch has been seen the least vestige by any modern traveller. Within twenty-one miles distance along the Euphrates, and twelve miles across it in breadth, I was unable to perceive any thing that could admit of my imagining, that either a wall or ditch had existed within this extensive area."

Keppel relates, that he and the party who accompanied him, " in common with other travellers, had totally failed in discovering any trace of the city walls." And he adds: " The divine predictions against Babylon have been so totally fulfilled in the appearance of the ruins, that I am disposed to give the fullest signification to the words of Jeremiah THE BROAD WALLS OF BABYLON SHALL BE UTTERLY BROKEN."

It was predicted that " Babylon should be an astonishment. Every one that goeth by Babylon shall be astonished." How exactly this accords with the feelings of modern travellers, may be learned from their own language. Porter says, " I could not but feel an indescribable awe, in thus passing, as it were into the gates of fallen Babylon." "I cannot portray," says Mignan, "the overpowering sensation of reverential awe that possessed my mind, while contemplating the extent and magnitude of ruin and devastation on every side." In another place Porter adds the following interesting remarks, expressive of his feelings while surveying the scene. "The whole view was particularly solemn. The majestic stream of the Euphrates, wandering in solitude, like a pilgrim monarch, through the silent ruins of his devastated kingdom, still appeared a noble river, under all the disadvantages of its desert-tracked course. Its banks were hoary with reeds: and the gray osier willows were yet there, on which the captives of Israel hung up their harps; and, while Jerusalem was not, refused to be comforted. But how is the rest of the scene changed since then! At that time those broken hills were palaces—those long undulating mounds, streets. This vast solitude, filled with the busy subjects of the proud daughter of the east. Now wasted with misery, her habitations are not to be found, and for herself, 'the worm is spread over her.'"

The Rev. Alexander Keith, concludes with these pertinent remarks: "Has not every purpose of the Lord been performed against Babylon? What mortal shall give a negative answer to the questions subjoined by the author of these very prophecies? Who hath declared this from ancient time? Who hath told it from that time? Have not I the Lord? And there is no God beside me—declaring the end from the beginning, and from ancient time the things that are not yet done. Saying, my counsel shall stand, and I will do all my pleasure." Is it possible there can be any attestation of the truth of prophecy, if not witnessed here? "The records of the human race, it has been said with truth, do not present a contrast more striking than that between the primeval magnificence of Babylon, and its long desolation. How few spots are there on earth of which we have so clear and faithful a picture as prophecy

gave of fallen Babylon, when no spot on earth resembled it less than its present desolate, solitary site Or could any prophecies respecting any single place be more precise, or wonderful, or numerous, or true or more gradually accomplished through many generations?"

TYRE.

Tyre is another famous ancient city, which was the object of some very particular and remarkable prophecies, which have been most exactly fulfilled. Isaiah uttered his prediction concerning Tyre when she was in her glory, and flourishing in all the pride and luxury, which were sustained by the richest commerce in the world, at least a century before any danger threatened the place. The reason which the prophet assigns for God's judgments was the pride of this wealthy city. "The Lord of hosts hath purposed it, to stain the pride of all glory, and to bring into contempt all the honourable of the earth." (Isaiah xxiii. 9.) Ezekiel employs three whole chapters in describing the luxury, wealth, commerce and destruction of Tyre.*

The following particulars are clearly included in the divine predictions concerning Tyre.

1. That this luxurious and populous city should be taken by the Chaldeans; who, at the time of the prophecy, were an inconsiderable people. Ezekiel not only predicts that the ruin of this city should be by the Chaldeans, but names the prince by whom it should be taken: "Thus saith the Lord God, I will bring upon Tyrus, Nebuchadnezzar, king of Babylon, a king of kings, from the north, with horses, and with chariots, and with horsemen. He shall slay thy people with the sword, and thy strong garrisons shall go down to the ground."† Josephus informs us, that Nebuchadnezzar besieged Tyre for thirteen years while Ithobal reigned there, and for his authority quotes Menander the Ephesian. The Phenician ar

---

* Ezek. xxvi. xxvii. xxviii.   † Ezek. xxvi. 7—11.

nals, as Dr. Prideaux has shown, agree exa tly with this account.

2. It was predicted that the inhabitants should pass over the Mediterranean sea, to the islands and countries adjacent. Isaiah says, "Pass ye over to Tarshish, howl ye inhabitants of the isle.* Arise, pass over to Chittim, there also shalt thou have no rest." Ezekiel foretells the same thing. "The isles that are in the sea shall be troubled at thy departure." Bishop Newton has shown from ancient authors, that the Tyrians planted colonies in many places over sea, and among them were the cities of Carthage in Africa, and Tartessus in Spain, which last is the Tarshish of the prophets.

3. It was predicted, that after seventy years Tyre should be restored. Isaiah is express in the mention of this period. "And it shall come to pass in that day, that Tyre shall be forgotten for seventy years, according to the days of one king;"† in which reference is made to the duration of the Chaldean dynasty, which was to continue only seventy years. Jeremiah intimates this to be the length of the Babylonish power. "These nations shall serve the king of Babylon seventy years."‡

4. It was foretold that Tyrus, after being restored, should be destroyed again. When Nebuchadnezzar took the city, the people took their effects and went into their ships, and escaped, with much of their wealth; so that God promised Egypt as a recompense for his hard service and poor reward in besieging Tyre. When the inhabitants returned, they did not build on the old site, but went to an island separated from the main land by a strait of the sea. Here the new city arose and flourished in commerce and wealth. The prophets not only foretold the overthrow of old Tyre, but of this new city, built, as it were, "in the midst of the sea." Isaiah says, "Howl ye inhabitants of the isle." Ezekiel, "What city is like Tyrus, like the destroyed in the midst of the

* Isa. xxiii. 6.   † Jer. xxv. 11, 12.
‡ Isa xxiii. 15—17

sea.* Zechariah, who had lived long after the first destruction, and must refer to the second, says, "And Tyrus did build himself a strong hold, and heaped up silver as the dust, and fine gold as the mire of the streets. Behold the Lord will cast her out, and he will smite her power in the sea, and she shall be devoured with fire."† This new city was truly a strong hold, for not only was the sea a defence, but her walls were one hundred and fifty feet in height. Ezekiel also plainly predicts, that the second destruction of Tyre should be by fire. "I will bring forth a fire from the midst of thee, and it shall devour thee, and I will bring thee to ashes on the earth in the sight of all them that behold thee." Accordingly, Alexander the Great besieged and took the city, and set it on fire. This is expressly asserted by Quintus Curtius.‡

For a while, the insular situation of Tyre and her command of the sea, hindered the approach of Alexander's army to the walls; but he took the stones and rubbish of the old city, and made a causeway across the arm of the sea which lay between the island and the continent; thus fulfilling the prophecy of Ezekiel, "They shall lay thy stones, and thy timber, and thy dust in the midst of the water."§ This was a work of immense labour, and occupied his army for seven months. On this occasion also, the Tyrians betook themselves to their ships, and fled across the sea. Both Diodorus Siculus, and Quintus Curtius, testify, that during the siege, they sent away their wives and children to Carthage; and when the city was taken, the Sidonians contrived to carry off fifteen thousand persons in their ships. And they were happy who thus escaped, for the conqueror exercised unbounded cruelties upon such as remained. Eight thousand were slain in taking the city, two thousand were crucified, and thirty thousand sold for slaves.

Although Tyre was again rebuilt, and for a con siderable time flourished; yet the unchangeable de

* Ezek. xxvii. 32.   ‡ L. 4. c. 3.
† Zech. iii. 1.   § Ezek. xxvi. 12.

cree of the Almighty had been published and record
ed by the prophets, that this once proud city, the
mistress of the sea, should become a perfect desola
tion.　Ezekiel, who has given so vivid and so particular a description of the wealth and commerce of
Tyrus, and of the pride of her kings and merchants,
also furnishes the most exact prediction of her ruin
and utter desolation.

"Thus saith the Lord God, behold I am against
thee, O Tyrus, and will cause many nations to come
up against thee, as the sea causeth his waves to come
up, and they shall destroy the walls of Tyrus and
break down her towers.　I will also scrape her dust
from her, and make her as the top of a rock.　It
shall be a place for the spreading of nets in the midst
of the sea, for I have spoken it saith the Lord."　And
to show the absolute certainty of this total desolation
of Tyre, he repeats what was last mentioned in the
fourteenth verse.　"I will make thee like the top of
a rock, thou shalt be a place to spread nets upon;
thou shalt be built no more; for I have spoken it,
saith the Lord God.　And again, I will make thee a
terror, and thou shalt be no more, though thou be
sought for, thou shalt never be found again, saith the
Lord God."

Now, to show how exactly this is fulfilled, let us
hear what account modern travellers give of this
famous city.

Cotovicus, a Dutch traveller, who visited Syria in
1598, writes, "that this city so often restored after
being overthrown, now at length appears to be
utterly ruined; so that it has ceased to be any longer
a city, and only some inconsiderable vestiges of her
former ruins are now visible.　If you except a few
arches and baths, and some ruined walls, and col-
lapsed towers, and mere rubbish, there is now nothing of Tyre to be discerned."　And then he refers
to the prophecy of Ezekiel.

Dr. Shaw visited Tyre, but could find nothing
like a port or secure harbour any where in the neighbourhood.　But Maundrell's account is the most

exact and striking. " This city, standing in the sea, on a peninsula, at a distance, promises something very magnificent; but when you come nearer, you find no similitude of that glory for which it was so renowned in ancient times, and which the prophet Ezekiel describes in the 26th, 27th, and 28th chapters of his prophecy. On the north side, it has an old ungarrisoned Turkish castle, besides which you see nothing but a mere Babel of broken walls, pillars, vaults, &c., there being not so much as one entire house left; its present inhabitants only a few poor wretches, harbouring themselves in the vaults, and subsisting chiefly on *fishing*, who seem to be preserved in this place, by divine Providence, as a visible argument how God has fulfilled his word concerning Tyre, that it should be 'as the top of a rock a place for fishers to dry their nets on.' "

And even Volney seems to be constrained to add his testimony to confirm the fulfilment of the divine prediction, respecting Tyre. After contrasting its former glory with its present desolation, he says " The whole village of Tyre contains only fifty or sixty poor families, who live obscurely on the produce of their little ground and a *trifling fishery.*" And Bruce describes Tyre, in the very language of the prophet, as " a rock whereon fishers dry their nets." Several of our missionaries have visited the site of this once populous, refined, and wealthy city, and add their testimony to that of other travellers, of its present desolate condition.

Thus we see how remarkably prophecies, committed to writing above two thousand years ago, are at this day literally fulfilled, in the utter desolation of some of the richest and strongest cities which ever existed in the world

The prophecies recorded in the book of Daniel are very wonderful. There we have described the rise and fall of four successive monarchies or empires, and a prophecy concerning the conquests of Alexander the Great, and concerning his successors, embracing so many particulars that it assumes the

14

appearance of a history of the events which it predicts. Porphyry, an early and learned opposer of Christianity, was so struck with the coincidence between the predictions, and the history of the events by which they are fulfilled, that he declared that the prophecy must have been written after the events occurred. The infidel can make no complaint of obscurity here, as he commonly does when prophecies are adduced; the objection now is, that the prediction is too explicit and circumstantial. This objection of Porphyry induced Jerome to use the following pertinent language: *Cujus impugnatio testimonium veritatis est. Tanta enim dictorum fides fuit, ut propheta incredulis hominibus non videatur futura dixisse, sed narrasse præterita.* The meaning of which is, " This objection is a testimony of the truth; for such is the perspicuity of the language, that the prophet in the opinion of infidel men, seems rather to be narrating past events, than predicting those which are future."

It will be sufficient to observe, that there is not the least foundation for this opinion of Porphyry, that the book of Daniel was written after the time of Antiochus Epiphanes. Josephus relates that the prophecies of Daniel were shown to Alexander the Great, when he visited Jerusalem; and that this was the reason of his granting so many privileges to the Jewish people. However this may be, Daniel is spoken of, in the first book of Maccabees; and Josephus himself reckons him among the greatest of prophets. If this book had been written at that late period, it never could have found a place in the Jewish canon, as the prophecies of Daniel. These prophecies are also recognized and quoted by Jesus Christ as the productions of Daniel.

CHAPTER XI.

PROPHECIES RESPECTING MESSIAH—PREDICTIONS OF CHRIST RESPECTING THE DESTRUCTION OF JERUSALEM.

The prophecies which relate to the Messiah are so numerous and interesting, and involve so much critical discussion, that to exhibit them in their proper light, a volume would scarcely be sufficient. I must, therefore, be contented to refer to the most remarkable of these predictions, in a very brief and general way.

1. It is plain, from a cursory perusal of the Old Testament, that frequent intimations are given of the coming of a remarkable personage. From these, the Jewish nation have been led, in all ages, to entertain the expectation of a Messiah; and from them, the idea of a distinguished person who was to proceed from Judea, seems to have pervaded the surrounding nations. Some of the passages of Scripture, on which this opinion was founded, were, the promise of " the seed of the woman;" " the seed of Abraham in whom all nations should be blessed;" " the Shiloh who was to come out of Judah, before the dominion of that tribe should depart;" " the prophet like unto Moses, whom the Lord would raise up;" " the king whom the Lord would set upon his holy hill;" " the priest after the order of Melchisedek;" " the anointed one, or Messiah;" " the righteous branch;" " the corner stone;" " the desire of all nations;" " the Shepherd of Israel."

2. The time of the arrival of the Messiah is designated in prophecy. He was to come before the sceptre departed from Judah; at the end of seventy prophetic weeks, or four hundred and ninety years, from the time of the going forth of the command to restore and build Jerusalem, and while the second temple was yet standing.

3. The place of his birth, and the family from wh.ch he was to descend, were also explicitly mentioned in prophecy. From the evangelical history, and from the acknowledgment of the Jews, it is evident, that they well know that the Messiah was to be born at Bethlehem, and to be of the family of David.

4. Things of an apparently contradictory nature are predicted concerning the Messiah. At one time he is represented as a king and conqueror, whose dominion would be co-extensive with the earth, and who would flourish in righteousness and peace for ever; at another he is exhibited as one "despised and rejected, a man of sorrow and grief, as wounded and bruised, as cut off out of the land of the living, and as pouring out his soul unto death." These apparently irreconcilable characters led the Jews at one time to entertain the opinion that two Messiahs were predicted; the one a triumphant conqueror, the other a persecuted and patient sufferer. But, however great the apparent inconsistency, there is an exact accomplishment of both characters in Jesus of Nazareth. And certainly, the same cannot be said of any other person who ever lived.

5. It is predicted of the Messiah, that he should be A LIGHT TO THE GENTILES; and that under his administration, the face of the world should be changed, and that peace and righteousness should prevail. Although this prophecy is only in part fulfilled, yet so much has been accomplished in the call of numerous Gentile nations to the standard of the Messiah and in the benign and salutary influence of Christianity, that we must conclude that it was uttered under the influence of inspiration.

6. It was not only predicted that Messiah should be cut off, but it is expressly stated that he should die as a vicarious sacrifice, an expiatory victim for sin and transgression. "Thou shalt make his soul an offering for sin."

For the fulfilling of these predictions, I need only refer to the recorded testimony of the evangelists

That there is a remarkable coincidence between the language of the prophets and the history of the evangelists, cannot be denied, however it may be accounted for. The fifty-third chapter of Isaiah has a counterpart in the sufferings and death of Christ which has forced conviction on the minds of many unbelievers.

But there are also many particular facts and circumstances foretold respecting the Messiah, which it may be proper briefly to mention. His forerunner, John the Baptist, is predicted by Isaiah and Malachi. His miracles, his uncomplaining meekness and tranquil submission under cruel sufferings, by Isaiah. His riding on an ass, and a colt the foal of an ass; his being pierced where the wound should be visible; his being sold for thirty pieces of silver which should be appropriated to buy the Potter's Field, by Zechariah. It is predicted in the Psalms, that they would " part his raiment and cast lots for his vesture ;" and that vinegar would be given him to drink. The very words too which he uttered on the cross, when forsaken of God, are set down in the twenty-second Psalm.

It was also predicted in the Law of Moses, by an expressive type, " that not a bone of him should be broken ;" the fulfilment of which was wonderful, since the legs of both those crucified with him were broken. Isaiah foretold that he should make his " grave with the wicked, and with the rich in his death," which was literally accomplished when Jesus Christ was suspended on the cross between two thieves, and when he was taken down from the cross by a rich man and buried by him in his own new tomb.

The most of these particulars were fulfilled by the free actions of the enemies of Jesus, who had no idea that they were fulfilling any divine prophecy. It is impossible, that so many circumstances, literally predicted, should have been fulfilled by a mere fortuitous concurrence.

The whole ritual law is in fact a prophecy of JESUS. To him the Old Testament dispensation had

4*

reference. The Law, the Psalms, and the Prophets all testify of him. As said the angel to St. John, THE TESTIMONY OF JESUS IS THE SPIRIT OF PROPHECY.

CHRIST himself delivered, while upon earth, many clear and remarkable prophecies. Most of his parables have a prophetic character and in a striking manner represent the progress of the gospel, the rejection of the Jews, the calling of the Gentiles, and the future condition of the Church. He also foretold, in express words, the treatment which his followers should receive from the world, the treachery of Judas Iscariot, the conduct of Peter in denying him three times in one night, the particular circumstances and exact manner of his own death, and his resurrection on the third day. But I must pass over all these at present, and confine my attention to that astonishing prophecy, which Jesus delivered to his disciples on Mount Olivet, concerning the utter destruction of the temple of Jerusalem, and of the whole Jewish nation. This prediction was uttered about forty years before the events occurred, and was recorded by Matthew, according to the common opinion of early writers, thirty, or at least twenty years before it was fulfilled. The same was recorded by Mark and Luke, a few years after the writing of Matthew's gospel, but several years before the occurrence of these prodigious things which are foretold in it. The testimony of antiquity is, that both these evangelists were dead before the invasion of Judea by the Romans. John was the only one of the evangelists, or perhaps of the apostles, who lived to witness the fulfilling of the Lord's prophecy; and it is remarkable, that in his gospel this subject is never mentioned.

Let it be remembered, that when this prophecy was delivered by our Saviour, there was not the least human probability of such an event, as the destruction of Jerusalem. The Jews were in a state of profound peace, and the power of the Romans was such that it could not have been conjectured, that one small nation would think of rebelling against them.

The words of this prophecy may be read in the twenty-fourth chapter of the gospel of Matthew; also in the thirteenth chapter of the gospel of Mark; and in the seventeenth and twenty-first chapters of the gospel of Luke.

I will first collect into one view all the most remarkable particulars of this prophecy, and then show how they were fulfilled. The predictions relate, 1. To the signs and precursors of the desolation of the holy city; 2. To the circumstances of its siege and capture; 3. To the consequences of this tremendous catastrophe.

1. The signs and precursors of this event were to be false Christs; seditions and wars; famines, pestilences, earthquakes, and extraordinary appearances in the heavens; the persecution of Christians; the apostasy of professors, and the great want of charity, and depravation of morals among the people.

2. The circumstances of this tremendous judgment of Heaven, are such as these: that the event should occur before the existing generation had completely passed away; that it should be brought on by a war waged against the Jews, by a heathen nation, bearing idolatrous ensigns; that Jerusalem should be utterly destroyed, and the temple so completely demolished, that one stone of that sacred edifice should not be left on another; that multitudes should perish by the sword; that great numbers should be carried away captives; that the distress should exceed any thing which had ever occurred in the world; and that the divine wrath should be manifest in all these calamities, as it is called the day of vengeance, and it is said that there should be wrath against the people.

3. The consequences of the destruction of the temple of Jerusalem, as predicted by Christ, were to be the dispersion of the Jews through all the nations the total overthrow of the Jewish commonwealth, which is expressed by the prophetic symbols of "the sun being darkened, the moon not giving her light, and the stars falling from heaven;" the rejection of the Jews and the calling of the Gentiles; the

rising of false prophets and false Messiahs; the ex
tent and continuance of these judgments on the Jew
ish nation; with some intimation of their restoration.
The escape of the Christians from these calamities is
also foretold, and directions given for their flight;
and on their account it is promised, that those days
should be shortened; and finally, it is predicted that
the gospel should be preached among all nations.

Let us now proceed to inquire, in what manner
these numerous and extraordinary predictions were
accomplished; and we cannot but remark, that i
seems to have been ordered specially by Providence
that the history of the series of events by which this
prophecy was fulfilled, should be written by a man
who was not a Christian: and who was an eye-witness of the facts which he records. I allude to the
Jewish historian, Josephus, who is an author of high
respectability, and whose testimony is of great value
in the cause of Christianity.

1. In regard to false Christs, of which the prophecy speaks so emphatically, we learn from the historian just mentioned, that impostors and magicians
drew multitudes after them into the wilderness, promising to show them signs and wonders, some of whom
became insane, and others were punished by Felix,
the procurator. One of these impostors was that
Egyptian spoken of in the Acts of the Apostles, who
drew multitudes of people after him to Mount Olivet,
promising that he would cause the walls of Jerusalem to fall down at his word.

Theudas was another who pretended to be a prophet, and gave out that he would divide the waters
of Jordan; but he was quickly routed by Cuspius
Fadus, and all his followers scattered. The impostor
himself was taken alive, and his head cut off and
brought to Jerusalem. In the reign of Nero, and
during the time that Felix was procurator of Judea,
impostors arose in such numbers, that the historian
informs us, "many of then were apprehended and
killed every day."

There were also, at this time, great commotions

and horrible seditions and wars, in various places, as at Cesarea, Alexandria, and Babylon. There were great contentions between the Jews and Samaritans; and also between the Jews and people of other nations who dwelt in the same cities with them. Both Josephus and Philo give a particular account of these disturbances, in which multitudes of the people were slain.

Famines, pestilences, and earthquakes, are mentioned by Suetonius, and by several other profane historians, who are cited by Eusebius, by Josephus, by Tacitus, and by Seneca.

That prodigies were frequent, is expressly asserted by Josephus and Tacitus. The former declares that a star hung over the city like a sword, for a whole year; that at the ninth hour of the night, a bright light shone round the altar and the temple, so that for the space of half an hour it appeared to be bright day; that the eastern gate of the temple, which it required twenty men to shut, and which was fastened by strong bars and bolts, opened of its own accord; that before sunset, there was seen in the clouds, the appearance of chariots and armies fighting; that at the feast of Pentecost, while the priests were going into the inner temple, a voice was heard, as of a multitude, saying, "Let us depart hence." And what affected the people more than any thing else was, that four years after the war began, a countryman came to Jerusalem, at the feast of Tabernacles, and ran up and down crying, day and night, "A voice from the east, and a voice from the west, a voice from the four winds, a voice against Jerusalem and the temple. Wo wo to Jerusalem!" It was in vain that by stripes and torture the magistrates attempted to restrain him; he continued crying, especially at the public festivals, for seven years and five months, and yet never grew hoarse nor appeared to be weary, until during the siege, while he was crying on the wall, a stone struck him and killed him instantly. Tacitus, the Roman historian, joins his testimony to that of Josephus

"Armies, says he, "were seen engaged in th nea-
vens, the glittering of arms was observed; and suddenly the fire from the clouds illuminated the temple; the doors of the inner temple were suddenly
thrown open and a voice more than human was
heard proclaiming, 'The gods are departing;' and at
the same time, the motion of their departure was
perceived." Men may form what judgment they
please of these narratives; but one thing is certain,
that the minds of men were, about this time, much
agitated and terrified with what appeared to them
to be prodigies. There were "fearful sights and
great signs from heaven."

2. The circumstances attending the siege and cap
ture of the city, were as exactly foretold as the preceding signs. " The abomination of desolation,"
spoken of by Daniel the prophet, was nothing else
than the Roman armies, whose ensign was an eagle
perched upon a spear, which ensigns were worshipped as divinities. These stood where *they ought
not,* when they were planted not only in the holy
land, but on the consecrated spot where the temple
had stood. But the Christians had been warned, at
the first appearance of this desolating abomination,
immediately to betake themselves to flight, which
they did, and, instead of going into the city, retired
to Pella beyond Jordan.

The distress of the Jews within the city, during the
siege, where two or three millions of people were
crowded into a narrow space, almost exceeds belief.
What with their continual battles with the Romans;
what with intestine feuds and tumults; what with
famine and pestilence, the sufferings which they
endured cannot now be conceived. No such distress
was ever experienced by any people before or since.

Jerusalem was hemmed in on all sides by the besieging army, and notwithstanding the great strength
of its fortifications, was taken. Although Titus had
given express orders that the temple should be preserved, the mouth of the Lord had declared that it
should be otherwise; and accordingly it was burnt

to the ground, and the very foundation dug up by the soldiers with the hope of finding hidden treasures. After the city had been destroyed, Titus ordered the whole space to be levelled like a field; so that a person approaching the place would hardly suspect that it had ever been inhabited.

The number slain in the war has already been mentioned, to which we may now add that the captives amounted to ninety-seven thousand. Josephus, in relating these events, adopts a language remarkably similar to that used by Christ in the prophecy. "The calamities of all people," says he, "from the creation of the world, if they be compared with those suffered by the Jews, will be found to be far surpassed by them." The words of Christ are: "There shall be great tribulation, such as was not from the beginning of the world to this time; no, nor ever shall be."

That these unparalleled calamities proceeded from the vengeance of heaven against a people whose iniquities were full, was not only acknowledged by Josephus, but by Titus. After taking a survey of the city, the height of its towers and walls, the magnitude of the stones, and the strength of the bands by which they were held together, he broke out into the following exclamation: "By the help of God, we have brought this war to a conclusion. It was God who drew out the Jews from these fortifications; for what could the hands or military engines of men avail against such towers as these?" And he refused to be crowned after the victory, saying that he was not the author of this achievement, but *the anger of God against the Jews*, was what put the victory into his hands.

3. Finally, the consequences of this catastrophe were as distinctly predicted, and as accurately fulfilled, as the preceding events. The Jews who survived were dispersed over the world, in which condition they continue till this day. The Christians, availing themselves of the warnings of their Lord, escaped all the calamities of the siege. Jerusalem

was trodden down of the Gentiles, and continues to be trodden down until this day.

Jerusalem was rebuilt by Adrian, but not precisely on the old site, and was called Ælia, which name it bore until the time of Constantine. The apostate Julian, out of hatred to Christianity, and with the view of defeating the prediction, "Jerusalem shall be trodden down of the Gentiles," determined to restore the Jews, and rebuild their temple. Immense sums were appropriated for the work, the superintendence of which was assigned to one of his lieutenants; and the governor of the province to which Jerusalem belonged, assisted in it. But horrible balls of fire, bursting forth from the foundations, rendered the place inaccessible to the workmen, who were often much burnt, so that the enterprise was laid aside. The account now given is attested by Julian himself, and his favourite heathen historian Ammianus. The witnesses are indeed numerous and unexceptionable· "Ammianus Marcellinus, a heathen; Zemach David, a Jew, who confesses that Julian was *divinitus impeditus*, providentially hindered in his attempt; Nazianzen and Chrysostom among the Greeks; Ambrose and Rufin among the Latins; all of whom flourished at the very time when this wonderful event occurred. Theodoret, Socrates, Sozomen, and Philostorgius, respectable historians, recorded it within fifty years after the event, and while the eye-witnesses of the fact were still surviving."* That part of the prophecy which relates to the restoration of the Jews, remains to be accomplished, and we hope the accomplishment is not far distant. When this event shall take place, the evidence from this prophecy will be complete and almost irresistible. This shall occur when "the times of the Gentiles shall be fulfilled." The circumstances of this glorious event are more particularly described by Paul, in his Epistle to the Romans (chap. xi.) "If the fall of them be the riches of the world, and the diminishing of them the riches of the Gentiles, how much more their

---

* See Whitby's General Preface to the New Testament.

fulness? For I would not, brethren, that ye should be ignorant of this mystery, that blindness in part is happened to Israel, until the fulness of the Gentiles be come in; and so all Israel shall be saved." The preaching of the gospel to all nations has been considered in another place.

After this concise review of some remarkable prophecies contained in the Bible, is there any one who can persuade himself that all these coincidences are accidental, or that the whole is a cunningly devised fable? That man must indeed be blind, who cannot see this "LIGHT which shineth in a dark place; this SURE WORD OF PROPHECY which holy men of God spake as they were moved by the Holy Ghost."

CHAPTER XII.

NO OTHER RELIGION POSSESSES THE SAME KIND AND DEGREE OF EVIDENCE AS CHRISTIANITY; AND NO OTHER MIRACLES ARE AS WELL ATTESTED AS THOSE RECORDED IN THE BIBLE.

HAVING given a brief view of the external evidences of Christianity, it is now proper to inquire whether any system of religion, ancient or modern, is as well supported by evidence; and whether other miracles have testimony in their favour, as satisfactory as that by which the miracles of the gospel are accompanied.

The usual declamation of infidel writers on this subject is calculated to make the impression on unsuspicious readers, that all religions are similar in their origin; that they all lay claim to miracles and divine communications; and that all stand upon an equal footing. But when we descend to particulars, and inquire what religions that now exist, or ever did exist, profess to rest their claims on well attested miracles and the exact accomplishment of prophecy, none besides the Jewish and Christian can be produced. Among the multiform systems of Paganism there is not one which was founded on manifest miracles or prophecies. They had indeed their pro digies and their oracles, by which the credulous multitude were deceived; and their founders pretended to have received revelations or to have held communion with the gods. But what well attested miraculous fact can be produced from all the religions of the heathen world? What oracle ever gave responses so clear and free from ambiguity, as to furnish evidence that the knowledge of futurity was possessed? It is easy to pretend to divine revelation: this is done by every fanatic.

It is not disputed that many impostors have appeared in the world, as well as many deluded fanatics. But the reason why all their claims and pretensions may with propriety be rejected, is, that they were not able to exhibit any satisfactory evidence that they were commissioned from heaven to instruct mankind in religion.

In this we are all agreed. Of what use therefore can it be, to bring up these impostures and delusions, when the evidences of the Christian religion are under consideration? Can it be a reason for rejecting a religion which comes well attested, that there have been innumerable false pretensions to divine revelation? Must miracles supported by abundant testimony be discredited, because there have been reports of prodigies and miracles which have no evidence? And because heathen oracles have given answers to inquiries respecting future events, dark, indeterminate, and designedly ambiguous; shall we place no confidence in numerous authentic prophecies, long ago committed to writing, which have been most exactly and wonderfully accomplished?

It is alleged, that the early history of all ancient nations is fabulous, and abounds in stories of incredible prodigies; and hence it is inferred, that the miracles of the Old and New Testament should be considered in the same light. To which it may be replied, that this general consent of nations that miracles have existed, is favourable to the opinion that true miracles have at some time occurred. It may again be observed, that the history of Moses, which is more than a thousand years older than any profane history, has every evidence of being a true relation of facts; and moreover, that the age in which the miracles of the New Testament were performed, so far from being a dark and fabulous age, was the most enlightened period of the heathen world. It was the age of the most celebrated historians, orators, and poets. There never was a time when it would have been more difficult to gain a general belief in miracles which had no sufficient testimony than in the Augustan and succeeding age. Not only did learning flourish; but there was at that period a general tendency to skepticism and atheism. There can evidently therefore be no inference unfavourable to Christianity, derived from the belief of unfounded stories of miraculous events in the dark ages of antiquity. The only effect of the prevalence of false accounts of miracles should be, to produce caution and careful examination into the evidence of every report of this kind. Reason dictates that truth and falsehood should never be confounded. Let every fact be subjected to the test of a rigid scrutiny, and let it stand or fall, according as it is supported or unsupported by testimony. If the miracles of the Bible have no better evidence than the prodigies of the heathen, they ought to receive no more credit; but if they have solid evidence, they ought not to be confounded with reports which carry imposture on their very face, or at least have no credible testimony in their favour.

There is no other way of deciding on facts which occurred long since, but by testimony. And the truth of Christianity is really a matter of fact. In support of it, we have adduced testimony which cannot be invalidated; and we challenge our opponents to show that any other religion stands on the same firm basis. Instead of this, they would amuse us with vague declamations on the credulity of man, and the many

fabulous stories which have been circulated and believed. But what has this to do with the question?
We admit all this, and maintain that it does not furnish the semblance of an argument against the truth
of the well-attested facts recorded by the evangelists.
Because there is much falsehood in the world, is there
no such thing as truth? It would be just as reasonable to conclude that, because many men have been
convicted of falsehood, there are no persons of veracity in the world; or because there are many knaves,
all pretensions to honesty are unfounded.

The Mohammedan religion is frequently brought
forward by the enemies of revelation, with an air of
confidence, as though the pretensions and success of
that impostor would derogate from the evidences of
Christianity. It is expedient, therefore, to bring this
subject under a particular examination. And here
let it be observed, that we do not reject any thing,
respecting the origin and progress of this religion,
which has been transmitted to us by competent and
credible witnesses. We admit that Mohammed existed and was the founder of a new sect, and that
from a small beginning his religion spread with
astonishing rapidity over the fairest portion of the
globe. We admit also, that he was the author of the
Koran, which he composed from time to time, probably with the aid of some one or two other persons.
It is also admitted, that he was an extraordinary
man, and prosecuted the bold scheme which he had
projected, with uncommon perseverance and address.
Neither are we disposed to deny that the Koran contains many sublime passages, relative to God and his
perfections, and many sound and salutary precepts
of morality. That the language is elegant, and a
standard of purity in the Arabic tongue, has been
asserted by all Mohammedan writers, and conceded
by many learned Christians. But as to his pretended
revelations, there is no external evidence whatever
that they were real; and there is an overwhelming
weight of internal evidence that they are not from
God.

To bring this subject fairly before us, let the following considerations be impartially weighed:

1. The pretensions of Mohammed were supported by no miracles or prophecies. He was often called upon by his opposers to confirm his mission by this decisive proof; but he always declined making the attempt, and resorted to various excuses and subterfuges. In the Koran, God is introduced as saying, " Nothing hindered us from sending thee with miracles, except that the former nations have charged them with imposture: thou art a preacher only." Again, that if he did perform miracles, the people would not believe, as they had before rejected Moses, Jesus, and the prophets who performed them.

Dr. Paley* has enumerated thirteen different places in the Koran, where this objection is considered, in not one of which is it alleged that miracles had been performed for its confirmation. It is true, that this artful man told of things sufficiently miraculous; but for the truth of these assertions, we have no manner of proof except his own word, which, in this case, is worth nothing.

If it had been as easy a thing to obtain credit to stories of miracles publicly performed, as some suppose, surely Mohammed would have had recourse to this measure, when he was so pressed and teased by his enemies with a demand for this very evidence But he had too much cunning to venture upon an expedient so dangerous; his opposers would quickly have detected and exposed the cheat. At length, however, he so far yielded to the demand of his enemies as to publish one of the most extravagant stories which ever entered into the imagination of man, and solemnly swore that every word of it was true I refer to his night journey to Jerusalem, and thence to heaven, under the guidance of the angel Gabriel.

This marvellous story, however, had well nigh ruined his cause. His enemies treated it with deserved ridicule and scorn; and a number of his followers forsook him from that time. In fact, it ren

* Paley's Evidences.

dered his further continuance at Mecca entirely inex-
pedient; and having before despatched some of his
disciples to Medina, he betook himself with his followers to that city, where he met with a more cordial
reception than in his native place.

The followers of Mohammed, hundreds of years
after his death, related many miracles, which they
pretended that he performed: but their report is not
only unsupported by testimony, but is in direct contradiction to the Koran, where he repeatedly dis-
claims all pretensions to miraculous powers. And
the miracles which they ascribe to him, while they
are marvellous enough, are of that trifling and ludicrous kind commonly to be met with in all forgeries
in which miracles are represented as having been
performed; such as, that the trees walked to meet
him; that the stones saluted him; that a beam groaned
to him; that a camel made complaint to him; and that
a shoulder of mutton told him that it was poisoned.

It appears then that Mohammedanism has no evidence whatever but the declaration of the impostor.
It is impossible therefore that Christianity should be
placed in a more favourable point of light than in
comparison with the religion of Mohammed. The
one, as we have seen, rests on well attested miracles;
the other does not exhibit the shadow of a proof that
it was derived from heaven.

2. It is fair to compare the moral characters of the
respective founders of these two religions. And here
we have as perfect a contrast as history can furnish.
Jesus Christ was "holy, harmless, undefiled, and
separate from sinners." His life was pure, without
a stain. His most bitter enemies could find no fault
in him. He exhibited, through life, the most perfect
example of disinterested zeal, pure benevolence, and
unaffected humility which the world ever saw. Mohammed was an ambitious, licentious, cruel, and unjust man. His life was stained with the most atrocious crimes. Blasphemy, perjury, murder, adultery, and robbery, were actions of daily occurrence
in his life. And to shield himself from censure, and

open a door for unbridled indulgence, he pretended revelations from heaven to justify all his vilest practices. He had the effrontery to pretend that God had given him the privilege to commit at pleasure the most abominable crimes. The facts which could be adduced in support of these general charges, are so numerous and so shocking, that I will not defile my paper, nor wound the feelings of the reader, by a recital of them.

3. The Koran itself can never bear a comparison with the New Testament, in the view of any impartial person. It is a confused and incongruous heap of sublime sentiments, moral precepts, positive institutions, extravagant and ridiculous stories, and manifest lies and contradictions. Mohammed himself acknowledged that it contained many contradictions; but he accounted for this fact by alleging that what had been communicated to him in one chapter was repealed in a subsequent one: and so he charges his inconsistency on his Maker. The number of abrogated passages is so great, that a Mussulman cannot be easily confuted by proving the falsehood of any declaration in the Koran; for he will have recourse to this doctrine of *abrogation*. There is nothing in this book which cannot easily be accounted for; nothing above the capacity of impostors to accomplish. It is artfully accommodated to the religions of Arabia, prevalent at the time. It gives encouragement to the strongest and most vicious passions of human nature ; promotes ambition, despotism, revenge, and offensive war; opens wide the door of licentiousness ; and holds out such rewards and punishments as are adapted to make an impression on the minds of wicked men. It discourages, and indeed forbids all free inquiry, and all discussion of the doctrines which it contains. Whatever is excellent in the Koran, is in imitation of the Bible; but wherever the author follows his own judgment, or indulges his own imagination, we find falsehood, impiety, or ridiculous absurdity.*

* See Ryan's History of the effects of Religion on Mankind.

4. The means by which the religion of Moham
med was propagated were entirely different from
those employed in the propagation of the gospel. If
there is any point of strong resemblance between these
two systems, it consists merely in the circumstance
of their rapid and extensive progress and permanent
continuance.

But when we come to consider the means by
which this end was attained in the two cases, instead
of resemblance we find a perfect contrast. Mohammed did indeed attempt at first to propagate his religion by persuasion and artifice, and these efforts he
continued for twelve years, but with very small success. At the end of three years, he had gained no
more than fourteen disciples; at the end of seven
years, his followers amounted to little more than
eighty; at the end of twelve years when he fled from
Mecca, the number was still very inconsiderable. As
far, therefore, as there can be a fair comparison between the progress of Christianity and Mohammedanism—that is, during the time that Mohammed
employed argument and persuasion alone—there is
no resemblance. The progress of Christianity was
like the lightning which shineth from one part of
heaven to the other; extending in a few years, not
only without aid from learning and power, but in
direct opposition to both, throughout the whole Roman empire, and far beyond its limits. Mohammedanism for twelve years made scarcely any progress,
though it commenced among an ignorant and unciv-
ilized people. During this period, the progress was
scarcely equal to what might be expected from any
artful impostor. This religion never spread in any
other way than by the sword. As soon as the inhabitants of Medina declared in favour of Mohammed,
he changed his whole plan, and gave out that he was
directed to propagate his religion by force. From
this time he is found engaged in war. He began
by attacking mercantile caravans, and as his force
increased went on to conquer the petty kingdoms
into which Arabia was then divided.* Sometimes,

* See Prideaux's Life of Mohammed.

he p it all the prisoners to death, and at othe. times, sold them into slavery. At first, the order was to massacre every creature that refused to embrace his religion; but he became more lenient afterwards especially to Jews and Christians. The alternative was, "the Koran, death, or tribute."

But it is a great mistake to suppose that the con quests of Mohammed himself were very extensive He, never, during his life, extended his dominior beyond the limits of Arabia, except that he overran one or two inconsiderable provinces of Syria. It was by the Caliphs, his successors, that so great a part of Asia and Egypt were brought into subjection. But what is there remarkable in these successes more than those of other conquerors? Surely the propagation of Mohammedanism by the sword, however rapid or extensive, can never bear any comparison with that of Christianity, by the mere force of truth under the blessing of heaven.

5. The tendency and effects of Mohammedanism, when compared with the tendency and effects of Christianity, serve to exhibit the latter in a very favourable light. The Christian religion has been a rich blessing to every country which has embraced it; and its salutary effects have borne proportion to the care which has been taken to inculcate its genuine principles, and the cordiality with which its doctrines have been embraced. What nations are truly civilized? Where does learning flourish? Where are the poor and afflicted most effectually relieved? Where do men enjoy the greatest security of life, property, and liberty? Where is the female sex treated with due respect, and exalted to its proper place in society? Where is the education of youth most assiduously pursued? Where are the brightest examples of benevolence; and where do men enjoy most rational happiness? If we were called upon to designate the countries in which these advantages are most highly enjoyed, every one of them would be found in Christendom; and the superiority enjoyed by some over the others, would be found to bear

an exact proportion to the practical influence of pure Christianity.

On the contrary, if we take a survey of the rich and salubrious regions possessed by Mohammedans we behold a wide-spread desolation. The fairest portion of the globe, where arts, literature, and refinement formerly most flourished, are now blighted Every noble institution has sunk into oblivion. Despotism extends its iron sceptre over these ill-fated countries, and all the tranquillity ever enjoyed is the dead calm of ignorance and slavery. Useful learning is discouraged, free inquiry proscribed, and servile submission required of all. Justice is perverted or disregarded. No man has any security for life or property, and as to liberty, it is utterly lost wherever the Mohammedan religion prevails. While the fanatic ardour of making proselytes continued, the fury of the propagators of this faith rendered them irresistible. Indeed, their whole system is adapted to a state of war. The best work that can be performed, according to the Koran, is to fight for the propagation of the faith; and the highest rewards are promised to those who die in battle. There is no doubt that the principles of the Koran greatly contributed to the conquest of the Saracens, by divesting them of all fear of death, and inspiring them with an assurance of being admitted into a sensual paradise, if it should be their fate to be slain in battle. "The sword is the key of heaven and hell; a drop of blood shed in the cause of God, a night spent under arms, is of more avail than two months of fasting and prayer. Whosoever falls in battle, his sins are forgiven. At the day of judgment, his wounds shall be resplendent as vermilion and odoriferous as musk; and the loss of his limbs shall be replaced by the wings of angels and cherubims." But when they had finished their conquests, and a state of peace succeeded their long and bloody wars, they sunk into torpid indolence and stupidity. While other nations have been making rapid improvements in all the arts, they have remained stationary, or rather have been continually going backwards. They have derived no advantages from the revival of letters, the invention of printing, or other improvements in the arts and sciences. The people who have been subjected to their despotism without adopting their religion, are kept in the most degraded subjection.

At present,* the Greeks are making noble exertions to break the cruel yoke which has oppressed them, and though unsupported by Christian nations, have succeeded in expelling the Turks from a large portion of their country. God grant them success, and give them wisdom to make a good use of their liberty and independence when acquired and established!† Mohammedanism was permitted to prevail, as a just punishment to Christians for their luxury and dissensions. It is to be hoped, however, that the prescribed time of these "locusts of the abyss"‡ is nearly come to an end; and that a just God, who has so long used them as a scourge to Christians, as he formerly did the Canaanites to be thorns in the eyes and in the sides of the Israelites, will soon bring to an end this horrible despotism, founded on a vile imposture. The signs of the times give strong indications that the Mohammedan power will shortly be subverted. But it is not for us to "know the times and the seasons which the Father hath put in his own power."

The only thing further necessary to be considered, in this chapter, is, the miracles which have been brought forward as a counterpoise to the miracles of Christ and his apostles. This is an old stratagem, at least as old as the second century, when one Philostratus, at the request of Julia Augusta, wife of the emperor Severus, wrote a history, or rather romance, of Apollonius of Tyana, a town in Cappadocia. This Apollonius was nearly contemporary with Jesus Christ; but whether he was a philosopher or a conjurer cannot now be ascertained; for as to the

---

* A.D. 1825.
† The Greeks have now become an independent nation, 1836.
‡ Rev. ix. 3.

story of Philostratus, which is still extant, it is totally unsupported by any reference to eye-witnesses of
the facts, or any documents of credit, and has throughout as much the air of extravagant fiction as any
thing that was ever published. That the design of
the writer was to set up this Apollonius as a rival to
Jesus Christ, is not avowed, but is sufficiently evident from the similarity of many of his miracles to
those recorded in the gospels, borrowed from the
evangelical history. He is made to raise the dead,
to cast out demons, and to rise from the dead himself. In one instance, the very words of the demons
expelled by Jesus Christ, as recorded by St. Luke,
"Art thou come to torment us before the time?" are
put into the mouth of a demon, said to be cast out
by Apollonius. But in addition to these miracles,
his biographer pretends that he saw beasts with a
human head and a lion's body, women half white
and half black, together with phœnixes, griffins, dragons, and similar fabulous monsters.

In the fourth century, Hierocles, a bitter enemy
of Christianity, instituted a comparison between Jesus and Apollonius, in which, after considering their
miracles, he gives the preference to the latter. This
book was answered by Eusebius, from whose work
only, we can now learn how Hierocles treated the
subject, as the book of the latter is not extant. The
only conclusion which can be deduced from this his
tory of Apollonius is, that the miracles of Christ were
so firmly believed in the second century, and were
attended by such testimony, that the enemies of
Christianity could not deny the facts, and therefore
resorted to the expedient of circulating stories of
equal miracles performed by another.

Modern infidels have not been ashamed to resort
to the same stale device. Mr. Hume has taken
much pains to bring forward a great array of evidence in favour of certain miracles, in which he has
no faith, with the view of discrediting the truth of
Christianity. These have been so fully and satisfactorily considered by Dr. Douglass, Bishop of Salis-

bury, in his Criterion, and by Dr. Campbell, in his Essay on Miracles, that I need only refer to these learned authors for a complete confutation of Hume's arguments from this source.

For the sake, however, of those who may not have access to these works, I will lay down a few general principles by which we may distinguish true and false miracles; for which I am indebted principally to the author of the Criterion.

1. The nature of the facts should be well considered, whether they are miraculous. The testimony which supports a fact may be sufficient, and yet it may have been brought about by natural causes.

The miracles of Jesus Christ were such that there was no room for doubt respecting their supernatural character; but a great part of those performed by others, which have received the best attestation, were of such a nature that they may readily be accounted for, without supposing any divine interposition. The case of the man diseased in his eyes, said to have been cured by Vespasian's rubbing his hand over them, and the lame man cured by a touch of the emperor's foot, were no doubt impositions practised by the priests of the temple where they were performed. The emperor did not pretend to possess any miraculous power, and was induced, only after much persuasion, to make the experiment. It may be admitted that the facts as related by Tacitus, though he was not an eye-witness, are true. Such persons were probably brought forward and a cure pretended to be made, but there is no evidence that there was a real miracle. There was no one present who felt interested to examine into the truth of the miracle. The priests who proposed the thing had no doubt prepared their subjects; and the emperor was flattered by the honour of being selected by their god to work a miracle. How often do beggars in the street impose upon many, by pretending to be blind and lame! The high encomiums which Mr. Hume bestows on the historian Tacitus, in order to set off the testimony to the best advantage, can have no weight here; for he only related what he had heard from others, and showed pretty evidently that he did not credit the story himself.

The same may be said respecting the man at Saragossa, spoken of by Cardinal de Retz, who was represented as having been seen without a leg, but obtained one by rubbing the stump with holy oil. The Cardinal had no other evidence of his having ever been maimed, than the suspicious report of the canons of the Church; and he took no pains to ascertain whether the leg which he obtained was really flesh and blood, or an artificial limb.

A great part of the cures said to have been performed at the tomb of the Abbé Paris, were proved upon examination to be mere pretences; and those which were real may easily be accounted for, from the influence of a heated imagination and enthusiastic feelings; especially, since we have seen the wonderful effects of animal magnetism and metallic tractors.

The Abbé Paris was the oldest son of a counsellor of Paris, but being much inclined to a life of devotion he relinquished his patrimony to his younger brother, and retired to an obscure part of Paris, where he spent his life in severe penance, and in charitable exertions for the relief of the distressed poor. He was buried in the ground of the church of St. Medard, near the wall, where his brother erected a tombstone over the grave. To this spot many poor people who knew his manner of life, came to perform their devotions, as much, probably, out of feelings of gratitude as any thing else. Some, among the devotees who attended at this place, professed that they experienced a salutary change in their ailments. This being noised abroad, as the Abbé had been a zealous Jansenist all who were of his party encouraged the idea of miracles having been performed; and multitudes who were indisposed, were induced to go to the tomb of the saint; and some, as they confessed before a competent tribunal, were persuaded to feign diseases which they never had. It is a fact, however, that the greater part received no benefit, and that more diseases were produced than were cured: for, soon, many of the worshippers were seized with convulsions, from which proceeded the sect of CONVULSIONISTS, which attracted attention for many years.

It was soon found expedient to close up the tomb: but cures were still said to be performed by the saint on persons in distant places. The Jesuits exerted themselves to discredit the whole business, and the Archbishop of Paris had a judicial investigation made of a number of the most remarkable cases, the results of which were various, and often ludicrous. A young woman said to have been cured at the tomb of blindness and lameness, was proved to have been neither blind nor lame. A man with diseased eyes was relieved, but it appeared that he was then using powerful medicine, and that, after all, his eyes were not entirely healed. A certain Abbé who had the misfortune to have one of his legs shorter than the other, was persuaded that he experienced a sensible elongation of the defective limb, but on measurement no increase could be discovered. A woman in the same situation danced on the tomb daily to obtain an elongation of a defective limb, and was persuaded that she received benefit; but it was ascertained, that she would have to dance there fifty-four years, before the cure would be effected, at the rate at which it was proceeding; but as for the unfortunate Abbé, seventy-two years would have been requisite. In short, the whole number of cures, after examination, was reduced to eight or nine, all of which can be easily accounted for on natural principles; and in several of these instances, the cures were not perfect.

2. A second consideration of great weight is. that in true miracles we can trace the testimony to the very time when the facts are said to have occurred, but in false miracles the report of the facts originates a long time afterwards, as in the case of Apollonius, the miracles ascribed to Mohammed by Abulfeda, and Al-Janabbi, and the miracles ascribed by the

Jesuits to Ignatius Loyola their founder; which were never heard of until long after his death.

3. Another criterion of importance is, that the report of miracles should originate and first obtain credit in the place and among the people, where they are said to have been performed. This is too remarkably the fact, in regard to the miracles of the Bible, to require any proof. But many stories of miracles are rendered suspicious by the circumstance that they were first reported and believed in some place far from that in which they were alleged to have been wrought. The miracles ascribed by the Romanists to Francis Xavier, are condemned by both the rules last mentioned. In all his letters while a missionary in the east, he never hints that miracles had been wrought; and a reputable writer who gave some account of his labours nearly forty years after his death, not only is silent about Xavier's miracles, but confesses that no miracles had been performed among the Indians. These miracles were said to be performed in the remote parts of India and Japan, but the report of them was published first in Europe Almost all the miracles ascribed by the Romish Church to her saints, fall into the same predicament. The history of them is written long after they are said to have been performed, and often in countries remote from the place where it is pretended they occurred or they are manifestly the effect of cunning contrivance and imposture.

4. Another necessary question in judging of the genuineness of miracles, is, whether the facts were scrutinized at the time, or were suffered to pass without examination. When the miracles reported coincide with the passions and prejudices of those before whom they are performed; when they are exhibited by persons in power, who can prevent all examination and put what face they please on facts, they may well be reckoned suspicious. The cures at the tomb of the Abbé Paris were not performed in these circumstances. The Jansenists were not in power, and their enemies not only had the opportunity to

examine into the facts, but actually did so with the utmost diligence. We have reason to believe, therefore, that we have now a true report of those occurrences. The defect of these miracles is in their nature, not in their evidence.

But, in most cases, the miracles which have been reported, took place when there was no opportunity of examining into the facts; when the people were pleased to be confirmed in their favourite opinions; or when the ruling powers had some peculiar end to answer.*

But supposing these miracles to be ever so well attested, I do not perceive how the evidence of divine revelation can be affected by them; for if it could be made to appear that these were supported by testimony as strong as that which can be adduced in favour of the miracles of the New Testament, the only fair conclusion is, that they who believe in Christianity should admit them to be true—but what then? Would it follow, because miracles had been wrought on some rare occasions, different from those recorded in the Bible, that therefore, these were of no validity as evidence of divine revelation? Would not the fact that other miracles had been wrought, rather confirm our belief in those which were performed with so important a design? Mr. Hume does, indeed, artfully insinuate that the various accounts of miracles which exist cannot be true, because the religions which they were wrought to confirm, are opposite; yet not one of those which he brings forward as being best attested, was performed in confirmation of any new religion, or to prove any particular doctrine, therefore they are not opposed to Christianity. If they had actually occurred, it would not in the least disparage the evidence for the facts recorded in the New Testament. And especially, it is a strange conceit, that miracles performed within the bosom of the Christian Church should furnish any proof against Christianity.

It is, however, no part of the object of those who

* On this whole subject, see Douglass's Criterion.

bring forward such an array of testimony in support
of certain miracles, to prove that such facts ever
occurred.   This is diametrically opposite to their
purpose.   Their des.gn is to discredit all testimony
in favour of miracles, by showing, that facts acknowledged to be false have evidence as strong as those
on which revealed religion rests.   But they have
utterly failed in the attempt, as we have shown: and
if they had succeeded in adducing as strong testimony for other miracles, we would readily admit their
truth, and that in perfect consistency with our belief
in Christianity.

The Romish Church and some other fanatical sects,
do still profess to work miracles; but these pretences
are never submitted to the test of an impartial examination by opposers.   Or if they are ever publicly
exhibited, as in the case of the liquefaction of the
blood of St. Januarius, it only serves to convince all
reasonable men that it is a gross imposture.

CHAPTER XIII.

THE BIBLE CONTAINS INTERNAL EVIDENCE THAT ITS ORIGIN IS DIVINE

As the Old and New Testaments are intimately connected, and form parts of the same system, it is unnecessary to make any distinction between them, in
considering this branch of the evidence of divine re
velation.

A late writer,* of great eminence and popularity,
has represented this species of evidence as unsatisfactory; as not capable of being so treated as to produce conviction in the minds of philosophical infidels;
and as opening a door to their most specious objections to Christianity.   But certainly this is not the most
effectual method of supporting the credit of the Scrip-

* Dr. Chalmers.

tures. Another popular writer,* has gone to the other extreme, and seems to set little value on the external evidences of Christianity, while he exhibits the internal in a light so strong that his argument assumes the appearance of demonstration.†

But these two species of evidence, though distinct are harmonious, and strengthen each other. There is, therefore, no propriety in disparaging the one for the purpose of enhancing the value of the other. I believe, however, that more instances have occurred of skeptical men being convinced of the truth of Christianity by the internal than by the external evidences. It is the misfortune of most infidels, that they have no intimate acquaintance with the Bible; and even many of those who have undertaken to write against it, appear never to have read it with any other view than to find some ground of objection.

No doubt it is necessary to come to the examination of this species of evidence, with a candid and docile disposition. If reason be permitted proudly to assume the seat of judgment, and to decide what a revelation ought to contain in particular; in what manner, and with what degree of light it should be communicated; whether it should be made perfectly at once, or gradually unfolded; and whether, from the beginning, it should be universal; no doubt, the result of an examination of the contents of the Bible, conducted on such principles, will prove unsatisfactory, and insuperable objections will occur at every step in the progress. It was wise in Dr. Chalmers to endeavour to discourage such a mode of investigation, as being most unreasonable; for how is it possible that such a creature as man should be able to know what is proper for the infinite God to do, or in what way he should deal with his creatures upon earth? To borrow the language of this powerful

* Soame Jenyns.
† The author has the pleasure of knowing that in his more recent publications, Dr. Chalmers recognizes the validity and importance of the internal evidence of Christianity, and has treated the subject in his usual forcible and convincing manner.

writer,* "We have experience of man, but we nave no experience of God. We can reason upon the procedure of man in given circumstances, because this is an accessible subject, and comes under the cognizance of observation; but we cannot reason upon the procedure of the Almighty in given circumstances." But when he speaks "of disclaiming all support from what is commonly understood by the internal evidence," and "saving a vast deal of controversy, by proving that all this is superfluous and uncalled for," I am constrained to think that, instead of aiding the cause of Christianity, the excellent author has attempted to take away one of its firmest props. The internal evidence of revelation is analogous to the evidence of the being and perfections of God from the works of creation : and the same mode of reasoning which the deist adopts relative to the doctrines and institutions of the Bible, the atheist may adopt, with equal force, against the existence of a God. If men will be so presumptuous as to determine, that if God makes a world he will form it according to their idea of fitness, and that the apparent imperfections and incomprehensibilities in the material universe could never have proceeded from a being of infinite perfection, atheism must follow of course. But if, notwithstanding all these apparent evils and obscurities, there is in the structure of the world the most convincing evidence of the existence of an all-wise and all-powerful being, why may we not expect to find the same kind of evidence impressed on a revelation from God? Upon Dr. Chalmers' principles we ought to depend simply on historical testimony, for the fact, that God created this world; and "disclaim all support" from what may, without impropriety, be termed the internal evidence of the existence of God, derived from the contemplation of the work itself. The truth however, is, that every thing which proceeds from God, whatever difficulties or obscurities accompany it, will contain and exhibit the impress of his charac

* Chalmers' Evidences.

ter. As this is resplendently visible in the heavens
and in the earth, it is reasonable to think that it will
not be less manifest in his word. If the truths contained in a revelation be worthy of God, they will
be stamped with his image; and if this can be in
any measure discovered, it undoubtedly furnishes the
most direct and convincing evidence of their divine
origin. This is, without being reduced to the form
of a regular argument, precisely the evidence on
which the faith of the great body of Christians has
always rested. They are incapable of appreciating
the force of the external evidence. It requires an
extent of learning which plain Christians cannot be
supposed commonly to possess. But the internal
evidence is within their reach; it acts directly upon
their minds whenever they read or hear a portion of
the word of God. The belief of common, unlearned
Christians, is not necessarily founded on the mere
prejudice of education; it rests on the best possible
evidence. And as there is a faith which is saving
and to which a purifying efficacy is ascribed; if we
inquire on what species of evidence this depends, it
must be answered, on internal evidence, not indeed
as perceived by the unaided intellect of man, but as
it is exhibited to the mind by the illumination of the
Holy Spirit. We cannot consent, therefore, to give
up this species of evidence, as " superfluous and uncalled for;" but must consider it, if not the most
effectual to silence gainsayers, yet certainly the most
useful to the real Christian; and if unbelievers could
be induced to attend to it with docility and impar-
tiality, there is reason to think that they would experience its efficacy, in the gradual production of
a firm conviction of the truth of Christianity. The
internal evidence of the truth of the Scriptures cannot be fully brought into view, in any other way
than by a careful study of the Bible. It cannot
easily be put into the form of logical argument, for it
consists in moral fitness and beauty; in the adaptation of truth to the human mind; in its astonishing
power of penetrating and searching the heart and

affecting the conscience. There is a sublime sanctity in the doctrines and precepts of the gospel; a devotional and heavenly spirit pervading the Scriptures;
a purity and holy tendency which cannot but be felt
by the serious reader of the word of God; and a
power to sooth and comfort the sorrowful mind; all
which qualities may be perceived, and will have
their effect, but cannot be embodied and presented,
with their full force, in the form of argument. But
although this evidence, from the nature of the case,
cannot be exhibited in its entire body, to any but
those who study the Scriptures and meditate on their
truths day and night, it is possible to select some
prominent points and present them to the reader in
such a light as to produce a salutary impression.
This is what will be briefly attempted in the following remarks, which might without difficulty be greatly enlarged.

1. The Scriptures speak of God and his attributes
in a way which accords with what right reason
would lead us to expect in a divine revelation. He
is uniformly represented in the Bible as ONE, and as
a being of infinite perfection; as eternal, omnipotent,
omniscient, omnipresent, and immutable. And it is
truly remarkable, that these correct and sublime
views of theology were entertained by those who
possessed the Scriptures, when all other nations had
fallen into the grossest polytheism and most degrading idolatry. Other nations were more powerful,
and greatly excelled the Israelites in human learning; but in the knowledge of God all were in thick
darkness, whilst this people enjoyed the light of truth.
Learned men and philosophers arose in different
countries, and obtained celebrity on account of their
theories, but they effected no change in the popular
opinions; indeed, they could not enlighten others,
when they were destitute of the light of truth themselves. However deists may deride and scoff at the
Bible, it is a fact capable of the clearest proof, that
had it not been for the Scriptures, there would not
at this time be such a thing as pure theism upon

earth. There is not now in the world an individual who believes in one infinitely perfect God, whose knowledge of this truth may not be traced directly or indirectly to the Bible.

How can it be accounted for that the true theology should be found accompanying the Scriptures in all ages, while it was lost every where else, unless we admit that they are a revelation from God? If the knowledge of the true God, as received by the Jews, was the discovery of reason, why was it that other nations advanced far beyond them in learning and mental culture, never arrived at the knowledge of this important truth?

It is true, indeed, that the Scriptures sometimes represent God as having bodily parts and human passions; but a little consideration will show the attentive reader, that all these expressions are used in accommodation to the manner of speaking among men Human language is inadequate to express the attributes and operations of the Supreme Being. He is infinitely above our conceptions, both in his essence and his mode of existence and acting. We can do no more than approximate towards just ideas on this subject. When we speak of him we are under the necessity of conceiving of his perfections with some relation to the operations of the human mind, and to employ language expressive of human acts and feelings; for all other language would be unintelligible. The necessity of this accommodation extends much further than many seem to suppose. It exists not only in relation to words which, taken literally, convey the idea of bodily members and human passions, but also in regard to those which express the operations of will and intellect. This mode of speaking therefore, instead of being an objection against the Bible, is an argument of the wisdom of its Author, who has spoken to man in the only way in which he could be understood.

Again, it is seen by the most cursory reader that truth is not taught in the Bible in a scientific or systematic order. We have no profound metaphysical

disquisitions of philosophical principles; no array o
artifical dialectics; no systematic arrangement of the
subjects treated.   In all this there may be great
wisdom, and whether we can see the reason or not,
the objection to revelation on this ground is not
greater than the one which may be made to the
natural world, because the materials for building
which it contains, are not found erected into houses;
and because all its fields and forests are not placed
in the order of an artificial garden or regular orchard.

The method of speaking of God, in the sacred
Scriptures, is at once most simple and sublime.   Few
words are employed, but these are most significant.
When Moses wished to receive an appropriate name
which he might mention to Pharaoh, he was directed
to say, I AM THAT I AM, hath sent me.   And when on
another occasion, the name of the Most High was
declared to Moses, it was in the following remarkable
words: THE LORD, THE LORD GOD, MERCIFUL AND
GRACIOUS, LONG-SUFFERING AND ABUNDANT IN GOOD-
NESS AND TRUTH; KEEPING MERCY FOR THOUSANDS;
FORGIVING INIQUITY, AND TRANSGRESSION, AND SIN;
AND THAT WILL BY NO MEANS CLEAR THE GUILTY.
If the most perfect simplicity, united with the highest
sublimity, would be received as a proof that the
writers of these books were inspired, we could adduce
hundreds of passages of this description; but we
mean not to lay any undue stress on the argument
derived from this source.

The glory of the Scriptures is the revelation which
they contain of the moral attributes of God.   These
are manifested with but a feeble light in the works
of creation; but in the Bible they shine with trans-
cendent lustre.   It would by no means comport with
the intended brevity of this work, to enter much into
detail on this subject, but I must beg the indulgence
of the reader while I endeavour to bring distinctly
into view the account which the Scriptures give us
of the HOLINESS and the GOODNESS OF GOD.

These two attributes are stamped on the pages
of the Bible, and form its grand characteristic.   It is

of no importance whether we consider these as distinct or as expressive of two aspects in which the same infinite excellence is exhibited. Who can open this sacred book without perceiving that the God of the Bible is HOLY? All his laws, institutions, and dispensations are holy; even those laws which are ceremonial have this characteristic. Every person, edifice, and utensil employed in his worship, must be solemnly consecrated; and all must approach God with caution and reverence, because he is HOLY. The very ground where he occasionally makes himself known is rendered holy. Every external sign and emblem of profound reverence, is required in them who worship him; and when he manifests himself with more than usual clearness, the holiest men are overwhelmed and become as dead men under a sense of their own vileness. And not only so, but even the heavenly hosts who are free from every stain of sin, seem to be overwhelmed with the view of the HOLINESS of God. They not only cry to one another, as they worship around his august throne, HOLY, HOLY, HOLY, but they are represented, as falling prostrate at his feet, and veiling their faces in token of profound veneration. All those passages of Scripture which speak of the WRATH, the INDIGNATION, the FURY, the JEALOUSY, or the ANGER of the Almighty, are no more than strong expressions of his infinite holiness. All his severe judgments and threatenings; all the misery which he ever inflicts on his creatures in this world or the next; and above all, the intense and ineffable sufferings of Christ, are exhibitions of the holiness of God.

Now if there be a God, he must be holy; and if he make a revelation of himself, it will be marked with this impress of his character. Wicked men would never have made this attribute so prominent; they would have been disposed rather to keep it entirely out of view. There is no truth more evident to the attentive observer of human nature than that men do not naturally love holiness, although they are obliged to acknowledge its worth. This, I believe, is the true reason why the Scriptures, although they contain the highest excellence in composition, both in prose and poetry, of which a good taste cannot be insensible, are neglected by literary men, or rather studiously avoided. A mere fragment of any other book, if it could claim an equal antiquity with the Bible, and especially if it possessed any thing like its excellence of composition, would be sought after with avidity by all men of taste; but the Bible remains almost as much unstudied by men of this description as the Koran. This has often appeared to me paradoxical; but I am now persuaded that the true reason is the awful holiness of God, as exhibited in this book and impressed on almost every page. This glares upon the conscience of an unholy man, as the meridian sun on diseased eyes. GOD IS A CONSUMING FIRE. This common dislike of the Bible, even in men of refined taste and decent lives, furnishes a strong argument for its divine origin. The question before us, is, who composed this book, inspired men or wicked impostors? The characteristic which we have been considering, will accord perfectly with the former supposition; it never can be reconciled with the latter. There is a moral certainty that base impostors never would have written a book, the most remarkable trait of which is HOLINESS.

The GOODNESS OF GOD, or that benevolence which he exercises towards his creatures, as it appears in the providence which sustains and feeds so great a multitude of sentient beings, and which is conspicuously manifested to the human family, is often celebrated in the Scriptures. Some of the most beautiful and sublime poems which were ever written, are employed in celebrating the praise of God for his marvellous goodness. The reader is requested to turn to the 34th, 103d, 104th, 145th, 147th, and 148th Psalms, as an exemplification of this remark.

There is another and a peculiar view of the divine goodness given in the Scriptures. It is that form of goodness called MERCY. It is the love of creatures who had forfeited all claim to any kindness It is the bestowing of pardon and salvation on those who are condemned to death by the righteous laws of God; and this without showing himself less displeased with their sins than if he had punished them for ever. This is the view of divine goodness which is peculiar to the Bible. Reason could not have formed a conjecture concerning it. It is the development of a trait in the divine character before unknown. To reveal the mercy of God, may with truth be said to be the principal object of the Bible. But our idea of this divine goodness is very imperfect until we learn in what way it was manifested. No words can express this so well as those of Christ himself: "God so loved the world, that he gave his only begotten Son, that whosoever believeth on him should not perish, but have everlasting life."

To many, perhaps, it will appear that this love is so extraordinary, that it rather forms an objection against the Bible than an argument in its favour. If the wonderful and unparalleled nature of any thing were an objection to it, then I acknowledge that there would be some ground for this opinion. But what is there which is not full of wonders, when we come to contemplate it attentively? It is wonderful that there should exist such a creature as man, or such a body of light as the sun; but shall we therefore refuse to believe in their existence? To come nearer to the subject, what is there in the character of God or his works, which is not calculated to fill the mind with surpassing wonder? His eternity, his omniscience, his omnipresence, his creating power, his universal providence are so wonderful, that we are at a loss to say which is most wonderful; or whether any thing else can be more wonderful. But is this any argument against their reality? And if God is so wonderful in his other attributes, shall we expect to find nothing of this kind in his LOVE, which is his highest glory? There is, indeed, no goodness of this sort among men; but shall we make our faint and limited shadow of perfection the measure by which to judge of the character of the infinite God? How unreason

able such a procedure   The objection derived from
the insignificance of man, the object of this wonderful
love, is delusive; for the same objection would lie, if
his powers were increased ever so much.   In comparison with God, all creatures may be considered as
on a level; in this view all distinctions among them
are, as it were, annihilated.   On the same principles,
how easy would it be to construct an argument
against the providence of God!   There are innumerable myriads of animalcules, invisible to man, all of
which have a perfect organization, and no more than
an ephemeral existence.   It might be said these
minute creatures are too diminutive to occupy the
attention of an infinite being.   It might be said that
the display of so much skill in the organization of
creatures of a day, was unsuitable to the wisdom of
God.   But however plausible such objections may
be made to appear, they are all founded in a presumptuous intrusion into what does not appertain to
us, and concerning which we have no ability to form
any correct judgment.   Man has an infinitude below
him as well as above him, in the gradation of being.
I do not mean to say that creation is absolutely infinite, but that we can fix no bounds to the possibility
of a continual existence of creatures in the scale of
perpetual diminution, any more than we can to the
possibility of creatures still increasing in magnitude
above us.   In this respect, as in others, we stand
between two infinitudes, the great and the small.   A
ingle drop of liquid contains myriads of perfectly
organized creatures; and who knows but every par
ticle of the blood of these invisible animalcules may
contain other worlds of beings still more minute,
without its being possible for us to fix any limit to
the diminution in the size of creatures?

   But to return; unless it can be shown, that such
love as that exhibited in the gospel is impossible,
which will not be pretended, or that it is repugnant
to the moral attributes of God, its wonderful nature
can never be used as an argument against its existence.   It should be rather argued, the more won-

ful, the more like God; the more wonderful, if no appearance of human weakness accompany it, the more unlikely to be the invention of man.

And here I would suggest an idea, which, if cor rect, would shed light on the subject; namely, tha wonder is congenial to the constitution of our minds The soul of man never enjoys more elevated emo tions and more exalted pleasure, than in the contem plation of objects so great and vast as to be perfectly incomprehensible. This is the foundation of that perpetual adoration which occupies the inhabitants of heaven. An incomprehensible God is the object of contemplation and wonder to every creature.

2. The account which the Bible gives of the origin and character of man accords, very exactly, with rea- son and experience. Indeed, this is the only source of our knowledge respecting the circumstances in which man was placed when he came from the hand of his Creator. Here we learn the origin of many things which we observe, but the reason of which we never could have discovered. The Bible teaches us that the wickedness which has existed in all ages and among all people, originated in the apostasy of the first man. It tells us the reason of covering the body with clothing, which is the custom of all nations, even where clothing is unnecessary to preserve the body from the effects of cold. Here we learn the cause of the earth's producing briers and thorns spontaneously, while useful grain and fruits must be cultivated. Here we learn the origin of marriage, and of the curse which has followed the female sex through all ages. Moses has also given us the ori- gin of that species of religious worship which was anciently practised among all people, but of which reason can teach us nothing. I mean the sacrifice of animals on an altar, and the offerings of grain, of incense, &c. He has also related the fact of a universal deluge, of which we have so many ocular proofs in every country and on every mountain, as well as so many ancient traditions.

The dispersion of the human family over the face

7*

of the earth, and the origin of the several nations of antiquity, are recorded in the Bible; and although this record is contained in a single short chapter, and has to us much obscurity, yet Bishop Watson declared, that if we had no other evidence of the authenticity of the Pentateuch besides the tenth chapter of Genesis, he would deem that alone satisfactory.*

The origin of the diversity of language is also found in the Bible, and not learned from any other source. Indeed, the origin of language itself, concerning which philosophers have disputed so much, is very evident from the history of Moses. Many learned men have thought that alphabetical writing took its rise from the writing of the decalogue by the finger of God upon the tables of stone; and I believe it would be found very difficult to prove by any authentic documents, that this art existed before. Be this as it may, it must be admitted that the earliest specimen of alphabetical writing now extant is contained in the Bible.

To these particulars it may be added that we have an account in the Bible of those nations and people, concerning whom the earliest profane historians treat, long before their histories commence; and when his tory comes down to that period when the affairs of nations are described by others, it receives ample corroboration from their narratives, as well as gives great light to enable us to understand many things which they have imperfectly recorded.

But the account which the Bible gives of the moral condition of man is that which is now most to our purpose. In all ages and circumstances the human race are represented as exceedingly depraved and wicked. Every man is declared to be a transgressor, and the root of this depravity is placed in the heart. Many of the gross crimes to which we all are inclined, and into the practice of which many fall, are enumerated; and where these are avoided and concealed, the heart is described as deceitful and despe-

* See Watson's Address to Scoffers.

rately wicked; and that pride and hypocrisy, which spread a false covering over the true character of man, are denounced as among the things most hateful to God. Now, if this picture is not taken from the life; if the character of man is entirely different from that delineated in the Scriptures, or if the vices of our nature are exaggerated; however difficult it may be to account for such misrepresentation, still it would furnish a strong argument against the inspiration of the writers of the several books of which the Bible consists. But on the other hand, if the character of man, as given in the Scriptures, is found exactly to correspond with universal experience and observation, it will be found an incontestable proof that the writers were guided by a strict regard to truth. To enter into a particular consideration of this subject, does not comport with the plan of this work; but for the truth of the representations of Scripture, I would appeal to all authentic history, and to every man's own observation and experience. The description which the apostle Paul gives of the vices of the heathen world in his time, is corroborated by all the historians and satirists who lived near that period. And who needs a laboured proof to show that men have generally a tendency to be wicked? Every civil institution, and all the most expensive provisions of civil government, are intended to set up barriers against the violence, injustice and licentiousness of man. Indeed civil government itself originated in nothing else than the necessity of protection against the wickedness of men. This, however, is a painful and mortifying conclusion, and it is not wonderful that pride and self-flattery should render us reluctant to admit it; nevertheless, every impartial man must acknowledge that the human character is correctly drawn in the Bible.

There is something wonderful in the power which the word of God possesses over the consciences of men. To those who never read or hear it, this fact must be unknown; but it is manifest to those who are conversant with the sacred volume, or who are in the habit of hearing it expounded. Why should this book, above all others, have the power of penetrating and searching the inmost recesses of the soul, and showing to a man the multitude and enormity of the evils of his heart and life? This may by some be attributed to early education, but I believe, if the experiment could be fairly tried, it would be found, that men who had never been brought up with any sentiment of reverence for the Bible, would experience its power over the conscience. The very best cure therefore for infidelity, would be the serious perusal of the Holy Scriptures. "The entrance of thy word giveth light." "The law of the Lord is perfect, converting the soul."

3. It deserves our special attention, in considering the internal evidences of Christianity, that the Scriptures contain explicit information on those points on which man stands most in need of instruction. These may be reduced to three: first, the doctrine of a future state of retribution; secondly, the assurance that sin may be pardoned, and the method by which this can consistently be done; thirdly, the means for restoring the depraved nature of man to a state of rectitude. We are not capable of determining in particular, as we have before shown, what a revelation should contain, but it is reasonable to think that if God gives a revelation, it will contain some instruction on these important points. And when we examine what the Scriptures teach on these subjects, it is found that the doctrine is worthy of God, and so adapted to the necessities of man, that it affords a strong argument in favour of their inspiration.

The certainty of a future existence to man, is a prominent feature in the New Testament. The connexion between our present conduct and future condition is clearly and expressly inculcated. Many interesting and momentous truths connected with the world to come, are presented in a light the best calculated to make a deep and salutary impression on the mind. It is revealed, that there will be a general judgment of all men, and that God hath appointed a day when this event shall take place. It is moreover taught in the New Testament, that not only will every man be judged, but every action of every individual, whether it be good or bad, will be brought under review; and the eternal destiny of all men will be fixed, agreeably to the judicial decision of this impartial trial. Some will be admitted to everlasting life, in the world above, while others shall go away into everlasting misery, into that place "prepared for the devil and his angels."

Another interesting fact revealed in the New Testament is, that there will be a general resurrection of the bodies of all men, previously to the final judgment. This fact reason could never have conjectured; it must, from its nature, be a matter of pure revelation. We may indeed discover some remote analogy to the resurrection, in the apparent death and resuscitation of vegetables and some animals; but this could never have authorized the conclusion, that the bodies of men, after being mingled with the dust of the earth, would be reorganized and re-animated by the same souls which were connected with them before their death. This doctrine however is very interesting, and to the pious must be very pleasing and animating, as we may learn from the beautiful and striking description of the resurrection given by Paul:—"It is sown in corruption, it is raised in incorruption; it is sown in weakness, it is raised in power; it is sown a natural body, it is raised a spiritual body; for this corruptible must put on incorruption, and this mortal must put on immortality."

It is worthy of remark that although the Scriptures express the joys of heaven, and the miseries of hell, by the strongest figures, they do not enter much into detail respecting the condition of men in the future world. There is true wisdom in this silence, because it is a subject of which we are at present incapable of forming any distinct conceptions. Paul, after being caught up to paradise and to the third heaven, gave no account of what he saw and heard

How different is this from the ridiculous description of the seven heavens, by Mohammed, and from the reveries of Emanuel Swedenborg. The account of a future state contained in the New Testament, is just that which is best suited to our present imperfect mode of conceiving, and at the same time adapted to make the deepest impressions on the minds of men.

The method of obtaining the pardon of sin, which is made known in the Scriptures, is so extraordinary, and yet so perfectly calculated to reconcile the forgiveness of the sinner with the justice and holiness of God, that it can scarcely be a mere human device. The mission from heaven of a person called the Son of God; his miraculous assumption of human nature; his holy and benevolent character; and his laying down his life as an expiation for the sins of men, are indeed wonderful events, but on that account not likely to be the invention of impostors. The death of Christ may be considered the central point in the Christian system. This was so far from being an incidental thing, or an event occurring in the common course of nature, that it is every where represented to be the very purpose of Christ's coming into the world. This, according to the gospel, is the grand means of obtaining all blessings for sinners. It is the great vicarious sacrifice offered up to God in behalf of the people, in consequence of which God can be just and the justifier of all who believe in Jesus. To know Christ crucified, is to know the whole gospel, to preach Christ crucified, is to preach the whole gospel; for all its doctrines are involved in this event. The plan of salvation revealed in the Scriptures is founded on the principle of receiving satisfaction for the transgressions of the sinner, from another person who is able to render to the law all that is required from the offender. This satisfaction was made by the obedience of Christ unto death, and is accepted by the Judge of all in place of a perfect obedience of the sinner, in behalf of all those to whom it shall be applied. This method of obtaining pardon is honourable to God, because while he receives the transgressor into favour, he expresses his hatred of sin in the strongest manner, and requires that the demands of his holy law be perfectly fulfilled; and it is suited to man, for it comes down to his impotence and wretchedness, and offers him a finished and gratuitous salvation, without works or merit of his own. And that there may be no room for an abuse of this doctrine of FREE GRACE, it is provided that all who hope for the benefits of this redemption shall yield a sincere obedience to the gospel, and thus evince their penitence for their sins, and their love to the Saviour. Ungodly men may pervert this doctrine and turn the grace of God into licentiousness, but this receives no encouragement from the principles of the gospel; it is merely the effect of the perverseness of sinful men.

This leads me to speak of the third thing important to be known by man, the means by which a depraved nature may be restored to rectitude, or thorough reformation of a sinner be effected. On this subject philosophy has never been able to shed any light. And this is not wonderful; for the most that human wisdom however perfect could effect, would be the direction and regulation of the natural principles and passions of men; but in this way no true reformation can be produced. Whatever changes are effected, will be only from one species of sin to another. In order to a radical restoration of the soul to moral rectitude, or to any degree of it, there is a necessity for the introduction into the mind of some new and powerful principle of action, sufficient to counteract or expel the principles of sin. It is in vain that men talk of producing a restoration to virtue by reason: the mere perception of the right way will answer no purpose, unless there is some inclination to pursue it. Now the want of virtuous affections, or to speak more correctly, of holy dispositions, is the great defect of our nature, in which our depravity radically consists; and the only way by which man can be led to love and pursue the course of obedience to the law of God, is by having love to God and to holiness excited or implanted in his soul. But to effect this, is not in the power of any creature: it is a work which requires a divine energy, a creating power; and therefore a true conversion from the ways of sin was never effected without super natural aid. There may be an external reformation. There may be, and often is, a change of governing principles. The man who in his youth was under the predominant influence of the love of pleasure, may in advanced years fall completely under the control of avarice or ambition; but in every such case, the change is effected by one active principle becoming so strong as to counteract or suppress another. It may be laid down as a universal maxim, that all changes of character are brought about by exciting, implanting, or strengthening, active principles, sufficient to overcome those which before governed the man.

Now let us inquire what plan of reformation is proposed in the Scriptures. It is such a one as precisely accords with the principles laid down. The necessity of regeneration by the power of God is taught in almost every variety of form, both in the Old and New Testaments. The effect of the divine energy on the soul is A NEW HEART, or new principles of moral action, the leading exercises of which are love to God and love to man. Let a philosophical survey be taken of the nature of man, with his complete system of perceptions, passions, appetites, and affections; and then suppose this powerful and holy principle introduced into the soul; all the faculties and propensities of man will be reduced to order, and the vices of our nature will be eradicated. Pretenders to reason and philosophy have often ridiculed this doctrine as absurd; whereas it is in every respect consistent with the soundest philosophy. It is the very thing which a wise philosopher, who should undertake to solve the problem, how depraved man might be restored to virtue, would demand. But ike the foundation which Archimedes required for his lever to raise the earth, the principle necessary for a sinner's reformaon is one which reason and philosophy cannot furnish. The Bible is the only book which ever taught the true method of purifying the soul from sin. A thousand ineffectual devices have been tried by philosophers and devotees of other systems. One of the most common has been to endeavour to extricate the soul from the influence of the body, by various methods of mortification and purgation; but all these plans have adopted the false principle, that the body is the chief seat of depravity, and therefore they have ever proved unsuccessful. The disease lies deeper, and is further removed from the reach of their remedies than they supposed. It is the gospel which teaches the true philosophy respecting the seat of sin and its cure. Out of the heart proceed all evils, according to the Bible. And if we would make the fruit good, we must first make the tree good. This necessity of divine agency to make men truly virtuous, does not, however, supersede the use of means, or exclude the operation of rational motives. When a new principle is introduced into a rational mind, the soul in the exercise of this principle is governed by the same general laws of understanding and choice as before. The principle of piety is pre-eminently a rational principle in its operation. God is loved because he is now viewed to be a most excellent and amiable being. Heaven is preferred to earth, because it is seen to be a far better and more enduring inheritance; and so of all other exercises.

I am naturally led from the consideration of this subject to speak of the moral system of the New Testament. I confine my remarks here to the New Testament, not because it teaches a different rule of moral duty from the Old, but because it teaches it more clearly. I need say nothing in general commendation of the moral precepts of the gospel; they have extorted the highest praise from many of the most determined enemies of Christianity. No man has been able to show how they could be improved in any one point. It has sometimes, indeed, been

18

objected that this system was not suited to man, because it requires a purity and perfection to which he
can never attain; but the objection concedes the very
point which we wish to establish—the absolute perfection of the gospel system of morality. It surely
requires no argument to prove that if God revealed
a rule for the regulation of his creatures, it will be a
perfect rule. It will never do to admit, that the law
must be lowered in its demands to adapt it to the
imperfection of creatures. This would be destructive
of all law.

It has again been objected, that in the precepts of
the New Testament many splendid virtues acknowledged by the heathen moralists have been omitted
Patriotism, friendship, bravery, &c., have been spe-
cified as belonging to this class. To which we reply,
that so far as patriotism and friendship are moral virtues, they are included in the general precepts of the
gospel, which require us to love our fellow men and
do them good; and in those which command us to
think of "whatsoever things are lovely, whatsoever
things are of good report;" but when the love of
country and attachment to a friend interfere with the
general obligation of loving all men, they are no
longer virtues, but vices.

The excellence of the moral system of the New
Testament will be manifest if we consider,

1. Its simple yet comprehensive character. All
moral duties which can be conceived as obligatory,
are here reduced to two grand principles, *the love of
God* and *the love of man.* The measure of the first
is the full extent of our capacity; of the second, the
love which we have for ourselves. "On these two,"
says Christ, "hang all the law and the prophets."
The duties which relate to temperance and self-gov-
ernment, do not need any additional principle. If
the soul be filled with love to man, self-love will be
so regulated and directed as to answer every purpose
in moving us to perform what has been called our
duty to ourselves.

2. The precepts of morality, in the New Testa

ment, although sometimes expressed in comprehensive language, are often applied to the actual relations and various conditions of men. We are not left to infer particular duties from general principles, but the duties of individuals, according to their circumstances, are distinctly enjoined. Parents and children, husbands and wives, magistrates and subjects, masters and servants, ministers and people, the rich and the poor, the friend and the stranger, have all their respective duties clearly marked out.

3 Moral duties which have been overlooked or misunderstood by other teachers, are here prominently exhibited and solemnly inculcated. The virtues of humility, meekness, forbearance, and the forgiveness of injuries, were not acknowledged by the heathen moralists; but in the New Testament they are made to assume their proper place, and much of true goodness is made to consist in their exercise. At the time of the advent of Christ, many false principles of morality had gained currency. The duty of loving all men had been circumscribed within narrow limits. Men charged with heresy, as the Samaritans, or notorious sinners, as the publicans, were by the Jews considered as properly excluded from all participation in their kindness or courtesy. The duty of subjection to a foreign power by which they had been conquered, and especially the duty of yielding obedience to a wicked tyrannical prince, was one on which it required much wisdom to decide aright. The people were divided among themselves on this point; it was therefore selected by a combination of both parties as a fit subject to entangle our Lord, by obliging him to decide one way or the other, and thus expose himself to the opposition of one of the parties. But when they asked him whether it was lawful to give tribute unto Cæsar or not, he called for a *denarius*, and looking at the image stamped upon it, asked whose it was; and upon being answered Cæsar's, made the following remarkable reply: "Render unto Cæsar the things that are Cæsar's, and unto God the things that are G d's." By which he decided that,

inasmuch as they permitted the coin of Cæsar to
circulate among them, which was an evidence of his
sovereignty over them, and availed themselves of
this money for purposes of trade, there could be no
impropriety in rendering to Cæsar what properly
belonged to him; and also that this was not incompatible with their allegiance to God. So that virtually in this answer, he reproved both the pharisees
and the Herodians; the former of whom made their
duty to God a pretext for refusing to pay tribute to
the Emperor; and the latter, to secure the favour of
the reigning powers, neglected their duty to God

Paul, living under the government of Nero, pre-
scribes obedience to the existing powers, not from
fear of suffering their displeasure, but for *conscience'
sake.* This is the general rule of duty on this difficult subject, than which none can be wiser; but it
must not be considered as inculcating passive obedience and non-resistance in all cases. Yet as long as
a government has authority, so long we are bound
to obey. Christianity is so constituted as not to interfere with any civil institution. It takes men as it
finds them, in all the relations of life, and teaches
them their duty. It never can therefore be the cause
of sedition and opposition to existing governments.
It considers all civil rulers as the ministers of God,
for the peace and good order of society, and for the
punishment of those that do evil. It is made the
duty of Christians therefore to be "subject unto the
higher powers, and not to resist the ordinance of
God; to render to all their dues; tribute to whom
tribute is due, custom to whom custom, fear to whom
fear, honour to whom honour."* But when they,
who have the right to change the government of a
country exercise it, and put down one set of rulers
and set up another the principle of Christian duty
remains the same. And if in any country Christians
form a majority of the nation, there is no reason why
they may not exercise this right of new-modelling
their government, or changing their rulers, as well as
others.

* Rom. xiii.

4. The moral system of the New Testament traces all virtue to the heart, and sets no value on the most splendid and costly offerings, or the most punctilious discharge of religious duties when the motives are not pure. The first inclination of the mind to an illicit object is denounced to be a violation of the law; and words of reproach, and all idle words, are among the sins for which an account must be given in the judgment. Prayers and alms proceeding from vain glory are represented as receiving no reward from God, however they may be applauded by men. The love of this world, and the love of money, are represented as radical sins, from which many others proceed. Pride and revenge are exhibited as not only odious, but incompatible with the divine favour. Purity of heart and heavenly-mindedness, with trust in God and submission to his will, are in this system, cardinal virtues.

5. The moral precepts of the New Testament were exemplified in the lives of the apostles and primitive Christians; but especially, and to the utmost perfection, in the example of Jesus Christ. It is impossible to conceive a character more perfect than that given by the evangelists, of the founder of the Christian religion; and it has already been observed, that this character, embracing every variety of excellence, often exhibited in delicate and difficult circumstances, is delineated by a simple narrative of facts. There is no panegyric, no effort or art to excite admiration; the writers merely inform us what Jesus said, did, and suffered. From this narrative we learn that he connected himself with no sect, and courted the favour of neither the rich nor the poor. He adopted none of the errors or prejudices of his nation; but by his discourses and his conduct showed that he acted from far higher views than national prejudices. The apparent sanctity of the Pharisees he denounced as hypocrisy; the traditions of the elders, as subversive of the law of God; the skeptical opinions of the Sadducees, as proceeding from ignorance of the true meaning of the Scriptures.

18*

Jesus Christ continually turned the attention of his hearers from earthly to heavenly things, as alone worthy of their attention and pursuits. Although he flattered no class of men, his attention was particularly directed to the poor; their spiritual necessities and their bodily afflictions excited his most tender compassion; and to them he addressed many kind and encouraging declarations. But his healing power was exerted in behalf of all applicants, rich and poor; and without regard to their sect or nation. Jews, Samaritans, heathens, publicans, and sinners, were the objects of his compassion. He was not deterred by the proud prejudices of the Scribes and Pharisees from associating with penitents, however vile and infamous they had before been. He graciously received returning sinners, and comforted them with the assurance of pardon, and permitted them to manifest their grateful affection to his person, by the most expressive signs and actions. He manifested the kindest sympathy with his friends in their afflictions, weeping with those that wept, and often exerting his omnipotence in raising their dear relations from the bed of sickness or from death. And although he often uttered severe rebukes against the incorrigibly wicked, and was sometimes grieved and angry with them, yet his compassion towards them never failed; and even when their day of grace was ended, he wept over them with the most affecting tenderness.

Jesus Christ was often brought into conflict with insidious, malignant, and learned adversaries. They attacked him with deliberate craft, and proposed to him questions on delicate and difficult subjects, to which he was required to return an immediate answer; but in no case of this sort was he ever confounded, or even puzzled by the cunning craftiness of his enemies. His answers were so appropriate and so fraught with wisdom, that his adversaries were commonly confounded and the audience filled with admiration.

The parables of Christ are unparalleled for beauty

and force, in the species of composition to which they belong. But this is the smallest part of their excellence. They contain so much important truth, and so happily adapted to the subject and the occasion, that the persons intended to be reproved by them were often constrained to give judgment against themselves. In these discourses, the leading doctrines of the gospel are exhibited in a beautiful dress of allegory, which rivets the attention and greatly aids us in understanding the fulness and freeness of the grace of the gospel. They are also prophetical of the rejection of the Jews and of the calling of the Gentiles; of the various reception of the gospel by different classes of hearers; of the mixture of sincere and unsound Christians in the Church; of the cruel persecutions which the followers of Christ should endure; and of the final overthrow and destruction of his enemies.

Jesus Christ spake, in all his discourses, as never man spake. He removed the false glosses which had been put on the law, and set its precepts in their proper light. He mingled the dogmas of no philosophical system with his instructions. He entered into no metaphysical and abstruse disquisitions, but taught the truth with simplicity and authority.

His zeal for the honour of God and for the purity and sanctity of his worship, and his dislike of all human inventions and will-worship, are manifest in all his conduct. A spirit of fervent and elevated devotion was a remarkable characteristic of Jesus of Nazareth. Whole nights he spent in prayer; and before day he would retire for the purposes of devotion. He was in the habit of praying and giving thanks on all occasions; but his devotion was free from all tincture of superstition or enthusiasm He taught that not the words, but the heart, not the length of prayers, but their spirit was regarded.

His benevolence, meekness, and laborious diligence, in promoting the welfare of men, were manifested every day of his life. But in his acts of mercy and in his most extraordinary miracles, there was no appearance of parade or ostentation. He went about doing good, but he sought no glory from men. He was humble, retired. and contented with the lowest state of poverty. When the people applauded him, he withdrew to some other place. When they would have made him a king, he escaped from their hands. When they asked curious questions, he directed them to something important. When they uttered unmeaning expressions of praise, he took occasion to announce some important truth or deliver some interesting discourse.

In nothing did he discover more profound wisdom, than in declining to interfere in any case with temporal concerns, and disputes about earthly possessions He showed by his conduct, what he solemnly declared on his trial, that "his kingdom was not of this world."

In his intercourse with his disciples, we observe a sweet mixture of dignity and gentleness, of faithfulness and humble condescension to their weakness and prejudices. No wonder that they should love such a Master. His last discourses with them before his passion, and the remarkable prayer offered on their behalf, for affectionate tenderness and the sweet spirit of consolation which pervade them, are altogether inimitable. How flat and unsatisfactory are the conversations of Socrates with his friends, when compared with those of Christ recorded in the fourteenth, fifteenth and sixteenth chapters of the gospel of St. John. Indeed it would be impossible to refer to any discourses, in any language, which could bear a comparison with this valedictory of Christ: and to enhance our admiration of the pure benevolence of the author, he was aware that his own sufferings were near and would be most cruel and ignominious; and yet his attention is turned to the case of his sorrowful disciples, and all that he says has relation to them. The institution of the EUCHARISTICAL SUPPER, intended to be commemorative of his death, was attended with circumstances which exhibit the character of Jesus in a very peculiar and interesting light.

This scene will be best understood by a perusal of the simple and affecting narrative of the evangelists.

The last thing in the character of Christ, which I shall bring into view at this time, is the patience and fortitude with which he endured sufferings intense and overwhelming beyond conception. There is something mysterious in this whole affair. The intense agonies which Jesus suffered, seem to have had no connexion with external circumstances. When he was betrayed, deserted, and arrested, he discovered no signs of fear or perturbation. He gave himself up, and submitted with unruffled composure to every species of contumely and insult. While his trial was going on before the Sanhedrim, and before Pilate, he maintained, for the most part, a dignified silence, uttering no reproaches or complaints; not even speaking in his own defence. When particularly interrogated by the judges, he answered directly to the questions proposed, and avowed himself to be the Messiah, the Son of God, and the King of Israel. Under the mockery and insult which were heaped upon him, he remained perfectly composed, and uttered not a word indicative of impatience or resentment. "As a sheep before her shearers is dumb, so he opened not his mouth." When he was bewailed by the daughters of Jerusalem, as he ascended the hill of Calvary, bearing his cross, he requested them not to weep for him, but for themselves and their children, on account of the calamitties that were coming on that devoted city. While suspended on the cross, he saw his beloved mother among the spectators, and knowing that she would need a friend and protector, he recommended her to the care of the disciple he most tenderly loved. Although no compassion was mingled with the vindictive feelings with which he was persecuted, he set a glorious example of that most difficult duty, love to enemies. As says the apostle Peter, "Because Christ also suffered for us, leaving us an example, that ye should follow his steps: who did no sin, neither was guile found in his mouth; who, when he was reviled,

reviled not again; when he suffered, he threatened not, but committed himself to him that judgeth right-eously." Among his last words, before he expired, was a prayer for those that were then engaged in crucifying him; " Father, forgive them, for they know not what they do." A penitent thief, who was crucified with him, implored his blessing and remem-brance, when he should come to the possession of his kingdom; he replied, " This day shalt thou be with me in Paradise." And finally, he said, "Father, into thy hands I commit my spirit," and bowed his head and died.

The moral excellence of the character of Christ is very remarkable, as uniting, in perfection, qualities which among men are considered almost incompati-ble. He exhibited a complete indifference to the possessions and glory of the world and a devout and heavenly temper, without the least mixture of aus-terity. He combined uniform dignity with humility and condescension; manifested strong indignation against all manner of sin and against impenitent sinners, but the most affectionate tenderness towards every humble penitent. He united the spirit of ele-vated devotion with a life of activity and incessant exertion. While he held free intercourse with men of all classes, he adopted the prejudices and spared the vices of none. On this subject, I will quote a passage from an excellent discourse of Dr. Channing, before referred to: " I will only observe," says the eloquent author, speaking of the character of Christ, " that it had one distinction, which, more than any thing, forms a perfect character. It was made up of contrasts: in other words it was a union of excellen-cies which are not easily reconciled, which seem at first sight incongruous, but which, when blended and duly proportioned, constitute moral harmony, and attract with equal power, love, and veneration. For example, we discover in Jesus Christ an unparalleled dignity of character, a consciousness of greatness, never discovered or approached by any other indi-vidual in history, and yet this was blended with a condescension, loveliness, and unostentatious simplicity, which had never before been thought consistent with greatness. In like manner, he united an utter superiority to the world, to its pleasures and ordinary interests, with suavity of manners, and freedom from austerity. He joined to strong feeling and self-possession, an indignant sensibility to sin, and compassion to the sinner; an intense devotion to his work, and calmness under opposition and ill success; a universal philanthropy, and a susceptibility of private attachments; the authority which became the Savior of the world, and the tenderness and gratitude of a son."

The salutary effects of Christianity on communities and individuals open a wide field for important remarks. It is a subject which we have not time to pursue, yet we must not pass it over in entire silence. The argument from this topic may however be reduced to a point. Take a survey of the whole world, at this time, and let an impartial judgment be formed of the condition of all the nations; and let the question be answered, whether Christian nations are in a less favourable or more favourable condition than others. And again, whether among Christians, those nations who have the free use of the Bible, and are carefully instructed in the doctrines of Christianity, are in a better or worse condition than those to whom the Scriptures are interdicted, and who are permitted to remain in ignorance of the religion which they profess? The answers of these questions are so obvious, that I cannot but presume, that all readers will be of the same mind. It may then be asked, would a vile imposture be the means of meliorating the condition of the world, and prove salutary in proportion as it is known and obeyed? "I speak as unto wise men, judge ye what I say."

We have moreover seen, in our own time, the wonderful effects of the gospel, in civilizing some of the most barbarous people on the face of the earth. Men who seemed to be sunk to a level with the beasts, have been reclaimed. enlightened, and exalt·

ed, to a participation of the blessings of civilized life, their ferocious temper being completely subdued and softened. Look at Greenland, at Africa, at the islands of the Pacific; and nearer home, at the Cherokees, Choctaws, and other Indian tribes, and see what the gospel can effect. I know not what infidels think of these things, but for my own part, I should not esteem one coming from the dead, or a voice of thunder from heaven, so undoubted an evidence of the truth of the gospel, as these effects. Will a series of falsehoods produce such effects as these?

I know that it has been objected, that Christianity has been the cause of many bloody wars and cruel persecutions; but this is impossible. That religion which breathes nothing but benevolence and peace, and which requires its disciples not to resist evil, but freely to forgive their most malignant enemies, can never be the *cause* of war and persecution. It may indeed be the *occasion*, and no doubt has been made the occasion of such evils; but it would be absurd to attribute to Christianity the evils of which it has been the occasion, when its own spirit is in direct opposition to those evils. As well might we charge civil government with all the wars and tumults which it has occasioned. As reasonably might we accuse liberty, as being the cause of all the atrocities of the French revolution. The wickedness of man is the cause of these evils; and the most excellent things in the universe, may be made the occasion of exciting it, or calling it into exercise. Christ foretold that his religion would be an occasion of family discord; and to express the certainty of the event predicted, he said, "Think not that I am come to send peace on earth; I came not to send peace, but a *sword*;" which some superficial readers have strangely misconstrued, as though he had signified that it was the tendency of his religion to produce strife among friends. No man can remain in error on this subject who will take the pains to read the New Testament. And I will venture to predict, or rather to repeat what is already predicted, that as soon as the world shall sincerely embrace the Christian religion, wars will cease to the ends of the earth. Then shall men beat their swords into plough-shares and their spears into pruning-hooks, and learn war no more.

But the salutary effects of the gospel on those individuals who cordially embrace it, furnish the most manifest proof of its divinity. How often, by the secret powerful influence of the truths of the Bible, have the proud been humbled; the impure rendered chaste; the unjust honest; the cruel and revengeful, meek and forgiving; the drunkard, temperate; the profane, reverent; and the false swearer and liar, conscientious in declaring nothing but the truth. Under the influence of what other system are such salutary changes effected? Will it be said that many who profess to experience such a change prove themselves to be hypocrites? Admitted; but does this evince that they who give evidence of sincerity by the most incontestable proofs, all their lives, are also hypocrites? All men wish to be thought honest; but if many are discovered to be knaves, does this prove that there is not an honest man in the world?

However this argument may affect those who have had no experience of the power of the gospel, it will have great weight with all who have, by means of the truth, been converted from the error of their ways. There are thousands who can attest that they have experienced the salutary efficacy of the Bible, in turning them away from their iniquities and enkindling within them the love of God and of virtue. They cannot but believe that the Christian religion is from God, and are persuaded that no imposture could so elevate and sanctify the mind, that no human device could possess such a power over the conscience and the heart, as they have experienced from the Scriptures. These persons, therefore, may truly be said to have the witness of the truth in themselves.

19

But there is an efficacy in the truths of the Bible not only to guide and sanctify, but also to afford consolation to the afflicted in body or mind. The gospel brings peace into every bosom where it is cordially received. When the conscience is pierced with the stings of guilt, and the soul writhes under a wound which no human medicine can heal, the promises of the gospel are like the balm of Gilead, a sovereign cure for this intolerable and deeply-seated malady. Under its cheering influence, the broken spirit is healed and the burden of despair is removed far away. The gospel, like an angel of mercy, can bring consolation into the darkest scenes of adversity; it can penetrate the dungeon, and sooth the sorrows of the penitent in his chains, and on his bed of straw. It has power to give courage to the heart, and to brighten the countenance of the man who meets death on the scaffold or on the gibbet, if its precious invitations to the chief of sinners be sincerely embraced. It mitigates the sorrows of the bereaved, and wipes away the bitter tears occasioned by the painful separation of affectionate friends and relatives. By the bright prospects which it opens, and the lively hopes which it inspires, the darkness of the tomb is illumined; so that Christians are enabled, in faith of the resurrection of the body, to commit the remains of their dearest friends to the secure sepulchre, in confident hope that after a short sleep they will awake to life everlasting.

The cottages of the poor are often blessed with the consolation of the gospel, which is peculiarly adapted to the children of affliction and poverty. It was one of the signs of Jesus being the true Messiah, "that the poor had the gospel preached unto them." Here it produces contentment, resignation, mutual kindness, and the longing after immortality. The aged and infirm, who, by the gradual failure of their faculties, or by disease and decrepitude are shut out from the business and enjoyments of this world, may find in the word of God a fountain of consolation. They may, while imbued with its celestial spirit, look upon the world without the least regret for its loss, and may rejoice in the prospect before them, with a joy unspeakable and full of glory. The gospel can render tolerable even the yoke of slavery and the chains of the oppressor. How often is the pious slave, through the blessed influence of the word of God, a thousand times happier than his master! He cares not for the short deprivation of liberty; he knows and feels that he is " Christ's freeman," and believes " that all things work together for his good," and that " these light afflictions which are for a moment, will work out for him a far more exceeding and eternal weight of glory!" Nay, this glorious gospel is an antidote to death itself. He that does the sayings of Christ shall never taste of death; that is, of death as a curse: he shall never feel the envenomed sting of death. How often does it overspread the spirit of the departing saint with serenity! How often does it elevate, and fill with celestial joy, the soul which is just leaving the earthly house of this tabernacle! It actually renders, in many instances, the bed of the dying a place of sweet repose. No terrors hover over them; no anxious care corrodes their spirit; no burden oppresses their heart. All is light; all is hope and assurance; all is joy and triumph.

The question to be decided is, whether a book which is replete with such sublime and correct views of theology; which exhibits the true history and true character of man, without flattery, distortion, or exaggeration; which possesses such an astonishing power of penetrating the human heart and affecting the conscience; which gives us information on the very points with which it is most important we should be acquainted; which opens to us the future world, and shows us how we may attain its felicity and glory; which exhibits a perfect system of moral duty adapted to our nature and circumstances, and free from all the defects of other systems of morality; forbidding nothing which is innocent, and requiring nothing which is not reasonable and virtuous; which reduces all duty to a few general principles, and yet

illustrates the application of these principles by a
multitude of particular precepts, addressed to persons
in every relation of life, and exemplifies them by
setting before us the lives of holy men, who are portrayed according to truth with such imperfections as
experience teaches us belong to the best men; which
delineates the character of Jesus Christ, the founder
of Christianity, with such a perfection of moral excel-
lency, by simply relating his words, actions. and sufferings, that nothing can be taken from it, or added
to it, without detracting from its worth; and finally,
which contains the true sources of consolation for
every species of human suffering, and comfort in
death itself:—whether such a book is the production
of vile impostors, and those impostors uneducated
fishermen.   Would such men have fallen into no
palpable blunders in theology or morality?   Could
they have preserved so beautiful a harmony and
consistency between all the parts?   Could they
have exhibited such a character as that of Jesus
Christ? and while they introduce him acting and
speaking so often, and in circumstances so peculiar
and difficult, never ascribe to him any error or
weakness, in word or deed?   Would impostors have
denounced all manner of falsehood and deceit, as is
done in the New Testament?   Would they have insisted so much on holiness, even in the thoughts and
purposes of the heart?   Could they have so perfectly
adapted their forgery to the constitution of the human
mind and to the circumstances of men?   Is it probable that they would have possessed the wisdom to
avoid all the prejudices of their nation, and all
connexion with existing sects and civil institutions?
And finally, could they have provided so effectually
for the consolation of the afflicted?   What man now
upon earth could compose even the discourses, said
by the evangelists to have been spoken by Jesus
Christ?

    If any man can bring himself, after an impartial
examination of the Scriptures, to believe that they
were written by unprincipled impostors, then he

may believe that an untutored savage might con
struct a ship of the line; that a child might have
written the ILIAD, or PARADISE LOST; or even that
the starry firmament was the work of mere creatures.
No: it cannot be that this is a forgery. No man or
set of men ever had sufficient talents and knowledge
to forge such a book as the Bible. It evidently trans-
cends all human effort. It has upon its face the impress of divinity. It shines with a light, which by
its clearness and its splendour, shows itself to be
celestial. It possesses the energy and penetrating influence which bespeak the omnipotence and omniscience of its author. It has the effect of enlighten-
ing, elevating, purifying, directing, and comforting
all those who cordially receive it. Surely then it is
THE WORD OF GOD, and we hold it fast as the best
blessing which God has vouchsafed to man.

O PRECIOUS GOSPEL! Will any merciless hand
endeavour to tear away from our hearts this best,
this last, and sweetest consolation? Would you
darken the only avenue through which one ray of
hope can enter? Would you tear from the aged
and infirm poor the only prop on which their souls
can repose in peace? Would you deprive the dying
of their only source of consolation? Would you rob
the world of its richest treasure? Would you let
loose the flood-gates of every vice, and bring back
upon the earth the horrors of superstition or the
atrocities of atheism? Then endeavour to subvert
the gospel; throw around you the fire-brands of
infidelity; laugh at religion, and make a mock of
futurity; but be assured that for all these things God
will bring you into judgment. But I will not believe that any who reflect on what has been said, in
these pages, will ever cherish a thought so diaboli-
cal. I will persuade myself that a regard for the
welfare of their country, if no higher motive, will
induce them to respect the Christian religion. And
every pious heart will say, RATHER LET THE LIGHT
OF THE SUN BE EXTINGUISHED THAN THE PRECIOUS
LIGHT OF THE GOSPEL.

CHAPTER XIV.

THE SCRIPTURES OF THE OLD AND NEW TESTAMENT WERE WRITTEN BY
THE INSPIRATION OF GOD ; AND THIS INSPIRATION, HOWEVER IT MAY
BE DISTINGUISHED, WAS PLENARY ; THAT IS, THE WRITERS WERE UN-
DER AN INFALLIBLE GUIDANCE, BOTH AS TO IDEAS AND WORDS : AND
YET THE ACQUIRED KNOWLEDGE, HABITS, AND PECULIAR DISPOSITIONS
OF THE WRITERS, WERE NOT SUPERSEDED.

HAVING endeavoured to establish the authenticity
of the Scriptures, I come now to say something respecting the inspiration of the writers of the several
books. These two subjects are, it is true, involved
in each other; and many of the arguments for the
former are conclusive in favour of the latter; but
still there is a distinction which it is important to
observe. A book may be authentic, without having
the least claim to inspiration, as are all true narratives of facts, written by men of veracity in the exercise of their unassisted powers. The gospel history
may be established on the common principles of
human testimony, in the same manner as any other
history. Indeed, this must be done, in the order of
proof, before any convincing argument can be formed
in favour of divine revelation. Accordingly, all judicious writers on the Evidences of Christianity first
attempt to establish the facts recorded in the Gospels,
by an appeal to mere human testimony. This distinction is so clear, and practically so important, that
many persons believe in the facts—miracles as well
as others—and yet have no conviction that the history of these events was written by divine inspiration. This is understood to be the case in regard to
most of those called Unitarians. Dr. Priestley, in
his " Institutes of the Christian Religion," has established the authenticity of the facts recorded by the
evangelists with great force of reasoning; and yet
in the same work, he utterly denies the plenary in

spiration of these writers; but alleges that they were men of veracity, and that their testimony should be received, just as we receive that of other credible historians, but without ascribing infallibility to them. The same opinions have been maintained by many others. The authenticity of the facts is sufficient to demonstrate that the Christian religion is of divine origin; but it does not follow, as a matter of course, that the historian who gives an account of the facts on which it rests was inspired. This is a distinct inquiry, and although not so vitally important as the former, is of great moment, and deserves a serious and impartial consideration.

It may be proper also in this place to distinguish between inspiration and that illumination which every true Christian must receive, and which is the foundation of that saving faith which is produced in the mind by the operation of the Holy Spirit. The distinction is, that the object of *inspiration* is commonly to reveal some new truths, or more clearly to reveal such as were before but obscurely revealed; or it is intended to direct the mind, in a supernatural way, to write and speak certain things, and so superintends or strengthens its faculties, that it is enabled to communicate, with unerring certainty, truths before unknown; or to form ideas and adopt expressions so sublime, as to be above the range of the natural powers of the person. The *illumination* of the Holy Spirit communicates no new truths, but enables the soul spiritually to apprehend truths, already revealed. Here then is the grand distinction between those spiritual influences which all Christians enjoy, and enthusiasm which claims something of the nature of inspiration. The sober Christian can appeal to the word of God, as containing all the ideas by which his mind is affected, in its highest elevations of joy and love; but the enthusiast departs from the written word, and trusts to impulses, impressions on the imagination, immediate suggestions, dreams or supposed visions. If these impulses or suggestions were from the Spirit of God, they would be strictly of the nature of inspiration. And, accord ingly, most fanatics believe themselves to be inspir ed; but however strong their persuasion, we are not bound to believe in their pretensions, unless they can exhibit those external proofs, by which God is pleased to attest such communications as he makes to men.

There is also a difference between inspiration and revelation. All revelations are not made by a suggestion of truth to the mind of an individual. God often spake to people of old by audible voices, and communicated his will by the mission of angels. Many persons have thus received divine revelations, who had no pretensions to inspiration.. All the people of Israel who stood before God at Mount Sinai, heard his voice uttering the ten commandments, and yet no one would say that all these were inspired. So also when Christ was upon earth, in more instances than one, a voice was heard declaring that he was the beloved Son of God. Indeed, all who had the opportunity of hearing Christ's discourses might be said to receive a revelation immediately from God; but it would be absurd to say that all these were inspired. Dr. Dick is of opinion, that the word *revelation* would be more expressive, as being more comprehensive, than *suggestion*, which last conveys the idea of an operation on the mind; whereas, truth, in many cases, was made known in other ways. But for the reason stated above, it would not do to substi tute the word *revelation* for *inspiration;* inasmuch as multitudes received revelations who had no claim to inspiration. And when inspiration is confined to those who wrote the books of Scripture, no other word would so clearly express the idea.

Inspiration has by theologians been distinguished into three kinds; that of *superintendence,* of *suggestion,* and of *elevation.* The first of these takes place, when an historian is influenced by the Holy Spirit to write, and in writing is so directed as to select those facts and circumstances which will answer the end proposed; and so assisted and strengthened in the narrative of events, as to be preserved from all error and mistake. The facts need not be revealed, because they may be well known to the writer from his own observation, and may be deeply impressed on his memory; but no man can avoid inaccuracies and mistakes in a narrative of facts, long past. If it is important that such a narrative be exempt from error, the writer must be inspired. But as the chief object of inspiration is to communicate truths before unknown, the inspiration of suggestion is requisite in all such cases; as when the prophets were inspired to predict the revolutions of empires, or to communicate a message from God to a whole people, or to an individual, the ideas must of course have been immediately suggested by the Holy Spirit. The third species of inspiration takes place, when, by a divine influence, persons are enabled to bring forth productions, in speaking or writing, far more sublime and excellent than they could have attained by the exercise of their own faculties. Thus women, under the inspiration of God, have instantly uttered, in elevated strains of poetry, discourses in praise of God, which, by their unassisted powers, they could never have produced. In these compositions, there may be no revelation of truth; nor is there a mere superintendence of the human faculties, as in the first case was described; but the powers of the mind are, for the occasion, wonderfully elevated above their common level, so that the conceptions are more vivid and sublime, and expressed in language more appropriate and striking, than would have naturally occurred to them. By an inspiration of this sort David wrote the Psalms, and Solomon the Proverbs, and the speakers, in the book of Job, the sublime discourses which are there recorded. Many things of this kind are also found in the writings of the prophets.

Here another question of some perplexity demands our attention. It is, whether the words of Scripture, as well as the ideas, were given by inspiration. On the one hand it is alleged, that there is no necessity for supposing that the words used in communicating

revealed truth should be suggested by the **Holy
Spirit;** and that the fact proves that no such inspiration existed, because the style of each of the writers
is peculiar, and accords precisely with his education,
disposition, and turn of mind. But on the other
hand it is argued, that unless the words were inspired as well as the ideas, we cannot be certain that
the writer has, in any case, ommunicated accurately the mind of the Spirit; for men are liable to mistake in the selection of appropriate words, as much
as in any thing else; and as men often fail in conveying their own ideas in language which correctly
expresses their meaning, they might make similar
mistakes in the use of language to express ideas received by inspiration, if in this matter they were left
to the guidance of their own minds. It has also been
plausibly urged in favour of inspiration extending to
the words, that we can scarcely conceive of a revelation of truths to the mind, without supposing that
they were clothed in language. We cannot even
think distinctly, much less reason conclusively, on
any subject, without the intervention of words.

It is probable, that in this controversy as in many
others, both parties are right; or rather, that the
truth will be fully possessed by adopting the views
entertained on both sides, and endeavouring to reconcile them. The same principles which apply to
the ideas may, without any alteration, be applied to
the words. When the truths revealed were before
unknown to the inspired person; and especially—as
seems often to have been the case with the prophets
—when they did not fully comprehend the import
of what was revealed, it is necessary to suppose that
the words, as well as ideas, were immediately sug
gested by the Holy Spirit. This was remarkably
the case, when the apostles and others received the
gift of tongues: which was nothing else but the inspiration of words, as they were needed, for the communication of the truths of the gospel.

But as in the narration of well-known facts, the
writer did not need a continual suggestion of **every**

idea, but only to be so superintended, as to be preserved from error; so in the use of language in recording such familiar things, there existed no necessity that every word should be inspired; but there
was the same need of a directing and superintending
influence as in regard to the things themselves.
Here, then, we see that the language of the sacred
writers might be preserved from impropriety and
inaccuracy, and yet all the characteristics of style
peculiar to each writer be retained.   Just as if a
master should so guide the hand of a child in writing,
that the pen should be actually moved by the pupil,
but governed and directed by the master, so as not
to transgress the limits prescribed.   Or this superintendence, both as to ideas and words, may be illus-
trated by the case of a father conducting a child along
a narrow path.   The child walks by its own activity,
and takes steps according to its ability; but the father
preserves it from falling, and keeps it in the straight
path.   Just so it is with men when under the superintending influence of the Holy Spirit.   Their own
powers of understanding, memory and invention are
not superseded, but only directed, and preserved from
inaccuracy and error; but the man pursues his own
peculiar method of thinking, reasoning, and expression.   He speaks or writes in the language which he
has learned, and uses that idiom and style which
have become habitual; so that inspired men will,
according to this theory, retain their peculiarity of
style and expression just as fully, as if they were
writing or speaking without inspiration.

Some object to this theory of superintendence, under the impression that it is less perfect, than if every
thing were inspired by direct suggestion of the Holy
Spirit.   But there is really no foundation for this
objection.   It certainly is a matter of no consequence
how our knowledge is obtained, if it is only rendered
infallibly certain.   There are many things concerning which we could not acquire a greater degree of
assurance than we already possess, by inspiration of
any kind: and such knowledge acquired by the exer

cise of reason or intuition, is not the less valuable because it has been obtained in a natural way. In deed, these natural faculties, by which we are so constituted as to be capable of certain knowledge of the first principles of truth, are the gift of God as much as any inspiration can be: and the clear intuitive knowledge which we possess of certain truths, may be considered as a sort of permanent inspiration. Suppose a man by a constant plenary inspiration to be made absolutely sure of the truth of certain pro positions, so that he could not entertain any doubt respecting them, in what respect would there be any difference between this and the intuitive perception of self-evident principles, which every rational man by nature possesses? There would then be nothing gained by the inspiration of direct suggestion, in regard to our knowledge of those things of which we already possess intuitive certainty. It is also evident that in relation to all our knowledge acquired by experience or testimony, we only need such an influ ence as will enable us to communicate what ought to be recorded for the benefit of the church, and to do this without error, either as to matter or manner

Some, who do not deny the inspiration of the sacred writers, in general, have thought it necessary to make concessions on this subject which are not called for from the nature of the case, and have thus involved the cause which they defend in real difficul ties. They have granted that, while, in all matters of real importance, the penmen of the Scriptures were guided by a plenary inspiration, they were left to their own unassisted powers in trivial matters, and the relation of unimportant circumstances; and in such matters have, therefore, fallen into mistakes in regard to trivial circumstances. No evil or inconve- nience would result from this hypothesis, if the line could be definitely drawn between the parts of the book written by inspiration and those in which the writers were left to themselves. But as no human wisdom is sufficient to draw this line, the effect of it is opinion is to introduce uncertainty and doubt in a matter concerning which assurance is of the utmost importance. And it is in itself an improbable supposition, that the Spirit of God should infallibly guide a writer in some parts of his discourse, and forsake him in other parts. If we find a witness mistaken in some particulars, it weakens our confidence in his general testimony. And could it be shown that the evangelists had fallen into palpable mistakes in facts of minor importance, it would be impossible to demonstrate that they wrote any thing by inspiration.

The case of Paul is often adduced to prove that a writer who, for the most part, was inspired, may in particular cases be left to follow his own opinions.* If the meaning here ascribed to this apostle, and which is perhaps the most obvious, should be admitted, it would not authorize the opinion which we are now opposing. It would only follow that, in these few excepted cases, Paul was not inspired; which would leave us to enjoy full confidence in what he says in all other cases, as being spoken by divine inspiration. But it may well be doubted whether this was the true meaning of the apostle. It is much more probable, that all he intended to teach was, that our Lord Jesus Christ had delivered no opinion on the point which he was treating; but that he, by the aid of the Spirit which was in him, expressed an opinion which he evidently intended should be authoritative. And he plainly intimates that he spoke by inspiration, when he says, "And I think also that I have the Spirit of God." The import of this declaration, according to the usage of the New Testament, is, that Paul was persuaded that he was inspired in uttering the sentiments which he did. The words "I think," should not be interpreted as indicating any doubt or uncertainty, for that is not at all the meaning of the original; but as being the expression of the conviction of his own mind. There is, therefore, no need to suppose that Paul intended to intimate that he wrote any thing without the aid of divine inspiration. It would be strange indeed, if he

* See 1 Cor. vii. 12. 40.

20

who was inspired to all other purposes, had been left to himself in this one instance, as this is not to be reckoned among the least important matters which have fallen from his pen.

The true definition of inspiration, then, is, SUCH A DIVINE INFLUENCE UPON THE MINDS OF THE SACRED WRITERS AS RENDERED THEM EXEMPT FROM ERROR, BOTH IN REGARD TO THE IDEAS AND WORDS.

This is properly called PLENARY inspiration. No thing can be conceived more satisfactory. Certainty, infallible certainty, is the utmost that can be desired in any *narrative;* and if we have this in the sacred Scriptures, there is nothing more to be wished in regard to this matter.

That the Scriptures of the Old Testament were appealed to, and constantly spoken of as inspired, and free from error, is capable of the clearest proof. Christ said to the Jews, " Search the Scriptures, for in them ye think ye have eternal life, and they are they which testify of me." " For had ye believed Moses, ye would have believed me, for he wrote of me." On another occasion, he said, "Ye do err, not knowing the Scriptures," where it is evidently implied that the Scriptures are an unerring rule. In the same chapter it is recorded, that Jesus confounded the Pharisees by asking them how David could IN SPIRIT call Christ Lord, when he was his son. Again, Christ after his resurrection expresses this sentiment in the strongest terms: " These are the words which I spake unto you, while I was yet with you; THAT ALL THINGS MUST BE FULFILLED, which are written in the law of Moses, and in the Prophets, and in the Psalms, concerning me. Then opened he their understandings, that they should understand the Scriptures, and said unto them, Thus it is written, and thus it behoved Christ to suffer and to rise from the dead, on the third day." In the preceding part of the same discourse, this idea is also clearly exhibited: " Then he said unto them, O fools, and slow of heart 'o believe all that the prophets have spoken ought not Christ to have suffered these things, and to enter into his glory? And beginning at Moses and all the prophets, he expounded unto them in all the Scriptures the things concerning himself. And they said one to another, Did not our hearts burn within us while he talked with us by the way, and while he opened to us the Scriptures?" So also in the garden of Gethsemane, our Lord addressing Peter said, " Thinkest thou that I cannot now pray to my Father, and he shall presently give me more than twelve legions of angels? But how then shall the Scriptures be fulfilled, that thus it must be?" The same infallible authority is ascribed to the Old Testament by Christ, in his dispute with the Jews, recorded in the tenth chapter of John. "Jesus answered them, Is it not written in your law, I said, ye are gods? If he called them gods to whom the word of God came, and THE SCRIPTURES CANNOT BE BROKEN," &c. We have, besides, many passages, in which the evangelists refer to the Holy Scriptures as an infallible standard of truth. " But though he had done so many miracles before them, yet they believed not on him, that the saying of Esaias the prophet might be fulfilled which he spake—Lord, who hath believed our report, and to whom is the arm of the Lord revealed?" " Therefore, they could not believe, because that Esaias saith again—He hath blinded their eyes," &c. " For these things were done that the Scripture should be fulfilled, A bone of him shall not be broken. And again, another scripture saith, They shall look on him whom they have pierced."

The apostles are not less explicit than Christ and the evangelists, in testifying to the inspiration of the Scriptures of the Old Testament. Paul in his second epistle to Timothy put him in mind, that " from a child he had known the holy Scriptures, which were able to make him wise unto salvation, through faith which is in Christ Jesus;" and then adds, " all Scripture is given by inspiration of God, and is profitable for doctrine, for reproof, for correction, for instruction in righteousness; that the man o God may be perfect, thoroughly furnished unto all good works."

The Scriptures, which Timothy knew from his child hood, must have been the books of the Old Testament, for at that time no others had been written But when Paul goes on to declare, that "all Scripture was given by inspiration of God," he might have included under this general expression, all the books of the New Testament which had been published before his second imprisonment at Rome; and this would probably comprehend the first three Gospels, the Acts of the Apostles, and al this own epistles; for this seems to have been the last of Paul's writings; as he says in it, "I am now ready to be offered, and the time of my departure is at hand." That the writings of Paul were by the Church reckoned among the sacred Scriptures, we learn from the second epistle of Peter, which was probably written about this time or a little before. His words are remarkable, as containing the only clear testimony on record of one apostle to the writings of another. "Account," says he, "that the long-suffering of our Lord is salvation, even as our beloved brother Paul also, according to the wisdom given unto him, hath written unto you. As also in all his epistles, speaking in them of these things; in which are some things hard to be understood; which they that are unlearned and unstable pervert, as they do also the other Scriptures, to their own destruction." Hence it would appear, that Paul's epistles were now well known, and were reckoned among the other Scriptures, by the apostle Peter. Certainly then Paul himself might have included them, as well as the other published books of the New Testament, under the phrase "all Scripture;" and if so, this passage will contain a strong testimony to the inspiration of the whole of the Old Testament, and a large part of the New Testament. And admitting the facts of Paul's miraculous conversion, divine mission as an apostle, and endowment with the gift of tongues, of healing, of prophecy, &c., we cannot deny that he is a witness, in this case, on whom we may repose the most perfect confidence.

The apostle Peter has also given the most unequi

vocai testimony to the inspiration of the Old Testament prophets. He had been speaking concerning the wonderful scene of which he was a witness on the mount of transfiguration, whereupon he goes on to say: "We have a more sure word of prophecy whereunto ye do well that ye take heed, as unto a light that shineth in a dark place, until the day dawn and the day-star arise in your hearts; knowing this first, that no prophecy of Scripture is of any private interpretation. For the prophecy came not in old time by the will of man; but holy men of God spake as they were moved by the Holy Ghost." There is another testimony of this apostle in his first epistle: in which he clearly speaks of the inspiration of the prophets. "Of which salvation the prophets have inquired, and searched diligently, who prophesied of the grace that should come unto you; searching what or what manner of time the Spirit of Christ which was in them did signify, when it certified beforehand the sufferings of Christ and the glory that should follow. Unto whom it was revealed, that not unto themselves, but unto us, they did minister the things which are now reported unto you, by them that have preached the gospel unto you, with the Holy Ghost sent down from heaven."

That the Scriptures of the Old Testament were continually recognized by the apostles as given by inspiration of God, is so evident from every mention of them, that it may seem to be a waste of time to adduce the testimonies; but the subject is exceedingly important, and we cannot too frequently have these evidences set before our eyes.

In the epistle to the Hebrews, there are many clear testimonies, some of which I will bring forward. In the very first sentence it is said, "God, who at sundry times and in divers manners spake in time past unto the fathers by the prophets, hath in these last days spoken unto us by his Son." Whatever is spoken by the prophets is represented throughout this book as spoken by God himself. Thus in the same chapter it is declared. "A1 1 when he bring eth the first-begotten into the world, HE saith, And let all the angels of God worship him. And of the angels, HE saith, Who maketh his angels spirits. But to the Son, HE saith, Thy throne, O God, is for ever and ever." Now all these passages, where God is said to speak, are quotations from the Psalms. Certainly then we may conclude, that whatever is spoken in this book of Psalms is from the inspiration of God. The same is the fact, in the next chapter, where a large part of the eighth Psalm is quoted and applied to Christ. So also the Captain of our salvation is represented as saying certain things, which are found written in the Old Testament : " Saying, I will declare thy name unto my brethren:"—" And again, I will put my trust in him." In the third chapter of this epistle we have a quotation from the Psalms in the following remarkable words, " Wherefore, as the Holy Ghost saith, To-day if ye will hear his voice harden not your hearts." And in the fourth chapter the same style is used as before. "For HE spake in a certain place of the seventh day in this wise, And God did rest the seventh day from all his works." And in the fifth: " But he said unto him, Thou art my Son; to-day have I begotten thee. As he saith also in another place, Thou art a priest for ever after the order of Melchisedec." And God is represented as the speaker, not only in what is written in the Psalms, but in the prophets also. In the eighth chapter we have a long quotation from Jeremiah, which is declared to be the word of the Lord. "Behold the days come, saith the Lord," &c. One more testimony from this book shall suffice. In the tenth chapter, it is said, " Wherefore the Holy Ghost also is a witness unto us; for after that he had said before, This is the covenant that I will make with them after those days, saith the Lord," &c.

In short, as the writers of the Old Testament declared themselves to speak what they received from the Lord, so the whole of the Scriptures are continually referred to, and recognized as given by inspiration; nsomuch that .t would be difficult to find a single passage, in which these Scriptures are mentioned, where this idea is not expressed or clearly implied. And it will be shown hereafter, that the writers of the New Testament claim inspiration for themselves.

CHAPTER XV.

THE INSPIRATION OF THE BOOKS OF THE NEW TESTAMENT.

IF, as has been shown, the Old Testament was written by inspiration, and if the New Testament contains a revelation from God not less important, and is in fact the completion of the Old, can we believe that while prophets were inspired to write the former, the latter was left to be marred and obscured by the weaknesses of uninspired men?

To accomplish the purpose intended by revelation, it seems necessary that the writers who communicate it to posterity should be guided by inspiration. The end of revelation is to convey to men a certain knowledge of truth, to guide their faith and practice. But if the book which contains such a revelation is composed by erring, fallible men, we never can be sure, in any particular case, that we are in possession of the truth revealed. The men may be honest and faithful, but we know that all men are liable to errors and mistakes; and all men are more or less under the influence of prejudices and prepossessions. It is evident, therefore, that the purpose of giving a revelation would be in a great measure defeated, unless inspired men were employed to make the record by which it is to be transmitted to the various nations of the earth and to posterity.

Again, when we carefully consider the subject matter of the books of the New Testament, we cannot repose implicit confidence in what is taught, unless we have evidence that the pens of the writers were under the guidance of inspiration. To record the discourses which a man hears, and transactions which he sees, seems, at first sight, to require nothing more than veracity, and integrity in the historian. This might to a certain extent be admitted, if the witness instantly noted down what he heard or saw; but who can believe that after the lapse of eight, fifteen, or fifty years, the evangelists would be able to record with perfect accuracy, long discourses of their Master, and to relate correctly all the circumstances of the miracles of which they have given an account? It may be said, indeed, that they could give substantially the facts of which they were witnesses; but this is far from being satisfactory. Such a record would lose a portion of that reverence which it ought to possess, in order to give it a commanding authority over the conscience, and make it a solid foundation for unshaken confidence. In regard to the mysterious and sublime doctrines which the apostles teach in their epistles, if once we admit the idea that they were fallible men, we shall continually be liable to doubt: we shall be afraid they have misapprehended, or forgotten what they had heard; or, that, under the bias of prejudice or inclination, they may have been led insensibly to give a distorted view of the truths which they inculcate.

But we are not left to conclude from the necessity of the case merely, that the writers of the New Testament were inspired by the Holy Ghost. We have clear and abundant proof that our blessed Lord promised infallible guidance to his disciples whom he chose to be his witnesses to the world; and to whom he committed the propagation of his religion through all nations and all ages. "And I will pray the Father, and he shall give you another Comforter, that he may abide with you for ever; even the Spirit of truth, whom the world cannot receive, because it seeth him not, neither knoweth him; but ye know him, for he dwelleth with you and shall be in you." And that the Holy Spirit here promised was to guide the apostles in delivering their testimony, may be inferred from what is said in the fifteenth chapter of John: "But when the Comforter is come, whom I will send unto you from the Father, even the Spirit of truth, which proceedeth from the Father, he shall testify of me. And ye shall bear witness, because ye have been with me from the beginning." The promise of plenary inspiration is, however, more explicitly given in the sixteenth chapter. "Howbeit, when he, the Spirit of truth, is come, HE WILL GUIDE YOU INTO ALL TRUTH; for he shall not speak of himself; but whatsoever he shall hear, that shall he speak; and he will show you things to come. He shall glorify me; for he shall receive of mine, and shall show it unto you. All things that the Father hath are mine; therefore said I that he shall take of mine, and shall show it unto you." Christ also promised the inspiration of immediate suggestion to his disciples, when called to answer before kings and rulers, and commanded them not to premeditate what they should say, for it would be given to them at the moment what they ought to say. "For," said he, "it is not you that speak, but the Holy Ghost who speaketh in you." Now we may argue with irresistible force, that if plenary inspiration was granted to the apostles to enable them to make a proper defence when arraigned at a human tribunal, surely they would not be abandoned to their own weakness when preparing a record of Christ's words and actions, which was through all ages to be the guide of his Church. If the apostles were ever inspired, we may be sure that it was when directed to finish and record the testimony of God. The very idea that every book of the Old Testament was given by inspiration, but that the whole of the New was composed without this aid, is revolting to the reason of man. And this will appear the more unreasonable, when we consider, that the light of the new dispensation is seven-fold clearer than that of the old. The very forerunner of Christ was superior to all the prophets that preceded him. but the least in the king dom of heaven was greater than he. Then certainly, if all the prophets only spoke as they were moved by the Holy Ghost, the apostles who were the chosen witnesses of Christ and chief officers of his kingdom, were not left without this infallible guidance, when engaged in performing the most important part of the responsible duty assigned them; when executing that part of their commission which was most effectual in extending and perpetuating his spiritual kingdom. Accordingly, the apostles claim to be inspired men, and speak with an authority which would be arrogant, if they had not written under an infallible guidance. They do not merely express their own private opinions, and endeavour to support them by argument; they speak as men assured of the truth of what they deliver, and decide with authority and without hesitation, questions, which none but men inspired by the Holy Spirit could undertake thus positively to determine, without exposing themselves to the charge of dogmatism and self-sufficiency.

Besides, some parts of the New Testament, like much of the Old, are prophetic, and if true, could be written in no other way than by inspiration. The Apocalypse or Revelation given to John, is either a mere enthusiastic fable, or it was written by inspiration; and such is the majesty of the ideas here presented, and the awful sublimity of the style, that even Dr. Priestley was constrained to acknowledge that it bore on its face marks of a superhuman origin. If we had time to compare the prophetic representations of this singular book with authentic history, there would arise an evidence of its inspiration which could not be easily contradicted. Such men as Sir Isaac Newton, Dr. S. Clarke, Bishop Hurd, Bishop Newton, and a multitude of others, have seen in this book the most convincing proof of divine inspiration. The same may be said of all the prophecies of the Old and New Testament. If there is any truth whatever in them, they must be inspired; for none but inspired men can foretell future contingent events. Indeed, in all the cases where Moses and others

Jeclare that God spoke to them, and communicated instructions or laws, they must be considered as divinely directed, unless we deny their veracity. But we are now reasoning on the hypothesis, that the books are authentic and written by men of truth and honesty.

The style of the evangelists has often been adduced as an evidence of their inspiration: not that they write with an elegance and sublimity which cannot be imitated; but because they write as persons divested of the feelings which commonly belong to men. They write with an unaffected simplicity, and with an impartial, dispassionate regard to truth, which has no parallel, and has never been successfully imitated. How could illiterate men produce such works as the gospels without inspiration? Select a thousand sensible men, but unaccustomed to composition, and set them to write a simple history of the most remarkable transactions with which they have been conversant, and there will not be in any one of them an approximation to the characteristic manner of the evangelists. Others, and men possessed of more learning than the apostles, have undertaken, without inspiration, to write gospels, as if composed by some one or other of those holy men; but you cannot place the evidence of the inspiration of the genuine gospels in a stronger light than by contrasting them with any or all the apocryphal writings under the names of the apostles.

But we are in danger here of repeating what has already been said under the head of the internal Evidences of Christianity. The truth is, that the whole of the arguments from this source, for divine revelation, are directly in point to prove the doctrine of inspiration; and therefore, instead of going over the ground the second time, I would refer to what has been said on the subject of internal evidence.

Miracles also furnish the most conclusive proof of inspiration, where it can be ascertained that the writer of any book of Scripture possessed the power of performing such works; for the very end for which

miracles were exhibited, was, to prove that the person speaking was sent from God to deliver some
message. As Nicodemus properly said, "We know
that thou art a teacher come from God, for no man
can do the miracles which thou doest, unless God be
with him." If miracles are sufficient to prove the
truth of an oral communication, will they not also
be equally conclusive in favour of a written declaration? If there be any difference, it is in favour of the
latter, because it is much more important that a
written discourse intended for the instruction of all
ages should be well attested, than a discourse from
the lips, which is heard by few, and can never be recovered after it has been spoken.

In the whole of what has been said on the subject
of inspiration, the truth of the facts recorded in the
New Testament has been taken for granted; and also,
that the Scriptures contain a divine revelation. We
are not arguing with infidels, but with those who,
while they acknowledge the divine origin of the
Christian religion, doubt, or deny that the persons
who wrote the books of the Old and New Testament
were guided by a plenary inspiration. Now, as these
persons admit that the apostles and evangelists were
men of veracity and integrity, their testimony on this
subject ought to be decisive. If they claim inspiration, we cannot deny it to them, without invalidating
all the strongest evidences of the truth of Christianity. Why were they endowed with the power of
working miracles, but that full credence might be
given to what they testified? And when they declare
that they were moved by the Holy Ghost, and that
what they delivered was not the word of men, but the
word of God received by divine revelation, do not
these miraculous powers which they possessed. as
fully confirm what they wrote as what they spoke?

Having before shown that the apostles furnish ample testimony to the inspiration of the Old Testament,
we shall now adduce a few texts to prove that they
claimed inspiration for themselves. Their message
is every where called, THE WORD OF GOD. Paul

declares, that what he preached, he received not from man but "from the revelation of Jesus Christ;" that the things which he wrote were "the commandments of the Lord;" and that the things which he and his brethren taught, "God had revealed to them by his Spirit." He therefore declared, that he who despised the things which he taught, despised not men but God. Peter ranks the commandments delivered by the apostles with the words of the holy Prophets; and as has been before remarked, reckons the epistles of Paul with the other Scriptures. John says, " We are of God; he that knoweth God heareth us; he that is not of God, heareth not us. Hereby know we the spirit of truth, and the spirit of error."

The only thing wanting to complete the evidence of the inspiration of the New Testament, and consequently that of the Old, is to show that these writings were received unanimously by the Christian Church as inspired writings. But although there exists abundant evidence of this fact, to pursue it would lead us too much into detail, and would not comport with the studied brevity of this work. And I am the less inclined to enter on the labour of collecting this testimony here, because this will be done in a subsequent part of the work. I may say, however, that in the early ages of the Church, no Christian ever called in question the inspiration of the sacred volume; but all held this as a fundamental point in their religion. It was left for those who chose to style themselves rationalists, in modern times, to admit the authenticity of the facts recorded in the Bible, while they utterly deny the plenary inspiration of the writers But this is ground on which no consistent reasoner can long stand. If the miracles and prophecies of the Scriptures be acknowledged, and the divine origin of Christianity admitted, the inspiration of the writers of these books must follow as a corollary. It cannot be denied without the greatest inconsistency. And on the other hand, if inspiration be denied, the authenticity of the miracles and prophecies will soon be abandoned. The course of theological opinion among the neologists of Germany, for a number of years past, furnishes a striking illustration of the truth of the aforesaid observations. For a time the assault, in that country, was merely upon the doctrine of inspiration; but no sooner was that ground conceded than the critics directed their artillery against the authenticity of the miraculous facts and prophecies.

There is no end to the objections which may be started against the plenary inspiration of the Scriptures, just as is the fact in regard to the visible universe as the work of God; and it cannot be denied that there is a striking analogy between the mode of reasoning pursued by atheists and deists. But the foundation of all their arguments is human ignorance. They cannot form the conception of a creation by a being of almighty power and infinite wisdom, and of a supernatural revelation from such a being, which would not be liable to as great and much greater objections, than they are able to bring forward against his works and word, as they do actually exist. If such men could be induced in a calm and unprejudiced manner to examine this subject, I would recommend to them a careful perusal of Butler's *Analogy of Natural and Revealed Religion;* and to the deist I would especially recommend the seventh chapter of the second part, where the author, in a manner peculiar to himself, makes first some observations on the particular evidences of Christianity, and then, in the close, exhibits a view of the evidence arising from a general survey of the contents of the Bible. The argument, as presented in this last form, is so original and striking, that I would insert it in this place, were I not afraid of swelling this volume to an inconvenient size. The whole of the second book of the Analogy may be considered as the most satisfactory method of meeting the popular objections to divine revelation.

In regard to particular objections, arising from apparent discrepancies, from extraordinary facts, and from mysterious doctrines found in the sacred volume, it will be sufficient to refer the inquisitive reader to the first volume of *Horne's Introduction*, and to *Dick's* deservedly popular work on *Inspiration*, and also to learned commentators, some of whom have taken much pains to reconcile seeming contradictions, and to elucidate obscure passages, by an application of the rules of sacred criticism. I would only further remark in relation to the usual objections to the inspiration of the Scriptures, that they militate as fully against the authenticity of the facts as against the inspiration of the writers, and therefore do not require to be considered and obviated under this head.

A summary of the whole evidence for the plenary inspiration of the Scriptures of the Old and New Testament, is as follows : all the Internal Evidences of Christianity—whether arising from the peculiar excellence of the matter, or the simplicity and sublimity of the style; from the perfection of the character ascribed to Jesus Christ; from the continual recognition of the over-ruling providence of God, from the pure and elevated spirit of devotion which breathes through the sacred pages, from the penetrating and transforming efficacy of the holy Scriptures, and from their adaptation to the constitution of the human mind, and to the existing relations among men, go to prove, that they were written under the infallible guidance of the Holy Spirit.

Again, every prophecy which has been fulfilled, furnishes undoubted and independent evidence of the inspiration of that particular part of the Scriptures; and all the laws which proceeded from the mouth of Jehovah must be considered as infallible precepts, unless we call in question the whole truth of the narrative.

The writers, for the most part, were endued with the power of working miracles. These facts, it is admitted, prove that God spake by them; and if the prophets and apostles were inspired in the discourses which they delivered, then, *a fortiori*, they mus have been inspired in preparing those writings which were intended to guide the faith and practice of believers through all ages.

Moreover, the sacred writers generally lay claim to inspiration. They speak authoritatively in the name of the Lord. They call their message, the WORD OF GOD, and Christ has set his seal to the plenary inspiration of all the Scriptures of the Old Testament. The apostles and evangelists, in the most explicit manner, declare the same truth.

Besides, Christ promised plenary inspiration to his disciples, and they professed to be under the guidance of the Spirit in what they wrote.

And finally, while some of the apostles were living, their writings were classed with the divine Scriptures, and were universally received as inspired, and as the infallible word of God, by the whole primitive Church.

We cannot but conclude, therefore, that all the books of the Old and New Testament were written by the inspiration of God, and contain an infallible rule to guide the faith and practice of the church to the end of the world.

CANONICAL AUTHORITY

OF THE

BOOKS OF SCRIPTURE.

———————

CHAPTER XVI.

THE IMPORTANCE OF ASCERTAINING THE TRUE CANON OF HOLY SCRIPTURE.

THE Bible includes a large number of separa e books, published in different ages, during a space of more than fifteen hundred years. Each of these books, when first published, formed a volume; or at least, the writings of each author were, in the beginning, distinct: and if they had continued in that separate form, and had been transmitted to us in many volumes instead of one, their authority would not on this account have been less, nor their usefulness diminished. Their collection into one volume is merely a matter of convenience; and if any persons choose now to publish these books in a separate form, they cannot with propriety be charged with casting indignity on the word of God.

Hence it appears, that besides general arguments to demonstrate that the Bible contains a divine revelation, there is need of special proofs to evince that each of the books now included in that sacred volume, has a right to the place which it occupies, or does in reality contain a part of that revelation which God has given.

If, therefore, it could be shown (which, however it never can) that some particular book, now included in the Bible, was not authentic, the conclusion thence derived would only affect that single production, unless it were recognized as divine by the writers of the other books. The credit of the whole volume would not be destroyed, even if it could be proved that one half the books of which it consists were spurious. Infidels have much more to effect in overthrowing the Bible, than they commonly suppose. It is incumbent on them to demonstrate, not only that this or that book is false, but that every one of these productions is destitute of evidence that it has been derived from the inspiration of God.

On the other hand, it is manifest, that the advocate of divine revelation is bound to defend the claims of every separate portion of this volume, or to reject from it that part which has no evidence of a divine origin. It is necessary that he should be able to render a good reason why he admits any particular book to form a part of the inspired volume.

It is true, that the antiquity of this collection claims for it a high degree of respect: the transmission of this volume to us, through so many centuries, as HOLY SCRIPTURE, should teach us to be cautious how we question what is so venerable for its antiquity. But this only furnishes one presumptive argument in favour of each book. It by no means renders all further investigation unnecessary, much less, impious.

It is easy to conceive that books not written by the inspiration of God, might, by some casualty or mistake, find a place in the sacred volume. In fact, we have a striking example of this very thing in the Greek and Latin Bibles which are now in use, and held to be sacred by a large majority of those who are denominated Christians. These Bibles, besides the books which have evidence of being truly inspired, contain a number of other books, the claim of which to inspiration cannot be sustained by sound and satisfactory reasons. This inquiry, therefore, is far from being one of mere curiosity: t is in the highest degree *practical*, and concerns the conscience of every man capable of making the investigation. We agree, in the general, that the Bible is the word of God, and an authoritative rule; but the momentous question immediately presents itself, what belongs to the Bible? Of what books does this sacred volume consist? And it will not answer, to resolve to take it as it has come down to us, without further inquiry; for the Bible has come down to us in several different forms. The Vulgate Latin Bible, which alone was in use for hundreds of years before the era of the Reformation, and also the Greek version of the Old Testament, contain many books not in the copies of the Hebrew Scriptures. Now, to determine which of these contains the whole of the inspired books given to the Jews before the advent of Christ, and no more, requires research and accurate examination. The inquiry, therefore, is not optional, but forces itself upon every conscientious man; for as no one is at liberty to reject from the sacred volume one sentence, much less a whole book of the revelation of God, so no one has a right to add any thing to the word of God: and of consequence, no one may receive as divine, what others have without authority added to the HOLY SCRIPTURES. Every man, therefore, according to his opportunity and capacity, is under a moral obligation to use his best endeavours to ascertain what books do really and of right belong to the Bible. An error here, on either side, is dangerous, for, on the one hand, if we reject a part of divine revelation, we dishonour God, and deprive ourselves of the benefit which might be derived from that portion of divine truth; and, on the other hand, we are guilty of an equal offence, and may suffer an equal injury, by adding spurious productions to the Holy Scriptures; for thus we adulterate and poison the fountain of life, and subject our consciences to the authority of mere men.

I think, therefore, that the importance and necessity of this inquiry must be evident to every person of serious reflection. But to some it may appear that this matter has been long ago settled on the firmest principles; and that it can answer no good purpose to agitate questions which have a tendency to produce doubts and misgivings in the minds of common Christians, rather than a confirmation of their faith In reply to the first part of this objection, I would say, that it is freely admitted that this subject has been ably and fully discussed long ago, and in almost every age until the present time; and the author aims at nothing more, in this short treatise, than to exhibit to the sincere inquirer who may not enjoy better means of information, the substance of those discussions and proofs, which ought to be in the possession of every Christian. His object is, not to bring forth any thing new, but to collect, and condense in a narrow space, what has been written by the judicious and the learned, on this important subject. But, that discussion tends to induce doubting, is a sentiment unworthy of Christians who maintain that their religion is founded on the best reasons, and who are commanded to give to every man a reason of the hope that is in them. That faith which is weakened by discussion is mere prejudice, not true faith. They who receive the most important articles of their religion upon trust from human authority, are continually liable to be thrown into doubt; and the only method of obviating this evil, is to dig deep and lay our foundation upon a rock. If this objection had any weight, it would discourage all attempts to establish the truth of our holy religion by argument; and would also damp the spirit of free inquiry on every important subject. It is true, however, that the first effect of free discussion may be, to shake that easy confidence which most men entertain, that all their opinions are correct; but the beneficial result will be, that instead of a persuasion, having no other foundation than prejudice, it will generate a faith resting on the firm basis of evidence.

The word CANON is derived from a Greek word which literally signifies a rule, and is several times

used in the New Testament, as in Gal. vi. 6. Phil. iii. 16. And as the inspired books are the authoritative rule to regulate our faith and practice, the early fathers gave to them this name; all such books were called CANONICAL; and thus they have been denominated ever since. Thus Irenæus speaks of the Holy Scriptures as THE CANON OF TRUTH; Clement of Alexandria employs the appellation of THE TRUE EVANGELICAL CANON; Eusebius calls the Scriptures THE ECCLESIASTICAL CANON, and Athanasius speaks of the three sorts of books; 1. THE CANONICAL; 2. Such as might be read; And 3. The apocryphal. The council of Laodicea ordained, that none but CANONICAL books should be read in the Church, that is, the Scriptures of the Old and New Testament.

In the same language are the inspired books described by the other fathers and councils.

In treating this subject, it will be necessary to inquire into the claims which every book now received by Jews or Christians, Romanists or Protestants, has to a place in the canon. Where there is a universal agreement among all who receive the Scriptures, little need be said; but in regard to disputed points, it will be necessary to be more particular.

CHAPTER XVII.

THE CARE WITH WHICH THE BOOKS OF THE OLD TESTAMENT WERE PRE-SERVED — THEIR CANONICAL AUTHORITY—THE SANCTION GIVEN TO THESE BOOKS BY THE SAVIOUR AND HIS APOSTLES—AND THE METHOD OF ASCERTAINING WHAT BOOKS WERE IN THE CANON AT THE TIME OF CHRIST'S ADVENT.

IT would be reasonable to conclude, even if nothing had been said, that a book written by divine inspiration would, by all pious persons, be carefully preserved. But we are expressly informed, that when Moses had finished writing the LAW he "command ed the Levites which bore the ark of the covenant of the Lord, saying, Take this book of the LAW, and put it in the side of the ark of the covenant of the Lord your God, that it may be there for a witness against thee."*

Here, in the most sacred part of the sanctuary, the Pentateuch was preserved as a sacred deposite. On one occasion, indeed, it seems to have been displaced, and its integrity endangered, when in the reigns of Manasseh and Amon idolatry so prevailed, that the true worship of God was suspended. During this period of darkness, the LAW was cast out among the rubbish, where it was found in the reign of the pious Josiah.† But while the autograph of Moses was laid up by the side of the ark, we are not to suppose that there were no authentic copies of this sacred book among the people. Josephus relates, that every tribe, by the command of Moses, was furnished with a copy. And as it contained the liturgy for the public worship of God, the rites of which were very numerous, and the regulations very minute, the priests and Levites must have been supplied with copies, to enable them rightly to conduct the public service This book also contained the law of the land, and prescribed the duties of kings and rulers; on which account it was expressly commanded, that when there should be a king, "He shall write him a copy of this law in a book, out of that which is before the priests, the Levites."‡

It would, however, be unreasonable to expect that the autograph of Moses could last until this period of the world. What became of it is not known. The probability is, that it perished with the ark, in the destruction of the temple by Nebuchadnezzar. And this fact probably occasioned the tradition which was prevalent among the Jews, that the sacred Scriptures were utterly lost in the destruction of Jerusalem by the Chaldeans; and that they were restored by Ezra, by divine inspiration. Now it is probable

* Deut. xxxi. 25, 26.　　　　　† Deut. xv i. 18.
† 2 Kings xxii. 9, 10, 11

that the autographs were lost, and that Ezra the scribe, who was an inspired man, collected the scattered copies of the sacred books, corrected their errors, and thus restored the Scriptures to their original integrity. On account of this important and pious labour, the constitution of the canon of the Old Testament is by the Jews ascribed to Ezra; and they join with him, as assistants, "the men of the great synagogue," some of whom were prophets, by whose aid the sacred volume was prepared, and copies circulated among the people. In such a work, he would need many coadjutors; and no more holy or important work could have occupied the time and attention of inspired men. It is reasonable to believe, therefore, that all who were qualified to render effectual aid in this service, would be ready to assist Ezra in correcting and preparing the Holy Scriptures, for general use.

That all the copies of the LAW were not lost, is as evident as any thing can be; for Daniel in the captivity had possession of the prophecies of Jeremiah. And Ezra himself was a "ready scribe in the LAW;" and 'n the sixth chapter of Ezra we read, that the functions of the priests were regulated after the second temple was finished, "as it is written in the book of Moses;" and this was many years before Ezra came to Jerusalem. And in the eighth chapter of Nehemiah it is said, that Ezra "brought the LAW before the congregation, and read therein from morning until mid-day."

In regard to the other books, little is said. We read, however, that the writings of Joshua were annexed to the law, and of course deposited with it by the side of the ark; and we may take it for granted, as a matter of course, than when any prophet or inspired man had finished a writing intended for general use, it was added to the volume of the law, and preserved with it.

How carefully the writings of Moses were read and accurately remembered, appears from the frequent reference made to the facts there recorded by the writers who came after Moses; especially, by the holy men who composed the book of Psalms. And that this knowledge was commonly possessed by men not inspired, will appear from the full and accurate recapitulation of the history recorded in the law, in the complete and eloquent answer given by Jepthah to the king of the Ammonites.* The writings of the prophets also abound in references to facts recorded in the law of Moses.

On what *material* the Scriptures were written, in what character or alphabet, whether bound up in a single volume or in several; whether preserved in rolls, as in the synagogues now, or in the common form of our books, are inquiries which are worthy the attention of the biblical student, but no way necessary to our purpose, at present.

That which is of the utmost importance is, to know that the Lord Jesus Christ and his inspired apostles, gave their unqualified sanction to the SCRIPTURES which were in use and read in the synagogues, in their time. Christ severely censures the Scribes and Pharisees and Lawyers for neglecting to obey the Scriptures, and for misrepresenting them and rendering the law of God void by their vain traditions: but he never hints that they had corrupted the sacred text. On the contrary, he refers to the SCRIPTURES, then extant among the Jews, as an infallible standard. "Search the SCRIPTURES," said he; "for in them ye think ye have eternal life, and they are they which testify of me."† Again, "Ye do err, not knowing the SCRIPTURES."‡ He proves his doctrine by the Scriptures, "which cannot be broken,"§ and it is asserted repeatedly, that certain things came to pass, "that the Scriptures might be fulfilled."‖ Yea, Christ himself declares "they must be fulfilled."¶ And Paul says, "All Scripture is given by inspiration of God."** They are also by this apostle called "the

*Judges xi.
† John v. 39.
‡ Matt. xxii. 29.
§ John x. 35.

‖ Mark xiv. 49.
¶ Matt. xxvi. 54.
** 2 Tim. iii. 16.

ORACLES OF GOD,* THE WORD OF GOD."† And Peter says, "the PROPHECY came not in old time by the will of man, but holy men of God spake as they were moved by the Holy Ghost."‡ And James speaks of the SCRIPTURES with equal confidence and respect "And receive with meekness," says he, "the ingrafted word, which is able to save your souls"§—"And the SCRIPTURE was fulfilled which saith," &c.||

Thus it appears, that we have the best possible evidence that the SCRIPTURES which were in use when Christ was upon earth, were entire and uncorrupted, and were an infallible rule; and that men erred from not knowing or understanding them. Whether these SCRIPTURES were included in one book or in several, is of no consequence. In one place, our Lord refers to the Scriptures of the Old Testament under the name of MOSES and the PROPHETS.¶ They seem, however, to have been divided into three parts, called by our Saviour, "the LAW, the PROPHETS, and the PSALMS."** This exactly corresponds with the ancient division of the Jews, into the Law, Prophets, and Hagiographa, which is mentioned by Josephus. But whether there were three separate volumes, or only one, is a matter of no manner of consequence, any more than it is now, whether the canonical Scriptures are included in one or two volumes.

The only difficulty which remains is, to ascertain what books were actually extant, at that time, under the name of SCRIPTURES. If we can settle this point satisfactorily, the proof of the canon of the Old Testament will be complete.

In the first place, then, it may be observed, that the most important parts of the Old Testament are expressly quoted. We have seen that our Lord mentions the Law, the Prophets and the Psalms;

* Romans iii. 2. Heb. v. 12.
† Rom. ix. 6. x. 17. 1 Cor. xiv. 36. 2 Cor ii. 17. Ephes vi. 17 Col. i. 25. 1 Thess ii. 13. 1 Tim. ii. 9.
‡ 2 Peter i. 21.
§ James i. 21. 22
|| James ii 5
¶ Luke xvi. 29, 31.
** Luke xxiv. 44.

and several of the prophets are named, and citations
are made from others. Now, as far as this evidence
goes, it is complete; but it must be acknowledged
that several books now in the canon of the Old Testament, are not named nor quoted. In regard to
these we must resort to other evidence.

The next proof is derived from the copies of the
Hebrew Bible in the hands of the Jews. If our
canon is not the same as the one in use in the time
of Christ, the alteration must have been made by the
Christians, either by adding or taking away some
books. But if this had been done, the fraud could
easily have been detected by referring to the Jewish
Scriptures; for no one can suppose that they would
join in collusion with Christians, to mar or adulterate
their own sacred volume. Such has been the hostili-
ty between the Jews and Christians from the beginning, that they have been mutually safeguards of the
inspired books, to preserve them from alteration by
one party or the other. All that is necessary, there
fore, is to compare our copies of the Hebrew Scriptures with those found among the Jews. The result
of this comparison is, that in regard to this point,
there is a perfect agreement between the Jews and
Protestant Christians. We claim a place for no book
in the canon which they do not acknowledge to be
inspired; and they bring no accusation against Protestants for having mutilated the sacred volume by
abstracting from it any book or chapter.

But again, we are able to approach very near to
direct and full proof of the point in hand, from a
most unsuspected quarter. Josephus, who was contemporary with the apostle Paul, and himself not
only a learned man, but a priest, has left on record
a testimony which every impartial man will consider
satisfactory. "We have," says he, "only two and
twenty books which are to be believed as of divine
authority. Of which, FIVE are the books of Moses.
From the death of Moses to the reign of Artaxerxes,
the son of Xerxes, king of Persia, the prophets, who
were the successors of Moses, have written in THIR-

TEEN books. The remaining FOUR books contain hymns to God, and instructions of life for the use of men." Here the number and the description of the books, considered of divine authority, furnish satisfactory testimony, that the canon of the Jews in the time of our Saviour corresponds entirely with ours.

At first view it might seem, that we had many more than two and twenty books in the volume of the Old Testament; but this difficulty will be easily removed, when it is considered, that the Jews always reckoned the twelve minor prophets as one book; and the book of Ruth they considered an appendage to Judges, and the Lamentations of Jeremiah an appendage to his prophecy. Thus the number will be reduced exactly to twenty-two.

We have, besides, the direct testimony of early Christian writers. MELITO, bishop of Sardis, who lived in the second century, took the trouble of making a journey into Judea, to inquire into this matter; and although his own work has not come down to us, Eusebius has preserved his catalogue of the books of the Old Testament: from which it appears that the sacred canon contained then the very same books which are now included in it.

To Melito we may add the testimony of Origen, who spent much of his time in a place near to Judea, and who was skilled in the Hebrew tongue. This learned man has left a catalogue of the books of the Old Testament, which perfectly corresponds with our canon, except that he has omitted the twelve minor prophets; which book, however, he recognizes in other places as a part of the sacred volume.

Besides having catalogues by many other of the fathers, we have the testimony of two councils; that of Laodicea, and of Carthage; both of which made out catalogues of the books of the Old Testament, which are in perfect accordance with the canon as now constituted.

If other proof were needed, it might be found in the Samaritan Pentateuch, as far as the law is concerned; and in the Septuagint version, which contains al. ne books which are now in the Old Testament, in the Hebrew Bibles. This version was made nearly three centuries before the birth of Christ, and had long been in general and familiar use, even in the land of Judea. It is true, that this version, as it has come down to us, while it comprehends all the books now in the canon, includes what is called the apocrypha; therefore, while it furnishes full proof that nothing has been taken away, we cannot refer to it for proof that nothing has been added. But the inquiry respecting the apocryphal books, which claim a place in the canon, will be taken up in the next chapter.

Further proof of the canon of the Old Testament might be derived from the early versions made soon after the commencement of the Christian era; particularly the Syriac, and Latin Vulgate; as also from the quotations of the early Christian writers; from the Targums, which contain a paraphrase of all the books of the Old Testament in Chaldee. And abundant evidence of the same thing might be drawn from the Talmud, which contains the oral law of the Jews. But as what has already been adduced is sufficient, we deem it unnecessary to multiply proofs in a matter so evident.

Having shown that our canon of the Old Testament is the same as that which existed in the time of our Saviour, to which he gave his full and emphatic approbation, it follows of course, that none of the books which ever made a part of the sacred volume have been lost. But here we are met with an objection derived from the Old Testament itself, where several books are spoken of and referred to, which cannot now be found. For example, it is said of Solomon, " that he spake three thousand proverbs, and his songs were a thousand and five. And he spake of the trees, from the cedar in Lebanon even unto the hyssop that springeth out of the wall; he spake also of beasts, and of fowl, and of creeping things, and of the fishes."*

* 1 Kings iv. 32, 33.

We read also of "the book of Samuel the seer," and "the book of Nathan the prophet;" and "the book of Gad the seer."* Mention is also made of the book of "Jasher;" and of the book of "the wars of the Lord," &c.†

In answer to this objection it will be sufficient to remark, that there is no evidence that these compositions of Solomon were ever written, as the text only says, that he *spake* these things; but supposing them to have been written, there is no evidence that they were ever intended to be a part of the sacred canon; or that these compositions were inspired: for it is not necessary to suppose that either prophets or apostles had inspiration to direct them in all matters of common life, or in writing on subjects of natural science.

But in regard to the books of certain prophets and seers, it is highly probable, that those men assisted in writing the historical books of Samuel, Kings, and Chronicles.

And as to the book of Jasher, and the book of the wars of the Lord, too little is known about them to authorize us to think that they formed a part of the ancient canon; unless we adopt the opinion, that we still possess them under other names. Here it may with propriety be observed, that the Hebrew word for *book*, is used to signify any list or genealogy; and, accordingly, it is the opinion of judicious commentators, that the "book of the wars of the Lord," was nothing but *a muster-roll* of the army. And the book of "Jasher" (rectitude) may have been a compend of moral rules derived from the Scriptures; or a manual (not inspired,) composed by the wise for the conduct of life. The mere mention of a book, or citation of a sentence from it, by no means gives it a place in the canon.

There is no probability that any of the canonical books could have been lost from the Old Testament, when we consider with what religious, and even superstitious care, they have been kept and transcribed by the Jewish scribes.

* 1 Chron. xxix. 29 30. † 1 Sam. i. 18 Num. xxi. 14.

22*

The Rabbis among the Jews view this matter as we do: they never complain, nor even hint, that the sacred volume had been mutilated.

And the unqualified testimony in favour of the Old Testament scriptures by Christ and his apostles, already referred to, ought to be decisive on this point, if all other evidence was wanting.

CHAPTER XVIII.

THE BOOKS DENOMINATED APOCRYPHAL HAVE NO JUST CLAIM TO A PLACE AMONG THE CANONICAL SCRIPTURES OF THE OLD TESTAMENT.

THE word Apocrypha probably signifies that which is *hidden, obscure, without authority.* It is employed to designate such writings as claim a place in the canon, without possessing sufficient evidence to substantiate their claims. This word is said to have been first used by Melito, bishop of Sardis, in the second century. The subject acquires great importance from the fact, that it was formerly and is now a matter of earnest controversy, between Romanists and Protestants, whether certain books which are frequently included in Greek and Latin copies of the Bible, are canonical, or should be considered apocryphal. The number of books in dispute is six, namely, TOBIT, JUDITH, WISDOM, ECCLESIASTICUS, BARUCH, and the TWO BOOKS OF MACCABEES; and also, some additional chapters annexed to the book of Esther, which are not in the Hebrew; and to the book of Daniel, the *History of Susannah*, and *the Song of the Three Children* are prefixed, and *the History of Bel and the Dragon* is annexed. These books, and portions of books, are likewise placed at the end of the Old Testament, in our larger English Bibles, under the name APOCRYPHA.

The council of Trent, which sat in the sixteenth

century, have given a catalogue of the canonical books of Scripture, in which those above mentioned are included; and they are inserted promiscuously with the other books, in the editions of the Latin Vulgate, and in all other versions prepared by members of the Roman Catholic Church. They consider all copies of the Bible imperfect and mutilated, in which these books are not found; and this has created a great obstacle to the circulation of the Scriptures among the people of that persuasion, as Protestant Bible societies have come to a resolution not to circulate Bibles which contain those books which they deem apocryphal.

To show that these books are not canonical, but apocryphal, the following arguments are deemed sufficient.

1. These books are not found in the Hebrew Bible; nor are they written in the Hebrew tongue, but in the Greek or Chaldaic. For the proof of this fact we have the testimony of Jerome, a competent witness, who translated several of them into Latin. There is strong reason to believe, that all these books were composed originally in the Greek language, which was unknown to the Jews until after the canon of the Old Testament was closed. It has been always the current opinion, both among Jews and Christians, that Malachi was the last of the Old Testament writers; and books written by uncertain authors after the spirit of prophecy had ceased, have no just claim to a place in the sacred canon. The date of the composition of these books cannot be accurately fixed; but that it occurred long after the time of Ezra and Malachi, there can be no ground of reasonable doubt.

2. A second argument is, that these disputed books have never been acknowledged by the Jews to be of divine authority, nor have by them been admitted into the canon; and they are the best judges of what books properly belonged to their sacred Scriptures. If these books had been of divine authority, the fact would have been known to the Jewish Church, to which "the oracles of God were committed." And

if they had ever belonged to the canon, they would not have been left out afterwards.

The opinion of the ancient and modern Jews on this point is the same; and there is among them no diversity of opinion respecting this matter. Josephus, in a passage already quoted, declares, "that no more than twenty-two books were received as inspired by his nation." And although Philo Judæus refers often to the Old Testament, and comments largely on its contents in his writings, he never makes the least mention of any one of these books.

But if the ancient Jews knew any thing of these books as a part of their sacred canon, we should certainly find it in the voluminous writings of the Talmud; but not one of these books is recognized as canonical in this great body of Jewish traditions. It may certainly be inferred, therefore, that they were not considered canonical by the ancient Jews.

And the more modern Jews are so far from acknowledging them, that their testimony is expressly against them. Rabbi Azariah says, "they are received by Christians, not by us." He means Romanists, who acknowledged them as we have seen. And Rabbi Gedaliah, as quoted by Hottinger, has the following testimony. After giving a catalogue of inspired books received by the Jews, he goes on to say, "It is worth while to know, that the nations of the world wrote many other books which are included in their systems of sacred books, but are not in our hands." To which he adds, "They say that some of these are found in the Chaldee, some in the Arabic, and some in the Greek language."

Rabbi Azariah, before mentioned, ascribes THE WISDOM OF SOLOMON to Philo. And Rabbi Gedaliah observes, "That if Solomon ever wrote it, it must have been in the Syriac language, to send it to some of the kings in the remotest part of the east." "But," says he, "Ezra only put his hand to such books as were published by the prophets under the guidance of the Holy Spirit, and written in the sacred language. And our wise men prudently and delib erately resolved to sanction none but such as were established by him." "Their wise men," says Buxtorf, "pronounced this book to be apocryphal."

The book called ECCLESIASTICUS, is expressly numbered among apocryphal books in the Talmud; where it is said, "In the book of the son of Sirach it is forbidden to read." And Manasseh ben Israel, one of the most learned of the modern Jews, observes, "that those things which are alleged from a verse in Ecclesiasticus, are nothing to the purpose, because this is an apocryphal book." In the same way, they are wont to speak of all these books; and Jerome informs us, that he heard one of the Jews deriding the history of Susannah, who said it was invented by some Greek, he knew not whom." It is unnecessary to add further testimonies, because the fact that the Jews never did receive the apocrypha as a part of their canon, cannot be denied.

3. The third argument against the canonical authority of the aforementioned books, is, that they are never cited or referred to as a part of sacred Scripture, in the whole of the New Testament. We are aware that on this point we are at issue with the Roman Catholics. They even pretend to prove their right to a place in the canon, from quotations said to be made from them by Paul. One of the passages alleged is, " For who hath known the mind of the Lord, or who has been his counsellor?"* And the other is, "For before his translation he had this testimony, that he pleased God."† But both these passages are taken from the canonical books of the Old Testament; and there is no reason to think that the apostle had any thought of the apocrypha when he cited these texts.

4. The fourth argument against the divine authority of these books is, that they were not received as inspired by the Christian fathers; but were expressly rejected from the sacred canon, almost with one consent, by those who were best qualified to judge of their claims. In all the catalogues drawn up by

* Rom. xi. 34.　　　　　　　　　† Heb. xi. 5.

fathers and councils, for the very purpose of teaching the Church what books should be recieved as of divine authority, these are uniformly omitted. Justin Martyr, Origen, Athanasius, Hilary, Gregory Nazianzen, Jerome, Epiphanius, and Cyril, together with the councils of Laodicea and Carthage, have left catalogues of the canonical books of the Old Testament, among which, not one of these is to be found. And they almost all number the books agreeably to the Jewish custom, and make the number twenty-two, according to the number of letters in the Hebrew Alphabet. And not only so, but many of these learned fathers make express mention of these books, and explicitly reject them from the sacred canon. This is especially the case in regard to Jerome, who wrote prefaces to most of the books of the Old Testament, and in these he takes occasion to mention those now in question, and declares them all to be apocryphal. And this continued to be the common opinion among the most learned theologians down to the time of the Reformation, as Dr. Cosins has abundantly shown in his "Scholastic History of the Canon of the Old Testament."

5. As the external evidence is unfavourable to the canonical authority of the books in question, so also is the internal evidence.

Books which contain palpable falsehoods; abound in ridiculous and incredible stories; which contradict the plain acknowledged doctrines of the Bible; and which can by no means be reconciled with the recorded history of the Jews, cannot be a part of the sacred volume. And when the books under consideration are tried by these principles, they manifestly appear to be apocryphal.

In the book of Tobit an angel of God is made to tell a downright falsehood, by declaring that he was "Azarias the son of Ananias;" and in the same book, he declares, that he was "Raphael, one of the seven holy angels, which present the prayers of the saints, and go in and out before the glory of the Holy One."

Although Judith is celebrated for her devoted piety, and the book under her name was intended to exhibit her as a bright example of a person wholly consecrated to God; yet she is represented as speaking scarcely any thing else but falsehoods, to Holofernes; but what is still more inconsistent, she is made to pray to the God of truth, " Smite by the deceit of my lips, the servant with the prince, and the prince with the servant." She also commends the conduct of Simeon in the cruel slaughter of the Shechemites, of which God has expressed his strong disapprobation in various ways. Besides the objections to the book of Judith, already mentioned, there is another of great weight arising from the difficulty of finding any room for such transactions and such a state of things as are therein described, in any period of the Jewish history; nor is it easy to identify the places mentioned in this book. These difficulties have led some of its advocates to maintain, that the whole is an allegory, and that by BETHULIA, we should understand the Church of God, and by Nebuchadnezzar, the enemies of the Church; and that the victory achieved by the courage and address of Judith, is intended to teach us, that the church's deliverance is not to be accomplished by human power, &c. This perhaps is as favourable a view as can be taken of this extraordinary story; but no one ought any longer to claim a place for this book in the sacred canon.

In the second book of Maccabees, Razis, an elder of Jerusalem, is much commended for destroying his own life, to avoid falling into the hands of his enemies; but surely suicide has not the approbation of God.

Between the two books of Maccabees there are irreconcilable discrepancies; and some statements respecting Jeremiah's taking the ark and the golden altar to mount Pisgah, and hiding them in a cave, are manifestly fabulous.

The book of Wisdom is written under the name of Solomon, the son of David, and he talks about his being appointed to build the temple of the Lord;

whereas it has been clearly shown by Jerome, that this book never could have been written by Solomon

The absurd story in Tobit, of driving away the devil by the smoke of the liver of a certain fish, and of healing blindness by its gall, could not have been given by divine inspiration.

There are several things in the book of Baruch, not reconcilable with the sacred record: and the account given of Mardocheus, in the chapters annexed to Esther, is not consistent with what is said of Mordecai in the genuine parts of that book; and in this apocryphal writing, Haman is declared to be a Macedonian, whereas in the canonical book of Esther, he is called an Agagite; and he is represented in the former to have entertained a design of transferring the kingdom of Persia to the Macedonians; which is utterly incredible; for at that time the kingdom of Macedon, if it existed, must have been most obscure, and, in all probability, unknown at the Persian court.

6. And finally, these books are not canonical, because they were not written by prophets, or inspired men; but by writers who speak of their labours in a way wholly incompatible with divine inspiration.

The uniform belief of Jews and Christians is, that the spirit of prophecy ceased among the Jews after the time of Malachi. He has, therefore, been denominated *the seal of the prophets.*

We know not the author of the books of Maccabees. Both Jerome and Eusebius ascribe them to Josephus; but they can scarcely be believed to have the same author, as they contradict one another. By tne "Compiler of Jewish History," quoted by Drusius, these books are placed after the writings of Josephus. The second book of Maccabees is professedly an abridgment of the work of one Jason of Cyrene, in which, five volumes are reduced to one If the original work of Jason was not inspired, neither is this abridgment.

The book of WISDOM is the only one which claims to have been written by an inspired man. But this very claim condemns it; for 't may be demonstrated

hat it was composed long after the death of King
Solomon. It contains manifest allusions to Grecian
customs, and to Grecian philosophy. The author
praises himself, and flatters the Jewish nation, in a
style entirely foreign to that of the inspired prophets.
It has been by some ascribed to Philo Judæus; but
it is more probably the work of some other Jew. If
Solomon had written it, it would have been in the
Hebrew, and always inserted in the Jewish canon.

The book of ECCLESIASTICUS is the most valuable
of those denominated apocryphal, and would have
the best claim, as far as internal evidence is concerned, to a place in the canon; but the modest writer
of this book is so far from pretending to be inspired,
that he professes merely to have reduced to order a
work of his grandfather, which he received from
Sirach his father. And he entreats the reader to
peruse his work with indulgence, and to pardon him
if he should be found coming short in some words
which he attempted to interpret. Evidently the writer was conscious of no divine inspiration.

To evade the force of the above arguments, the
Roman Catholic writers have invented a distinction
between *primary* and *secondary* canonical books;
but this is a delusive distinction. A book is either
inspired, or it is not; it belongs to the canon, or it
does not. There is no conceivable medium in this
case. There may be an intermediate class of books,
between the canonical and spurious; that is, human
compositions, which though not inspired, nor claim-
ing a place in the canon, may be read with profit,
on account of the history or moral lessons which they
contain. Some of the fathers made this distinction,
and call these *Ecclesiastical*, in contradistinction both
from the canonical and supposititious. Such books,
too, were read in some churches in the early ages,
not as of authority, but merely for edification; and
thus they became mingled with the canonical books
The Greek fathers were accustomed to use the Sep
tuagint version of the Old Testament, and several of
these books, now in question, being also in Greek

became mixed with the canonical books, in the copies of this version. The oldest Greek MSS. of the LXX contain them intermingled with the other books, so that they must have become so at an early period But from the testimonies of the fathers, and the catalogues of canonical books which they have left, these books do not appear to have been included in the sacred volume, in the very earliest ages of the Christian Church. These books, indeed, were known to the fathers; but they are careful to distinguish them from the canonical books. And as some of them even disapproved of their being read, and warned their hearers against them, it cannot reasonably be supposed, that they were then included in the volume of Holy Scripture.

These books, called apocryphal, may be read with profit by the judicious; but they ought by no means to be placed on a level with THE ORACLES OF GOD, nor should they be bound up in the same volume with the canonical books, nor publicly read as a part of Scripture.

CHAPTER XIX.

CANON OF THE NEW TESTAMENT—METHOD OF SETTLING IT—TESTIMONY OF THE CHURCH—CONSTITUTION OF THE CANON—WHENCE THESE BOOKS DERIVE THEIR AUTHORITY—SOLICITUDE OF EARLY CHRISTIANS TO OBTAIN THESE BOOKS—THEIR CARE TO DISTINGUISH THEM FROM OTHERS—AUTOGRAPHS, &c.

THREE methods of determining what books of the New Testament are canonical, have been adopted by different persons. The first is the authority of the Church, that is, the Church of Rome, which arrogates this authority to herself. The second is internal evidence, which some have deemed sufficient, without the aid of external testimony. The third is to refer to historical testimony, as has been done in regard to the Old Testament. Some distinguished men among the Roman Catholics have asserted, that the Scriptures owe all their authority to the Church; so that if she did not give her attestation to the gospels, they would have no more authority than Æsop's Fables. But when asked how the Church can establish her authority, they must answer, that it is proved by the testimony of the Scriptures. This is a perfect example of the sophism called "a circle," for they prove the authority of the Scriptures by the Church, and the authority of the Church by the Scriptures. Some Protestants, to avoid having recourse to the testimony of the Church at all, have verged to the other extreme, and have insisted that internal evidence is sufficient to enable us to determine what books belong to the canon. The Reformed Church of France went so far as to make this an article in her public Confession of Faith. Now it ought not to be doubted that the internal evidence of the Scriptures is exceedingly strong; and that when the mind of the reader is truly illuminated by the Spirit of God, it derives from this source the most unwavering and soul-satisfying evidence of their truth and authority; but in regard to particular books, that every sincere Christian should be able to judge by this evidence alone whether they are canonical or not, cannot be admitted. For example, suppose the books of Ecclesiasticus and of Ecclesiastes were put into the hands of any plain, intelligent man, is it probable that he would be able to determine which of them had a right to a place in the canon? To adopt this principle would have a tendency to unsettle the canon, and there would be no certainty as to the rule of our faith. While, therefore, internal evidence ought not to be rejected, but may afford much light as an auxiliary source of evidence, our principal reliance must be upon historical testimony: and it is a matter of thankfulness that this is so complete, as to leave little more to be desired for the satisfaction of every impartial inquirer. The question to be decided is a matter of fact. It is, whether the books which compose the New Testament, were written by inspired men; that is, by the men whose names are affixed to them, the apostles and disciples of our Lord, who were eye-witnesses of the facts which they have recorded.   And the proper method of deciding this question, is to inquire whether there was a general agreement among those fathers who lived nearest to the times of the apostles, on this point; for it can scarcely be supposed, that there could be a general error among them in regard to a point of this kind.   A general consent of the early fathers, and of the whole Christian Church, scattered all over and beyond the Roman empire, furnishes the best evidence which the nature of the case admits of, and is that species of evidence which is least liable to fallacy.   The learned Huet has, therefore, laid it down as a rule on this subject, "THAT EVERY BOOK IS GENUINE, WHICH WAS ESTEEMED GENUINE BY THOSE WHO LIVED NEAREST TO THE TIME WHEN IT WAS WRITTEN, AND BY THE AGES FOLLOWING, IN A CONTINUED SERIES."

The reasonableness and certainty of this rule will appear more evident, when it is considered, in what high esteem these books were held, with what diligence they were sought after, how constantly they were publicly read, and how soon they were quoted, and translated into other languages.

The early Christians were neither careless nor credulous on this subject.   They pursued the only certain method of ascertaining the facts in the case. They searched into the records of the Churches, and learned by the testimony of all, what books had been received into the sacred volume, from the times of the apostles; and some of them even travelled into Judea, to learn accurately all that related to the origin and transmission of these sacred writings.

The question is often asked, *when* and by what authority was the canon of the New Testament constituted?   It seems to be assumed as true in such inquiries, that these books could not be of authority until sanctioned by some council or other ecclesiastical body; whereas, they were of authority, as far as known, from the day of their publication. Their right to a place in the canon does not depend on the vote of any council, or the decision of any bishop, but upon the fact that they were given by inspiration; and this is known by the character of the men who wrote them. The appeal to testimony, therefore, is not to obtain the judgment of the Church, that these books were canonical; but to ascertain the fact, that they are indeed the productions of the apostles, to whom our Lord promised plenary inspiration. The Church confers no authority on these books. She merely testifies that they were written by the persons to whom they have been ascribed. And on this point, we seek testimony not only from the fathers of the Church, but from Jews, Heathen, and Heretics. Celsus, Porphyry, and Julian, Manes and Marcion, are our witnesses, as well as Irenæus, Tertullian, Origen, and Eusebius. The boast of the Romanists, therefore, is vain, that we are obliged to depend on the authority of the Church, for our sacred books. We defer nothing to this authority, but merely appeal to men of earning and probity who lived near the times when they were written, for their testimony, as to the source from which they were derived. That these witnesses were members of the Church is a mere incidental circumstance. If they had held no connexion with the Church, their testimony as to the origin of these books would not be invalidated, but rather strengthened; we call in witnesses from without the Church, wherever we can find them, and consider the testimony of such highly valuable, because altogether unsuspected. If by the constitution of the canon, be meant, the collection of the books of the New Testament into one volume, it is a question of no importance; for every one of these books had complete authority before such a volume was formed; and if they had remained separate, and never been included in a single volume, neither their importance nor authority would have been less. Indeed, the testimony of ancient fathers and manuscripts would lead to the conclusion, that

ir very early times, the books of the New Testamen.
were not included in one, but in two volumes; one
of which was denominated GOSPELS; the other APOS-
TLES.

Whenever all the inspired books were written and
published, then was the canon completed, whether
any one Church possessed the whole or only a part;
whether they were bound in one volume or two, or
emained each separate from the rest.

The Church or individual, to whom any book was
addressed, or for whom it was written, would of
course enjoy the privilege of the first possession; but
as these books were never locked up, but freely communicated, the nearest Churches would commonly be
first supplied with a copy, and thus the sacred books
would soon circulate through the whole Church.
Every Christian Church would be solicitous to obtain, as soon as possible, an authentic copy of every
writing known to be the production of an apostle, or
other inspired man. If, for example, they had ever
enjoyed the unspeakable privilege of hearing Paul
preach, how eager would they be to read his epistles? And if they had never seen this "chief of
the apostles," their desire to see his writings would
scarcely have been less.

It may occur to some reader, that the Churches
might have been imposed upon by writings, not the
genuine productions of the apostles. To guard against
every thing of this kind, and to give full assurance
of the genuineness of his epistles, Paul was accustomed to commit them to the custody of respectable
men, whose names he commonly mentions in the
epistle. And although he appears to have employed
an amanuensis in writing; yet he made it a point to
pen the concluding salutation *with his own hand;*
and this signature must have been well known among
all the Churches with which he held correspondence.
Accordingly, we read in the epistle to the Romans,
"I, Tertius, wrote this epistle." And in the first to
the Corinthians, "The salutation of me Paul with
mine own hand." In that to the Galatians, "You

see how large a letter I have written to you with mine own hand." To the Colossians, "The salutation by the hand of me Paul." And to the Thessalonians, "The salutation of Paul with mine own hand, which is the token in every epistle; so I write."

Thus, what at first view appears to be a mere form of salutation, is found to be an important circumstance in giving authenticity to his epistles; so that they could not be successfully counterfeited.

It may be inquired, what has become of the autograph of these sacred books, and why cannot the very hand-writing of Paul, by which his epistles were authenticated, be now exhibited? The answer is, that no autograph of any book, as old as the New Testament, can be produced; unless it has been preserved in some extraordinary way, as is the fact in regard to numerous manuscripts found in Herculaneum; very few of which however can be read. The autographs of the apostles could not have been preserved to this time without a miracle, and the occasion did not require such an interposition. And primitive Christians, although they appreciated the truths contained in these books above all price, had no great solicitude about the mere ink and paper A correct copy was as good as the original; and considering the tendency of men to superstition, and how every pretended relic of the apostles is venerated and even worshipped, it seems to have been a wise ordination of Providence, that these autographs should perish.

How long these originals continued in existence, we have no way of certainly knowing, but it is thought by many, that Tertullian refers to them, as extant in his time, where he says, that the *authentic letters* of the apostles might be seen by any that would take the pains to go to the Churches to which they were addressed. If he had referred to *authentic copies*, why send the inquirer to the Churches to which these epistles were addressed? Were there not copies to be found every where, in all the Churches, as well as these? And it would be rather wonderful if these autographs were not in existence when Tertullian wrote, who lived less than a hundred years after the last of the apostles: and we have now manuscripts of the New Testament, which cannot be much less than fourteen hundred years old, and are perhaps older. It is, therefore, a most probable supposition, that the Churches referred to had in possession the autographs of Paul, when Tertullian lived and wrote.

As there is no dispute among Christians, of any denomination, respecting the books which belong to the canon of the New Testament, it will be unnecessary to go into any discussion respecting the multitude of apocryphal books, which at a certain period, were put into circulation under the names of the apostles or companions of the apostles. Most of these have long since perished; and were, as soon as published, declared to be spurious by the Church. almost with one consent. Such of these spurious Gospels, Acts, Revelations, &c., as have come down to us, prove themselves to be apocryphal; and only serve by contrast, to reflect a brighter light on the genuine Scriptures.

The proof of the canonical authority of the books of the New Testament may be derived from the *catalogues* which have been left by the fathers and councils; from express testimony of competent witnesses; from the fact that they were read as scripture in the primitive Churches; from the quotations made from them, and appeals made to them as an authoritative rule of faith and practice; and from the early versions of the New Testament.

1. Catalogues of these books which are still extant, were made out by *Origen, Eusebius, Athanasius, Cyril, Epiphanius, Gregory Nazianzen, Philastrius, Jerome, Rufin, Augustin,* and by the ancient author who goes under the name of *Dionysius the Areopagite.* To these may be added the catalogues prepared by two councils; that of *Laodicea,* and that of *Carthage.* The catalogue found in the book entitled. "*Apostolical Constitutions,*" and ascribed to

Clement of Rome, and the catalogue of the council of Nice, are not referred to as testimony, because we are of opinion, that neither of these is genuine. But we have no need of additional evidence. We have here thirteen catalogues of the books of the New Testament, all of which were prepared by men the most distinguished, and who had bestowed great attention on this subject. Out of these thirteen, seven (a majority of the whole) agree perfectly with our canon; and several of the others differ only by the omission of the book of Revelation, because it was not read in the Churches, and had fallen into some discredit on account of the use made of it by the Millenarians. The catalogue of Origen has an omission of *James* and *Jude*, but this was merely accidental, for he mentions both these epistles in his other writings. The catalogues of Jerome, Eusebius, Epiphanius, Augustin and Rufin, who of all others were the most competent judges of this matter, are perfectly the same as our canon. That of the council of Carthage is also the same; and that of the council of Laodicea differs only by the omission of *Revelation*, the reason of which has already been assigned

2. These books were constantly read as Scripture in the Churches. The primitive Christians imitated the Jews, in publicly reading the writings which they considered divine in their assemblies. This practice seems to have been introduced as early as the days of Paul, who says to the Colossians, "And when this epistle is read among you, cause that it be read also in the Church of the Laodiceans, and that ye likewise read the epistle from Laodicea." (Col. iv. 16.) Indeed, as Paul's epistles were addressed to the people at large, they could in no way be so conveniently communicated to those to whom they were sent, as by the public reading of them, when the Churches assembled on the first day of the week. But we have express testimony on this point. Justin Martyr, who lived in the beginning of the second century, says, " On the day which is called Sunday, there is a meeting of all (Christians) who live either in cities or

country places; and *the memoirs of the apostles* anc writings of the prophets are read."* Tertullian is equally explicit; for in giving an account of the meetings of Christians for worship, he says, " They assemble to read the Scriptures and offer up prayers." And in another place, among the solemn exercises of the Lord's day he mentions " reading the Scriptures, singing psalms, &c."† Cyprian gives a similar testimony,‡ and so does the ancient writer under the name of Dionysius the Areopagite, and others. Now nothing can be conceived better calculated to prevent deception by the introduction of apocryphal books, than this practice of the weekly public reading of the Scriptures, for by this means the people would know what books were of authority.

It is true, that the writings of some men who had been the companions of the apostles, were also read in the Churches for the edification of the people; particularly the epistle of Clement to the Corinthians, and the " Shepherd" of Hermas; but the fathers were careful to distinguish these from the canonical Scriptures. They were accustomed to call such as were written by inspired men *canonical*, and the writings of other pious men, such as Clement, Barnabas, and Hermas, *ecclesiastical*.

3. Another evidence in favour of the canonical books is, that they were quoted as books of decisive authority by the doctors of the Christian Church, living in all parts of the world. Now, this can only be accounted for by supposing that they knew no other books which claimed to be canonical; or that they with one consent rejected such claims, and acknowledged the books now included in the sacred volume, as the only writings which were divinely inspired. The conclusion is clear, then, that those books which were alone cited as authority, to decide questions respecting faith or duty, and which were generally appealed to by the early writers of the Christian Church, are canonical. Thus, the first

---

* Apol. II. p. 93. † Cyp. Ep. 36, 39.
+ Tertullian de Anima

epistle of Peter is universally acknowledged to be the production of that apostle, and is cited as authority by all the fathers; but other books under the name of Peter, such as his Revelation, his Gospel, and his Acts, are never quoted as Scripture by any of the fathers. This argument is repeatedly used by Eusebius, and other ancient defenders of the canon of the New Testament; and if the premises are true, it is perfectly conclusive.

Those persons, therefore, such as Toland and Dodwell, who have endeavoured to unsettle our present canon, labour with all their might to prove that other books, now considered apocryphal, were as commonly cited by the fathers as those which are now deemed canonical. But learned men have thoroughly examined this subject, and have shown that this is not the fact; as Nye and Richardson, from an examination of all the passages in the fathers where other books are cited, have demonstrated.

4. The early versions of the New Testament furnish an additional argument in favour of the canonical authority of most of the books now admitted into the sacred volume.

As long as the gift of tongues remained with the ministers of the Church, the gospel could be preached to all the nations in their own vernacular language; but when miraculous gifts ceased, there was a great necessity that the sacred books should be translated into the languages of those people who did not understand Greek, in which the New Testament was originally written. Therefore learned men early applied themselves to this work; and although we have no exact information of the time when these versions were made, or the persons by whom the work was performed; yet we have good evidence that they were made very early. The Christians of Syria and Mesopotamia, who were accustomed to the use of the Syro-Chaldaic dialect, would not have remained long without a Syriac or Aramean version of the New Testament, and, as many of the learned in these countries were well acquainted with Greek, there exists a strong probability that a version into Syriac must have been at least begun, early in the second century, if not before the close of the first And the fact, that the Syriac version called *Peshito* omits some of the books which were for awhile doubted of by some, favours the opinion that this version must have been made at a very early period, and probably in the beginning of the second century. Marcion, the heretic, lived in this century, and was acquainted with the New Testament; there was then a version into Syriac, his own vernacular tongue Without such a translation, a large number of the primitive churches must have been entirely destitute of the Scriptures.

The New Testament was also early translated into Latin, and from the fragments that remain, it appears that there were several versions into this language, which were in use, when the Latin language prevailed; and especially in Italy. One of these is called by Augustine, *Itala*, and was the vulgate, before Jerome undertook a translation; but it was not long before versions were made into various other languages, as the Coptic, Ethiopic, Arabic, Armenian, &c. Now all these contain all the books which are now included in our canon, except the Syriac, which is probably the oldest of them all. The books omitted in this version are the *Revelation*, and some of the minor epistles which were not generally known when this version was made. As it relates to all the other books of the New Testament, this version furnishes a satisfactory proof of their canonical authority. J. D. Michaelis is of opinion, that this is the best translation of the New Testament ever made, and that it is referred to by Melito, bishop of Sardis. In the time of Jerome, the Scriptures were read in Syriac in all the Churches in that country, and in Mesopotamia.

When the council of Nice met, and other general councils, there was never any dispute among the venerable bishops who attended, about the canon of Scripture. In regard to this there seems to have een a perfect agreement. The only persons who

impugned the commonly received books were heretics; and even from the testimony of these, much
evidence may be derived in favour of our canon.
The Arians and Pelagians appealed to the same
Scriptures as the orthodox Church. It was impossible, after the Church was widely extended, and the
New Testament translated into divers tongues, that
any book could have been added to the sacred volume, or abstracted from it. Such an attempt, if it
could have proved successful in a single Church,
never could have prevailed to any extent. Detection
of such a fraudulent attempt would have been certain and immediate. We have, therefore, the utmost
certainty, that we now possess the identical Scriptures which were given to the Churches by the apostles and other inspired men. The learned John
David Michaelis has very needlessly stirred a question concerning the canonical authority of the writings of Mark and Luke, because they only of the
writers of the books of the New Testament were not
numbered among the apostles. But the ancient
Church never entertained any doubt on this subject,
and received their gospels with the same confidence
and veneration as the others. Indeed, they seem to
have esteemed the gospel of Luke just as if it had
been dictated by Paul, and that of Mark as if dictated by Peter. And when we look into these gospels,
we find no more evidence of human weakness or
error, than in those written by Matthew and John.
And we feel no hesitation in applying to this case the
rule already mentioned, that books universally received as inspired by those who lived nearest to the times
when they were published, ought to be considered
canonical by us. And according to this rule, these
gospels have as good a claim to a place in the canon
as any books in the volume.

It will, we presume, be satisfactory to the reader
to have some of the testimonies of the Christian
fathers in regard to each book, or each class of books
set before him This will be the subject of the next
chapter.

CHAPTER XX.

ALTHOUGH the precise time when these books were written is unknown, it has generally been believed, that Matthew's gospel is among the earliest. The uniform testimony of the fathers is, that Matthew wrote in Hebrew; that is, in the vernacular language of Judea. To this opinion, modern critics have made serious objections. They allege, that there is no clear evidence of the existence of the Hebrew codex; that the work has no internal evidence of being a translation; and that this opinion tends to destroy our idea of the integrity of the sacred canon; for, according to it, one inspired work which belonged to the canon is lost, and its place supplied by a translation, made nobody knows by whom. For these, and such like reasons, a large number of our ablest critics have declared in favour of a Greek original. But as a mere argument cannot stand against a body of combined testimony, the opinion of a Hebrew original is likely to maintain its ground, especially as numbers among its advocates are men as learned and sagacious as those who appear on the other side. To reconcile these discordant opinions, an ingenious and plausible theory has been invented, which is, that Matthew first prepared his gospel for the Jewish converts; but others who did not understand the Hebrew, naturally wishing for an authentic account of the life of our Lord from the pen of an apostle, prevailed with him before he left Judea, to put it into Greek; or to cause it to be translated under his own eye. The Hebrew copy being only in possession of the Ebionites and Nazarenes, was soon corrupted, and finally lost, when no Church of Hebrew Christians any longer existed. Thus they reconcile the testimony of the ancients with the opinion that the

Greek text is truly inspired, and therefore a part of the sacred canon. There is much internal probability in this theory, and all it wants to commend it fully to our acceptance is the want of external testimony But let us hear what the fathers say respecting Matthew as an Evangelist.

Papias, bishop of Hierapolis, who had seen and conversed with the apostle John, mentions Matthew's gospel, and says, " he wrote the divine oracles in Hebrew."* We learn from this in what esteem the writings of apostles were held in the very earliest times. Matthew's gospel is here denominated *the divine oracles*, by a man who was contemporary with John, and who, no doubt, spoke the sentiments of the Church, in that day.

Irenæus, bishop of Lyons, who was acquainted with Polycarp the disciple of John, says, " Matthew, then among the Jews, wrote a gospel in their language, while Peter and Paul were preaching at Rome."† In another place, he says, " The gospel of Matthew was delivered to the Jews."‡ Origen says, " According to the traditions received by me, the first gospel was written by Matthew, once a publican, afterwards a disciple of Jesus Christ, who delivered it to the Jewish believers, composed in their own language."§ Origen flourished about a hundred years after the death of John, lived most of his life near to Judea, and was thoroughly versed in biblical learning.

Eusebius may be placed a century after Origen. No man had taken more pains to search into ecclesiastical antiq ities. He gives the following testimony, " Matthew having first preached the gospel to the Hebrews, when about to go to other people, delivered to them in their own language, the gospel written by himself."‖

Thus, in the Synopsis ascribed to Athanasius, it is said, " Matthew wrote his gospel in Hebrew, and published it at Jerusalem."¶

* Lardner, Vol. III. p. 169.
† Adv. Hær. L. III. c. 1
‡ Euseb L. V. c. 8.
§ Lardner, Vol. III. p 160.
‖ Ibid.
¶ Ibid. p. 150.

Cyril of Jerusalem also testifies, " that Matthew
wrote in Hebrew." Epiphanius, Gregory Nazianzen,
and Ebedjesu, say the same.

Jerome, in his commentary on this gospel, says,
" Matthew the publican, surnamed Levi, wrote his
gospel in Judea, in the Hebrew language."*

Concerning the time when this gospel was published, there are several opinions; some placing it
eight years after the ascension of our Lord; others
bringing it down to the fifteenth year; and some so
'ow as the year of our Lord sixty-four. While, on
the other hand, some late critics carry it up to the
third or fourth year after the ascension.

The gospel of Mark is also noticed by Papias, in a
passage which has been preserved by Eusebius. He
says, " that when Peter had come to Rome, they
were so inflamed with love for the truths of Christianity, that they entreated Mark the companion of
Peter, and whose gospel we now have, praying him
that he would write down for them and leave with
them an account of the doctrines which had been
preached to them; and they did not desist from their
request, until they had prevailed on him, and pro-
cured his writing that which is now the gospel of
Mark.   That when Peter came to know this, he was
by the direction of the Holy Spirit pleased with the
request of the people, and confirmed the gospel which
was written for the use of the Churches."†   According to this testimony of an apostolical father, the
gospel of Mark received the sanction of Peter, and is
as apostolic as if this apostle had written it with his
own hand.   And as it was nothing else than the substance of Peter's preaching, it is all one as if he had
dictated it to an amanuensis.

Irenæus, however, states the matter a little differently, in some respects.   He says, " After their death
(Peter and Paul,) Mark, also the disciple of Peter,
delivered to us the things which had been preached
by Peter."‡

* See Lard. Vol. III, p 180.   ‡ Lard Vol. III. p. 177
† Ibid. p 177.

Augustine called Mark "the abridger of Matthew," on account of his relating things so much in the same style as that apostle; but this gospel is not properly an abridgment, for in some things he is more minute, and enlarges more than Matthew; and he has many particulars not recorded by Matthew.

The testimony of Clement of Alexandria is much to the same purpose as what has already been stated; which shows that a uniform tradition existed in relation to this matter. He says, "when Peter was publicly preaching the gospel at Rome, by the influence of the Holy Spirit, many of the converts desired Mark, as having been long a companion of Peter, and who well remembered what he preached, to write down his discourses. That upon this he composed his gospel, and gave it to those who made this request, which when Peter knew, he neither encouraged nor obstructed the work."*

Tertullian informs us, "that the gospel published by Mark may be reckoned Peter's, whose interpreter he was."† And Origen concurs in the uniform testimony; "Mark," says he, "wrote his gospel according to the dictates of Peter." And Jerome also tells us, "that Mark, the disciple of Peter, wrote a short gospel, from what he had heard from Peter, at the request of the brethren at Rome, which when Peter knew, he approved and published it in our Churches, commanding the reading of it by his own authority,"‡ which exactly agrees with what was cited from Papias. We see how full are the testimonies in favour of this gospel; and accordingly, we never hear in all antiquity of any doubt or scruple respecting its canonical authority.

The only information that can be depended on respecting the time when this gospel was published, is, that in the testimonies cited above, it is said, that it was written after Peter came and preached at Rome; and one witness says, after his death. We have, it is true, something said on this subject by

---

* Euseb. Ecc. Hist. Lib. VI. c. 4.
‡ Lard. Vol. III. p. 178   Lard. Vol. III. p. 178

writers who lived in the middle ages, but their testi
mony is of little worth on such a subject.   And one
of these writers asserts, that Mark wrote his gospel
at Rome, and in the Roman language; for which
opinion there is no ancient authority.   It was no
doubt written, like the other books of the New Testament, in Greek.

Luke the penman of the third gospel, was selected
by the Churches to travel with Paul, and was his companion during his confinement at Rome.   Concerning this evangelist, Irenæus also speaks in the same
passage in which he mentions Mark, saying, " that
Luke, the companion of Paul, put down in a book
the gospel preached by him."   In another place, he
says, " Luke was not only a companion but a fellow-
labourer of the apostles, especially of Paul."   " The
apostles," says he, " envying none, plainly delivered
to all, the things which they had heard from the
Lord; so likewise Luke, envying no man, has delivered to us what he learned from them, as he says,
" even as they declared them unto us, from the beginning, who were eye-witnesses and ministers of his
word."*   Eusebius informs us, that Clement of
Alexandria, in a work not now extant, bore ample
testimony to the gospel of Luke, as well as to the
other gospels.   And he mentions a tradition which
he had received from more ancient presbyters, " that
the gospels with genealogies were first written."
Tertullian speaks of Mark and Luke as " disciples of
the apostles," but he ascribes the same authority to
the gospels written by them, as to others.   " Luke's
Digest," says he, " is often ascribed to Paul."   And
Origen, in speaking of the four gospels, says, " The
third is that according to Luke, the gospel commended by Paul, published for the sake of the Gentile
converts."†

The testimony of Eusebius to Luke's gospel is
very full.   He says, " Luke, who was of Antioch,
and by profession a physician, for the most part a
companion of Paul, who had likewise more than a

* Lard Vol. III. p. 198.   † Lard. Vol. III. p. 198.

slight acquaintance with the other apostles, has left us, in two books divinely inspired, evidences of the art of healing souls, which he had learned from them. One of them is the gospel which he professeth to have written as they delivered it to him who were eye-witnesses and ministers of the word, with all of whom he had been perfectly acquainted from the first."* And in another place, he says, "Luke hath delivered in his gospel a certain account of such things as he had been assured of by his intimate acquaintance and familiarity with Paul, and his conversation with the other apostles." In the Synopsis ascribed to Athanasius, it is said, "that the gospel of Luke was dictated by the apostle Paul, and writ ten and published by the blessed apostle and phy sician Luke." To these testimonies it will be unne cessary to add any others, except that of Jerome, which is as follows: "Luke, who was of Antioch, and by profession a physician, not unskilful in the Greek language, a disciple of the apostle Paul, and the constant companion of his travels, wrote a gospel, and another excellent volume, entitled the Acts of the Apostles." It is supposed that Luke did not learn his gospel from the apostle Paul only, who had not conversed with the Lord in the flesh, but also from other apostles, which likewise he owns at the beginning of his volume, saying, "Even as they delivered them unto us, who from the beginning were eye-witnesses and ministers of the word."†

In another place, he says, "the third evangelist is Luke, the physician, a Syrian of Antioch, who was a disciple of the apostle Paul, and published his gospel in the countries of Achaia and Bœotia."

This gospel has from the time of its publication, been received as canonical by the whole Christian Church; has been constantly read in the Churches as a part of divinely inspired Scripture; has been cited as authority by all Christian writers; and has a place in every catalogue of the books of the New Testament which was ever published. Its canonical

* Lard. Vol. I I p. 198.   † Ibid. Vol. III. p. 200.

authority is therefore placed beyond the reach of reasonable doubt, notwithstanding the injudicious scruples which some learned moderns have entertained and published to the world respecting it.*

The fourth and last of the gospels was written by John, the beloved disciple. This evangelist, according to the universal testimony of the ancients, survived all the other apostles, and did not leave the world until about the close of the first century of the Christian era. The testimonies to the genuineness and canonical authority of this gospel are as full as could be desired.

Irenæus asserts, "that the evangelist John designed by his gospel to confute the errors which Cerinthus had infused into the minds of the people, and which had been infused by those called Nicolaitanes; and to convince them that there was one God who had made all things by his WORD, and not as they imagined, one who was the Son of the Creator, and another the Christ who was impassible and descended upon Jesus the Son of the Creator."† Jerome fully confirms this testimony of Irenæus. He says, "that when John was in Asia, there arose the heresies of Ebion and Cerinthus, and others who denied that Christ had come in the flesh, that is, denied his divine nature; whom he in his epistle calls antichrist, and whom Paul frequently condemns in his epistles. He was forced by almost all the bishops of Asia, and the deputations of many other Churches to write more plainly concerning the divinity of our Saviour; and to soar aloft in a discourse concerning the WORD, not more bold than felicitous." "It is related in Ecclesiastical history, that John, when solicited by the brethren to write, answered, that he would not do it unless a day of public prayer and fasting was appointed to implore the assistance of God: which being done, and the solemnity being honoured with a satisfactory revelation from God, he broke forth in the

---

* See a discussion respecting the inspiration of the gospels of Mark and Luke, in my work on the Canon.

† Lard. Vol. III. p. 22.

words with which his gospel commences, IN THE BEGINNING WAS THE WORD," &c.*

The same learned father, in his book of "Illustrious Men," says, "John wrote a gospel at the request of the bishops of Asia, against Cerinthus and other heretics, and especially against the doctrine of the Ebionites then springing up, who say that Christ did not exist before his birth of Mary; for which reason he was obliged to declare his divine nativity. Another reason of his writing is also mentioned, which is, that having read the volumes of Matthew, Mark, and Luke, he expressed his approbation of their history as true; but observed, that they had recorded an account of but one year of our Lord's ministry, even the next after the imprisonment of John [the Baptist,] in which also he suffered. Omitting, therefore, that year, (for the most part,) the history of which had been written by the other three, he related the acts of the preceding time before John was shut up in prison, as may appear to those who read the four evangelists; which may serve to account for the seeming difference between John and the rest."†

This ample testimony of Jerome is confirmed by Augustine, who says, "that this evangelist wrote concerning the co-eternal divinity of Christ, against heretics."‡

Lampe, Lardner, and Titmann, have called in question this account of the occasion of John's writing; but the plausible reasonings of ingenious men have little weight, when laid in the balance with the positive testimony of such men as those who have asserted the contrary. Whether this gospel was written before or after the destruction of Jerusalem, is a matter of dispute among the learned; but the opinion of the ancients, and most of the moderns is, that it was written afterwards; and with this, the internal evidence best agrees.

The Acts of the Apostles was undoubtedly written by Luke, for it is dedicated to Theophilus, the same excellent person to whom he had dedicated his gospel, and in this last dedication he refers to his former work. The fact is also confirmed by the testimony of the whole Christian Church, no one having ever called it in question.

This book was in great esteem among the early fathers, and is often mentioned in their writings, and always quoted as a part of inspired Scripture.

Irenæus says, " Luke's Acts of the Apostles ought to be equally received with the gospel." " In them he has carefully delivered to us the *truth*, and given us a sure rule for salvation." So also, Clement of Alexandria, Tertullian, Origen, Eusebius, and Jerome, all ascribe the Acts of the Apostles to Luke.*

In the Syriac version of the New Testament, the name of Luke is prefixed to this book; the same is also said to be the fact in some very ancient manuscripts.

It must have been early circulated among the Churches, for it is plainly referred to by Clement of Rome, the fellow-labourer of Paul. And Polycarp, in his epistle to the Philippians, has cited a passage from the Acts; as also Justin Martyr, in his " Exhortation to the Greeks." It is distinctly cited by Irenæus more than thirty times, and is expressly denominated Scripture, which is also true of Tertullian.

The Acts of the Apostles being found in all the catalogues of the books of the New Testament, having always been read in the Churches, uniformly quoted as Scripture, and possessing all the internal evidences of inspiration, as well as the express testimony of the early fathers, has an undoubted right to a place in the sacred canon.

* See Lardner, Vol. III. p. 207.

CHAPTER XXI.

CANONICAL AUTHORITY OF PAUL'S EPISTLES.

THE fourteen epistles of Paul constitute a very large and very important part of the canon of the New Testament, and the evidence of their canonical authority is complete. Indeed, no question has ever been agitated respecting the divine authority of any one of them; but as his name is prefixed to all, except the epistle to the Hebrews, it has been doubted whether indeed it was written by Paul. After a thorough investigation, however, the Church, both in the east and west, settled down in the full belief that this apostle was the writer.

Clement of Rome, in an epistle to the Corinthians, refers expressly to one of Paul's epistles to the same people. "Take," says he, "into your hands, the epistle of blessed Paul the apostle. What did he at first write to you in the beginning of the gospel? Verily he did by the Spirit admonish you concerning himself, Cephas, and Apollos, because that even then ye did form parties."* There are, in the epistle of Clement, several other passages cited from Paul, but this is the only one where his name is mentioned.

Hermas and Ignatius also cite words from Paul's epistles, but without designating the book from which they are taken. And Polycarp, the martyr, and disciple of John, when condemned to death, wrote an epistle to the Philippians, in which he makes express mention of Paul's first epistle to the Corinthians, and cites the apostle's words: "Do ye not know that the saints shall judge the world?† as Paul teaches." This venerable and apostolical father, in the same epistle, quotes a passage from Paul's epistle to the Ephesians as Scripture. "For I trust," says he, "that ye are well exercised in the Holy Scriptures, as in these

* Epist Clem. Rom. ad Cor.   † 1 Cor. vi. 2.

Scriptures it is said, ' Be ye angry and sin not; let not the sun go down upon your wrath.' "* He also cites passages from the second epistle to the Corinthians, from the epistle to the Galatians, from the first and second to the Thessalonians, from the epistle to the Hebrews, and from both of Paul's epistles to Timothy. But as was customary at that time, he does not refer to the book from which his citation in any particular instance is made.

Justin Martyr quotes many texts from Paul's epistles, and in the very words of the apostle, but does not mention his name, or the title of the epistle from which he makes his citations. Irenæus quotes passages from all the epistles of Paul, except the short letter to Philemon. It would fill too much space to put down all the texts cited by this father. Let the following suffice.† " This same thing Paul has explained, writing to the Romans, ' Paul, an apostle of Jesus Christ, separated to the Gospel of God.'‡ Again writing to the Romans, he says, ' Whose are the fathers, and of whom concerning the flesh Christ came, who is God over all blessed for evermore.'§ This also Paul manifestly proves in his epistle to the Corinthians, saying, ' Moreover, brethren, I would not that ye should be ignorant how that all our fathers were under the cloud.'|| Paul, in his second epistle to the Corinthians, says, ' In whom the god of this world hath blinded the eyes of them that believe not.'¶ The Apostle Paul says, in his epistle to the Galatians, ' Wherefore then serveth the law of works? it was added until the seed should come to whom the promise was made.'** As also blessed Paul says in his epistle to the Ephesians, ' For we are members of his body, of his flesh, and of his bones.'†† As also Paul says to the Philippians, ' I am full, having received of Epaphroditus the things which were sent from you, an odour of a sweet smell, a sacrifice acceptable, well pleasing unto God.'‡‡ Again, Paul

* Ephes. iv. 26.	§ Rom. ix. 5.	** Gal. iii. 19.
† Iren. adv. Haeret.	‖ 1 Cor. x. 1.	†† Ephes. v. 30.
‡ Rom. i. 1.	¶ 2 Cor. iv. 4.	‡‡ Phil. iv. 13.

says, in his epistle to the Colossians, 'Luke, the beloved physician, saluteth you.'* The apostle, in the first epistle to the Thessalonians, says, 'And the God of peace sanctify you wholly.'† And again in the second epistle to the Thessalonians, speaking of antichrist, says, 'And then shall that wicked one be revealed.'' ‡ In the beginning of his work against heresies, he says, "Whereas some having rejected the truth, bring in lying words, and 'vain genealogies rather than godly edifying, which is in faith, as saith the apostle.' "§ The first epistle to Timothy is very often quoted in the above work. When speaking of Linus, he says, "Of this Linus Paul makes mention in his epistle to Timothy, 'Eubulus greeteth thee, and Pudens, and Linus.'‖ As Paul says, 'A man that is a heretic, after the first and second admonition reject.' "¶

Thus Irenæus, who lived in the age next after that of the apostles, and who had conversed with men who had seen some of them, refers as familiarly and frequently to the writings of Paul, as we are accustomed to do now. The epistle to the Hebrews he does not cite in any of his writings, which are now extant, though Eusebius informs us that he had seen a work of his in which there are citations from this epistle; but he does not say that he quoted them as from Paul. Probably he participated in the prejudice o the western Church respecting the author of this epistle.

The epistles of Paul are quoted by Athenagoras, who lived in the second century; also, many times by Clement of Alexandria. A few examples only need be here adduced. " The apostle, in the epistle to the Romans, says, 'Behold, therefore, the goodness and severity of God.'** The blessed Paul, in the first epistle to the Corinthians, says, 'Brethren, be not children in understanding; howbeit in malice be ye

---

* Col. iv. 4.
† 1 Thess. v. 23
‡ 2 Thess. ii. 8.
§ 1 Tim. i. 4.

‖ 2 Tim. iv. 21.
¶ Tit. iii. 10. See Lard. Vol. III
** Rom. ix.

children, but in understanding be men.'* The apos
tle, says he, calls the common doctrine of faith 'a sa-
vour of knowledge.'† Hence also Paul says, 'Having
these promises, dearly beloved, let us cleanse our
hearts from all filthiness of the flesh and spirit, per
fecting holiness in the fear of God.'‡ Whereupon
Paul also writing to the Galatians, says, 'My little
children, of whom I travail in birth again until Christ
be formed in you.'§ The blessed apostle says, 'I testify in the Lord that ye walk not as other Gentiles
walk.'‖ Again, 'Submitting yourselves to one another in the fear of God.' "¶ He also quotes the
epistle to the Philippians expressly; and in another
place he refers to it in the following manner: " The
apostle of the Lord also exhorting the Macedonians,
says, 'The Lord is at hand; take heed that we be
not found empty.' " He also cites Paul's epistle to
the Colossians and to the Thessalonians. And from
the first epistle to Timothy he takes the following
words: " O Timothy, keep that which is committed
to thy trust, avoiding profane and vain babblings,
and oppositions of science falsely so called, which
some preferring have erred concerning the faith."**
On which he observes, that heretics reject both epistles to Timothy. The epistle to Titus is quoted several
times; and in one place he remarks, " That Paul had
cited Epimenides the Cretan, in his epistle to Titus,
after this manner, 'One of themselves, a poet of their
own, said, the Cretans are always liars.' "†† This
father of the second century also distinctly quotes the
epistle to the Hebrews, and unhesitatingly ascribes it
to Paul. " Wherefore writing to the Hebrews, who
were declining from the faith, Paul says, 'Have ye
need that any teach you again which be the first
principles of the oracles of God, and are such as have
need of milk and not strong meat?' "‡‡

Tertullian, who also wrote in the second century
furnishes many testimonies in favour of Paul's epis

---

* 1 Cor xiv. 20.   § Gal. iv. 19.   ** 1 Tim. vi. 20, 21
† 2 Cor ii. 14.   ‖ Ephes. iv. 17, 18. †† Tit. ii. 12, 13.
‡ 2 Cor vii. 1.   ¶ Phil. iv. 5.   ‡‡ Heb. v. 12.

tles. He expressly refers to Romans ix. 5, where
Christ is called " God over all, blessed for evermore,"
which he interprets as we do now. In his treatise on
monogamy he computes. that one hundred and sixty
years had elapsed since Paul wrote his epistle to the
Corinthians. He speaks also of the second epistle to
the Corinthians, and of the opinion entertained by
some, that it was the same person who was here forgiven, who, in the first epistle, was ordered to be
" delivered to Satan for the destruction of the flesh.'
" But of this," says he, " no more need be said, if it
is the same Paul who writing to the Galatians reckons heresy among the works of the flesh; and who
directs Titus to reject a man who was a heretic after
the first admonition, 'knowing that he that is such,
is subverted and sinneth, being condemned of himself.' "*   " I pass," says he, " to another epistle,
which we have inscribed to the Ephesians, but the
heretics to the Laodiceans."   "According to the true
testimony of the Church, we suppose this epistle to
have been sent to the Ephesians, and not to the
Laodiceans. but Marcion has endeavoured to alter
this inscription, upon pretence of having made a
more diligent search into this matter."   " But," says
he, " the inscriptions are of no value, for the apostle
wrote to all when he wrote to some."   Paul to the
Galatians says, " For we through the Spirit wait for
the hope of righteousness by faith."†   To the Philippians he says, " If by any means I might attain
unto the resurrection of the dead; not as though I
had already attained or were already perfect."‡ And
writing to the Colossians he expressly cautions them
against philosophy: " Beware lest any man spoil
you through philosophy and vain deceit after the
tradition of men, and not after the instruction of the
Spirit."§ And in his epistle to the Thessalonians,
the apostles adds, " But of the times and seasons
brethren ye have no need that I write unto you. For
yourselves know perfectly, that the day of the Lord so

---

* Tit. i. 10.   † Phil. iii. 11, 12.
† Gal. v. 5.   § Col. ii. 8.

cometh as a thief in the night."* And in his second
epistle to the same people he writes with greater
solicitude, " But I beseech you, brethren, by the
coming of our Lord Jesus Christ, that ye be not soon
shaken in mind nor troubled."† And this charge
Paul has given to Timothy: " O Timothy, keep that
which is committed to thy trust."‡

That remarkable passage of Tertullian, already
referred to, in which he is supposed to speak of the
autographs of Paul's epistles, may appropriately be
cited in this place, to show that he did certainly
write to those churches to which his epistles are now
inscribed. " Well," says he, " if you be willing to
exercise your curiosity profitably in the business of
your salvation, visit the apostolical churches, in which
the very chairs of the apostles still preside, in which
their truly authentic letters are recited, sending forth
the voice and representing the countenance of each
one of them. Is Achaia near you? you have Corinth. If you are not far from Macedonia, you have
Philippi; you have Thessalonica. If you can visit
Asia, you have Ephesus. And if you are near to
Italy, you have Rome, from whence also you may
be easily satisfied."§

Origen quotes Paul's epistles as expressly and frequently as any modern writer. To transcribe all the
testimonies which might be taken from this author,
would fill a volume, and would require us to set
down the greater part of all Paul's epistles. In one
passage in his work against Celsus, he refers to several of them in the following manner. " Do you first
of all explain the epistles of him who says these
things, and having diligently read and attended to the
sense of the words there used, particularly in that to
the Ephesians, to the Thessalonians, to the Philippians, to the Romans, &c."‖ Origen believed that the
epistle to the Ephesians was addressed to the Church
of Ephesus, for he cites it under that name. And
he uniformly ascribes the epistle to the Hebrews to

---

* 1 Thess. v. 1—3.   † 1 Tim. vi. 20.   ‖ Lard. Vol. I p. 535.
† 2 Thess. ii. 1, 2.   § De Praescriptione, c. xxxvi. p. 245.

Paul, from which he quotes many passages. And he not only expresses his own opinion on this point, out delivers the current opinion which had come down from the fathers who preceded him. His words are, " for it is not without reason that the ancients have handed it down to us as Paul's." Considering the nearness of Origen to the times of the apostles, and that he resided near the people to whom it was sent, perhaps in the very city, and that his knowledge of ecclesiastical and biblical matters was more extensive than that of any other man, his testimony that this epistle belongs to Paul ought to be decisive; especially as it is corroborated by that of all the Greek fathers. Eusebius, indeed, while he admits its canonical authority, expresses some doubt about its authorship; yet in his writings he often quotes it as Paul's.

Cyprian, Victorinus, Dionysius of Alexandria, Novatus, and Methodius, who all lived in the third century, refer frequently to Paul's epistles;[*] but we deem it superfluous to cite further testimonies on this subject, except the full and decisive testimony of Jerome. than whom a more competent witness could not be found. This father, in speaking of the writings of Paul, says, " He wrote nine epistles to seven churches. To the Romans one; to the Corinthians two; to the Galatians one; to the Philippians one; to the Colossians one; to the Thessalonians two; to the Ephesians one; to Timothy two; to Titus one; to Philemon one. But the epistle to the Hebrews is not thought to be his, because of the difference of argument and style; but rather Barnabas's, as Tertullian thought; or Luke's, according to some others; or Clement's. who was afterwards bishop of Rome, who being much with Paul, clotned and adorned Paul's sense in his own language. Or if it be Paul's, he might decline putting his name to it in the inscription, for fear of offending the Jews."[†] He seems to have entertained the idea that this epistle was writ-

---

[*] See Lardner's History of the Apostles.
[†] Epist. ad Paulinum.

ten by Paul in Hebrew, and that it was translated into Greek by some one possessed of a more elegant style than Paul. He says, " he wrote as a Hebrew to the Hebrews, it being his own language; whence it came to pass that being translated it has more elegance in the Greek than his other epistles. This they say is the reason of its differing from Paul's other writings. There is also an epistle to the Laodiceans, but it is rejected by every body."*

Although Jerome sometimes doubted of the authorship of the epistle to the Hebrews, which was published without the name of the author, yet he commonly quotes it as Paul's; and in his letter to Evangelius, he writes, " That all the Greeks and some of the Latins received this epistle."† He means, received it as Paul's; for we do not find that any were for rejecting it altogether from the canon. And in a letter to Dardanus, he says, " That it was not only received as Paul's by all the churches of the east, but by all the ecclesiastical writers in former times though many ascribe it to Barnabas or Clement."‡ He also testifies " that it was daily read in the churches; and if the Latins did not receive this epistle as the Greeks rejected the Revelation of John, yet he received both; not influenced so much by the present times, as the judgment of ancient writers, who quote both; and that not as they quote apocryphal books, and even heathen writings, but as canonical and ecclesiastical."§

Ambrose and Augustine received the fourteen epistles of Paul just as we do now,|| and since their time this has been the uniform opinion of all; except that some modern critics have revived the controversy respecting the author of the epistle to the Hebrews but the claim of the apostle Paul has been vindicated by many learned men with such ability, and with arguments so conclusive, that it may be hoped that this question will not be soon stirred again.

* Epist. ad Pa :linum.
† Lard. Vol. IJ p. 558.
‡ Ibid.
§ Lard. Vol. II. ⸲ 553
|| Ibid. p. 581.

The time when each of Paul's epistles was written, is a point not capable of any certain determination; and as is usual, in such cases, the learned are divided into various opinions and conjectures. It has commonly been thought that the epistles to the Thessalonians were first written, but of late a prior date has been claimed for the epistle to the Galatians. The subject is not important and may be left to be settled by the critics.

CHAPTER XXII.

THE CANONICAL AUTHORITY OF THE SEVEN CATHOLIC EPISTLES, AND OF THE BOOK OF REVELATION.

Why these epistles received the denomination of *Catholic*, various reasons have been assigned: but none of them are very satisfactory. Some have said that they were so called, because they contained the one Catholic doctrine which was communicated to the Churches, and delivered to the apostles by our Saviour, and which might be read by the universal Church. But surely this furnished no reason for distinctive appellation of those seven epistles, since the same may be said of all the other canonical epistles.

Others allege, that they received this name because they were not addressed to particular Churches or individuals, like the epistles of Paul, but to the Catholic Church. But this statement is not correct; for several of them are addressed to particular persons.

The opinion of Dr. Hammond and Dr. Macknight is, that this appellation was at first given to the first epistle of Peter and first of John, which were addressed to Christians generally, and were *universally* received. On which last account they suppose that they were originally called *Catholic*, to distinguish them from such as were not universally received, out, aftei awhile, the other five being uniι eisally received also, were included under the same name.

The first epistle of Peter and the first of John, appear to have been circulated and known at a very early period. The apostolic fathers, Ignatius, Polycarp and Papias, cite passages from them, without, however, indicating the source whence they were derived.

Justin Martyr quotes a passage which is no where else found, but in the second epistle of Peter.

Diagnetus has several passages taken from the first epistle of Peter and the first of John.

Irenæus cites from Peter the following: " Whom having not seen ye love," which he expressly refers to Peter. He also cites the second of Peter, and first and second of John. Several texts are also quoted by this father from the epistle of James, but without mentioning his name.*

Clement of Alexandria quotes the first epistle of Peter often; the second sometimes; and also the epistle of Jude.

Tertullian often cites the first epistle of John, and in one instance, that of Jude; but has no quotations from the others.

Origen has given a satisfactory testimony to the epistle of James, and refers to it in the following manner: " For though it be called faith, if it be without works it is dead, as we read in the epistle ascribed to James." And in the Latin translation of his works, by Rufin, this epistle is quoted as DIVINE SCRIPTURE, and is referred to " JAMES, the apostle, and brother of our Lord." This learned father often cites passages from the first of Peter; but not from the second, except in his Latin works, the originals of which are lost. In his book against Celsus, he says, " as it is said by Peter, Ye as lively stones are built up a spiritual house." And again, " Peter in his Catholic epistle, says, ' put to death in the flesh, but q ickened in the spirit.' " His testimony in favour of Jude is also strong. " Jude," says he,

* Lιrd. Voι. III p. 415.

" rrote an epistle of few lines indeed, but full of powerful words and heavenly grace; who, at the beginning, says, 'Jude, the servant of Jesus Christ, and brother of James.' "

Cyprian has copious citations from the first epistle of John, and first of Peter; but he makes no mention of the others.

Eusebius has a peculiar opinion respecting the epistle of James; he admits that it was written by James, a disciple of Christ, but not by the apostle James, yet in another place he cites the words, " Is any among you afflicted, let him pray; is any merry, let him sing psalms; as the sacred apostle says." But he is not consistent with himself, for where he distributes the books into classes, he places James among the supposititous, or such as were not canonical. The testimony which he gives in his history is important. " One epistle of Peter, called his first, is universally received. This the presbyters of ancient times have quoted in their writings, as undoubtedly genuine; but that called his second epistle, we have been informed, has not been received into the Testament; nevertheless, it, appearing to many to be useful, has been carefully studied with the other Scriptures."* And in another passage, " That called the first of John, and the first of Peter, are to be esteemed authentic. Of the controverted, yet well known and approved by the most, are, that called the epistle of James, that of Jude, and the second and third of John, whether they were written by the evangelist or another."

Athanasius quotes the epistle of James as the work of the apostle of that name; and cites also passages from the first and second of Peter, from the first and second of John, and also from Jude.

Jerome gives the following full testimony to the epistle of James: " James called the Lord's brother, surnamed Justus, as some think the son of Joseph by a former wife, but as I think, rather the son of Mary the sister of our Lord's mother, mentioned by

* La·d. Vol. III. c. xix. p. 415.

John in his gospel. Soon after our Lord's passion he was ordained bishop of Jerusalem, and wrote one epistle, which is among the seven Catholic epistles; which too has been said to be published by another in his name, but gradually, in process of time, it has gained authority. This is he of whom Paul writes in his epistle to the Galatians, and who is often mentioned in the Acts of the Apostles; and sometimes, in the 'gospels according to the Hebrews,' lately translated by me into Greek and Latin." Augustine received all the Catholic epistles. He quotes that of James, as the production of the apostle of that name. Both the epistles of Peter are often cited by him; also the three epistles of John; and he quotes Jude, and calls him an apostle.

In the works of Ephrem, the Syrian, who lived and wrote voluminously in the fourth century, there are found express quotations from the epistle of James, the second of Peter, the second and third of John, and from Jude, as well as abundant citations from first Peter, and first John; so that he received as SCRIPTURE, the whole seven Catholic epistles.

The book of *Revelation*, for a season, fell into considerable discredit in the ancient Church; principally on account of the support which it seemed to give to the extravagant doctrines of the Millenarians; and it is not found in a number of the ancient catalogues. But another reason why it was permitted to lie in obscurity was, the deeply mysterious nature of its contents; on which account, it was not commonly read in the Churches. And some modern writers have ventured to question its right to a place in the sacred canon. But when its evidence comes to be examined, it is found, that so far as early testimony goes, it is not inferior to that of any other book in the New Testament.

Both Hermas and Papias appear to have been acquainted with this book; as the former imitates several of its descriptions, and makes repeated mention of the "book of life," and of those, whose names are written in it; and the latter seems to have derived some of his opinions from a too literal translation of some things in this book.

But Justin Martyr is the first who makes explicit mention of the *Revelation.* His words are, " And a man from among us, by name John, one of the apostles of Christ, in the Revelation made to him, has prophesied that the believers in our Christ shall live a thousand years at Jerusalem, and after that shall be the general and indeed eternal resurrection and judgment of all men together."[*]

In the epistle of the Church of Lyons and Vienne, in France, which was written before the close of the second century, there is found an evident quotation from this book: " For he was indeed a genuine disciple of Christ, *following the Lamb, whithersoever he goeth.*"

Irenæus expressly quotes the Revelation, and ascribes it to John the apostle. " The visions in this book," he says, " were seen no long time before, at the end of the reign of Domitian."[†] And in a passage preserved by Eusebius, he speaks of " the exact and ancient copies of this book, which were confirmed, likewise, by the concurring testimony of those who had seen John."

Theophilus of Antioch, as we are assured by Eusebius, cited testimonies from the Apocalypse, in his work against Hermogenes. This book is also quoted by Clement of Alexandria. In one passage, he says, " Such a one, though here on earth he be not much honoured with the first seat, shall 'sit upon the twenty-four thrones,' judging the people, as John says in the Revelation."[‡] In another place, he cites from it as the work of an apostle. Tertullian also quoted many things from the Apocalypse; and seems to have entertained no doubt of its being the work of the apostle John.

Hippolytus, of the third century, who had great celebrity, both in the eastern and western Church,

* Lard Vol. III. c. xxii. p. 447   † Lard Vol. III. p. 449
† Ibid. p. 448.

not only received the Revelation as the work of the apostle John, but appears to have written a commentary on the book, as is manifest by the monument of this father, dug up in the city of Rome, in the year 1551. His name, it is true, is effaced from this monument, but it contains a catalogue of all the works ascribed to him by Eusebius and Jerome, and some not mentioned by them, among which is one '*of the Gospel of John, and the Revelation.*"

Origen, who was well acquainted with the Revelation, denominates the author, "Evangelist and Apostle," and on account of the predictions which it contains, "a prophet" also. Origen declared his purpose to write a commentary on this book; but if he carried his purpose into execution, the work has not reached our times, nor is there any mention of it by ecclesiastical writers who came after him.

But Dionysius of Alexandria, one of the most learned men of the age, has furnished more information respecting the canonical authority of this book than any other person. It is from him we learn the fact referred to above, that it was on account of the use made of this book by the Chiliasts or Millenarians that it fell into partial and temporary discredit. These errorists were numerous in the district of Arsinoe, in Egypt, where Dionysius visited them, and took great pains to reclaim them from their errors, and his efforts were not ineffectual, for he had the pleasure of seeing many of them return to the orthodox faith. He informs us, that before his time, many rejected this book altogether, and ascribed it to Cerinthus, the heretic. He professes for himself to believe, that the Revelation was an inspired book, and written by a man whose name was John, but a different person from the apostle John. The only reason which he assigns for this peculiar opinion is, the difference of the style from that of the apostle in his other works. In answer to which, the judicious Lardner remarks, that supposing the alleged difference to exist, it will not prove that the apostle John is not the writer, because the style of prophecy is altogether different from that of historical narrative, and equally so, from the epistolary style. But this learned and accurate writer denies that there is such a difference of style, as to furnish any solid reason for this objection; and in confirmation of his opinion, he descends to particulars, and shows, that there are some striking points of resemblance between the language of the Apocalypse, and the acknowledged writings of the apostle John.*

Cyprian received the book of *Revelation* as of canonical authority, as will appear by the following citations from it. "Hear in the Revelation, the voice of thy Lord reproving such men as these: ' Thou sayest, I am rich and increased in goods, and have need of nothing, and knowest not that thou art wretched, and miserable, and poor, and blind, and naked.' " Again: " So in the Holy Scriptures, by which the Lord would have us to be instructed and warned, is the harlot city described." " That waters signify people, the divine Scriptures show in the Revelation."†

That Lactantius received this book is evident from all his writings; especially those in which he attempts from its predictions to foretell " the future destinies of the Church."‡ Victorinus also, who lived towards the close of the third century, often quotes this book, and ascribes it to John the apostle.§

Thus it appears, that until the beginning of the fourth century, the book of Revelation was universally received as canonical; and only one man expresses any doubt about the apostle John being the author; and he ascribes it to another John, a disciple of our Lord, who also was an inspired man. And although it now fell into some neglect and discredit, yet no man of any authority in the Church, went so far as to reject it altogether. Eusebius, after giving

---

* Lardner, Vol. I. c. xliii. p. 633.
† Ibid. Vol. II. p. 26, 27.
‡ Ibid. Vol. II. c. lxiv. p. 292.
§ Ibid Vol. II p. 290.

a catalogue of the other books, says, " After these, if it be thought fit, may be placed the REVELATION, concerning which there are different opinions."

Athanasius gives the following testimony: " Domitian in the fourteenth year of his reign, raising the second persecution after Nero, John was banished into the isle of Patmos, when he wrote the Revelation which Irenæus and Justin Martyr explain."[*]

Augustine received the Revelation, and frequently quotes it. He also ascribed it to the same John who wrote the gospel and epistles. Jerome translated it into Latin with the other books of the New Testament. The evidence of the canonical authority of this prophetic vision is therefore as strong as that of any book in the New Testament; and the time is coming when the seals which have so long closed up its meaning shall be broken, and the Apocalypse will appear indeed to be a wonderful Revelation of events of the greatest importance, which are now future. The study of this portion of sacred Scripture should not be discouraged; for as the great wheel of Providence revolves, the mystic page will become more and more illuminated, and the events predicted will be so clearly developed, that all who are endued with spiritual understanding will clearly see, by the developments which will take place, that the sealed book is opened, and that the purposes of God towards his Church are in the progress of full and rapid accomplishment; even " the things that are, and the things which shall be hereafter."[†]

* Lardner, Vol. II. 401.   † Rev. i. 19.

CHAPTER XXIII.

THE subject of the canon of the New Testament may properly be concluded by a few general remarks.

1. The constitution of the canon of the New Testament did not require the judgment or sanction of any council, synod, or church, except as they might be witnesses that the books were written by men who were known to be inspired. Every book written by an apostle had a right to a place in the canon as soon as published. The sacred books were therefore canonical before they were collected together into a volume. One of Paul's epistles, as soon as received by the Church to which it was sent, had as much authority as it ever could have, and possessed this authority, if that Church were not at the time in possession of any other book. The canon was constituted, or compiled, when the last inspired volume was published. And as the apostle John undoubtedly survived the other apostles, and wrote last, when he produced his last writing, whichever it might be, the canon was closed. And as this must have been prior to his death, so it may be said with certainty, that the canon of the New Testament was completed before the death of John. And as all the books were in circulation while he was living, the Church could enjoy the unspeakable privilege of having his infallible opinion respecting any and all of these books. This will sufficiently account for the universal consent with which these books were received in every part of the Church. As he gave his sanction to the other three gospels, so doubtless he would do to the whole sacred canon. Accordingly, we find no controversy in the early ages of the Church, respecting the canon. Doubt was entertained by some respect

ing a few of those books now in the ca. on, which,
resulted in a general acquiescence in their claims
after the subject was impartially examined; but res
pecting all other books there was a unanimous consent.   This leads to the remark.

2. That the writings of the apostles were from
the beginning carefully distinguished from all other
books.   They were denominated, " SCRIPTURE," DI-
VINE SCRIPTURE — INSPIRED WRITINGS — THE GOS-
PELS—-THE APOSTLES—ORACLES OF THE LORD—DI-
VINE FOUNTAINS, &c., &c.   The fathers were not too
credulous in regard to this matter, but used all care
to search into the claims of such books as professed
to be from the apostles.

3. These books, when written, did not lie in obscurity, but were publicly read in the churches; and
were sought with avidity by the people, and read
with veneration, not only by the learned but by common Christians; for the idea of locking up the holy
Scriptures from the people seems to have occurred to
no one.   That these canonical books were thus read
in the churches may be proved by the testimony of
Justin Martyr, Tertullian, Eusebius, Cyprian, and
Augustine; and no other books received the same
veneration and attention—none others were spoken
of as SCRIPTURE —as inspired.   When any other
pieces were read in public for instruction, the fathers
were pointedly careful to distinguish these from the
canonical books.

4. In all the controversies which arose in the
Church, these books were appealed to by all parties,
as decisive authority, unless we except some of the
very worst heretics, who, to maintain their opinions,
mutilated the Scriptures, and rejected such as plainly
condemned their impious tenets.   But most of the
heretics endeavoured to maintain their opinions by
the writings of the New Testament.   This was the
case in regard to the Valentinians, the Montanists,
the Sabellians, he Artemonites, the Arians, the Pelagians, and the Priscillianists.   None of these called
in question the authority of the sacred books.

5. It is an argument of great force, that even the avowed enemies of Christianity, who wrote against the truth, refer to the books now in the canon, as those received as sacred by Christians. These enemies of the gospel refer to matters contained in these books, and some of them mention several of them by name.

Celsus, who lived and wrote less than a hundred years after the age of the apostles, says, as his words are quoted by Origen, who answered him, " I could say many things concerning the affairs of Jesus, and those, too, different from what has been written by the disciples of Jesus, but I purposely omit them." In another place he says, " These things, then, we have alleged to you of your own writings."

Porphyry also, from the fragments of his writings which remain, appears to have been well acquainted with the four gospels; for the objections which he brings against Christianity are directed against things still found in these gospels.

The emperor Julian, called the Apostate, mentions by name Matthew and Luke, and cites various things out of the gospels. He also mentions John, and says, " none of Christ's disciples besides has ascribed to him the creation of the world;" " and that neither Matthew, nor Luke, nor Mark, had dared to call Jesus, God;" " that John wrote later than the other evangelists, and at a time when a great number of men in the countries of Greece and Italy were converted." Now if these books had not been genuine, would not these learned and powerful opponents have known the fact, and would they not have exposed the fraud? But they silently acquiesce in the genuineness of the gospels, and speak of them as the writings of the disciples of Christ, with as little hesitation as Christians themselves.

6. The testimony which we have adduced is not only sufficient to demonstrate that these books were originally written by the men to whom they have always been ascribed, but also, that the books which were in the hands of early Christians contained the

same things which are now found written in them
Excepting about half a dozen texts, the genuineness
of which is disputed, because the manuscripts and
versions vary; as far as can be judged from numerous quotations, from all the early versions, and from
the ancient manuscripts which have come down to
us, no material change has taken place in these wri
tings. It is true, the fathers in some instances appear to have quoted from memory, and in others to
have interpreted the words of the sacred writers
differently from what we do, but all evidence goes
to show that the Scriptures of the New Testament
have come down to us in their original integrity,
save those errors which arose from the carelessness
or ignorance of transcribers; but even in regard to
these, by means of the multitude of copies of the
Greek text, and of early versions, with the help of
numerous quotations made in Africa, Asia, and Europe, the correct reading can usually be ascertained
with very considerable certainty. It is probable that
almost every sentence in some books of the New
Testament has been cited or referred to by one or
other of the fathers. Let any one only cast his eye
over a table of texts quoted by Cyprian, Origen, Tertullian, or any other extensive writer among them,
and he will be convinced that a large part of the
New Testament could be collected from their writings.

As the apocryphal books of the New Testament,
though very numerous, are never connected with the
sacred volume, and as none now plead for the canonical authority of any of these books, there is no
necessity, in treating of the evidences of Christianity,
to enter into any discussion respecting them. And
I would beg leave to refer any who may feel a curiosity to inquire into their character, and to have some
specimens of their style and spirit, to Jones' " New
method of settling the canon of the New Testament;"
or the volume which the present writer compiled on
the subject of the canon.

Having brought this " View of the Evidences

Christianity" to a close, I would entreat the reader
who has accompanied me thus far, not to suffer his
mind to be disturbed, or his faith unsettled, by objections which ingenious men may raise, which he may
not be able to answer. Objections may be made to
the most certain principles of science, and even to
what we know by consciousness, and the evidence
of our senses; but though we cannot remove all difficulties, yet we do not distrust our intuitive judgments, our senses, and the clear deductions of reason.
Many of the objections of infidels, however, are easily
answered, and have been fully answered again and
again; but they still throw back the blunted weapons,
so often repelled, as though they had never been
used before. There is no room in this brief outline,
to enter on a consideration of the popular objections
of deists. Such a work would itself require a volume,
and he who executes such a work skillfully, will
deserve well of the Christian community.

One word more to the candid reader. Rest not,
I entreat you, in a mere rational conviction of the
truth of the gospel, but speedily reduce your faith to
practice. *Embrace* the gospel, as well as assent to
its truth. If Christianity is true, it is the most important concern in the world. Avail yourselves of
its precious invitations; obey its salutary precepts,
and escape from the dangers of which it gives you
warning.

If the Bible is written by the inspiration of God,
how highly should we prize this sacred volume, and
how devoutly and diligently should we study its contents! "Search the Scriptures." Pray for divine
illumination, that you may understand them. That
man who is pronounced "blessed," meditates in the
law day and night. "The law of the Lord is perfect, converting the soul; the testimonies of the Lord
are sure, making wise the simple." What is said
at the beginning and at the close of the last book in
the canon, may be well applied to the whole Bible:
" Blessed is he that readeth, and they that hear the

words of this prophecy, and keep those things which are written therein.

" For I testify unto every one that heareth the words of the prophecy of this book, if any man shall add unto these things, God shall add unto him the plagues that are written in this book. And if any man shall take away from the words of the book of this prophecy, God shall take away his part out of the book of life, and out of the Holy City, and from the things which are written in this book."

Religion in America
Series II

An Arno Press Collection

Adler, Felix. **Creed and Deed:** A Series of Discourses. New York, 1877.

Alexander, Archibald. **Evidences of the Authenticity, Inspiration, and Canonical Authority of the Holy Scriptures.** Philadelphia, 1836.

Allen, Joseph Henry. **Our Liberal Movement in Theology:** Chiefly as Shown in Recollections of the History of Unitarianism in New England. 3rd edition. Boston, 1892.

American Temperance Society. **Permanent Temperance Documents of the American Temperance Society.** Boston, 1835.

American Tract Society. **The American Tract Society Documents,** 1824-1925. New York, 1972.

Bacon, Leonard. **The Genesis of the New England Churches.** New York, 1874.

Bartlett, S[amuel] C. **Historical Sketches of the Missions of the American Board.** New York, 1972.

Beecher, Lyman. **Lyman Beecher and the Reform of Society:** Four Sermons, 1804-1828. New York, 1972.

[Bishop, Isabella Lucy Bird.] **The Aspects of Religion in the United States of America.** London, 1859.

Bowden, James. **The History of the Society of Friends in America.** London, 1850, 1854. Two volumes in one.

Briggs, Charles Augustus. **Inaugural Address and Defense,** 1891-1893. New York, 1972.

Colwell, Stephen. **The Position of Christianity in the United States,** in Its Relations with Our Political Institutions, and Specially with Reference to Religious Instruction in the Public Schools. Philadelphia, 1854.

Dalcho, Frederick. **An Historical Account of the Protestant Episcopal Church, in South-Carolina,** from the First Settlement of the Province, to the War of the Revolution. Charleston, 1820.

Elliott, Walter. **The Life of Father Hecker.** New York, 1891.

Gibbons, James Cardinal. **A Retrospect of Fifty Years.** Baltimore, 1916. Two volumes in one.

Hammond, L[ily] H[ardy]. **Race and the South:** Two Studies, 1914-1922. New York, 1972.

Hayden, A[mos] S. **Early History of the Disciples in the Western Reserve, Ohio;** With Biographical Sketches of the Principal Agents in their Religious Movement. Cincinnati, 1875.

Hinke, William J., editor. **Life and Letters of the Rev. John Philip Boehm:** Founder of the Reformed Church in Pennsylvania, 1683-1749. Philadelphia, 1916.

Hopkins, Samuel. **A Treatise on the Millennium.** Boston, 1793.

Kallen, Horace M. **Judaism at Bay:** Essays Toward the Adjustment of Judaism to Modernity. New York, 1932.

Kreider, Harry Julius. **Lutheranism in Colonial New York.** New York, 1942.

Loughborough, J. N. **The Great Second Advent Movement:** Its Rise and Progress. Washington, 1905.

M'Clure, David and Elijah Parish. **Memoirs of the Rev. Eleazar Wheelock, D.D.** Newburyport, 1811.

McKinney, Richard I. **Religion in Higher Education Among Negroes.** New Haven, 1945.

Mayhew, Jonathan. **Observations on the Charter and Conduct of the Society for the Propagation of the Gospel in Foreign Parts;** Designed to Shew Their Non-conformity to Each Other. Boston, 1763.

Mott, John R. **The Evangelization of the World in this Generation.** New York, 1900.

Payne, Bishop Daniel A. **Sermons and Addresses,** 1853-1891. New York, 1972.

Phillips, C[harles] H. **The History of the Colored Methodist Episcopal Church in America:** Comprising Its Organization, Subsequent Development, and Present Status. Jackson, Tenn., 1898.

Reverend Elhanan Winchester: Biography and Letters. New York, 1972.

Riggs, Stephen R. **Tah-Koo Wah-Kan; Or, the Gospel Among the Dakotas.** Boston, 1869.

Rogers, Elder John. **The Biography of Eld. Barton Warren Stone, Written by Himself:** With Additions and Reflections. Cincinnati, 1847.

Booth-Tucker, Frederick. **The Salvation Army in America:** Selected Reports, 1899-1903. New York, 1972.

Satolli, Francis Archbishop. **Loyalty to Church and State.** Baltimore, 1895.

Schaff, Philip. **Church and State in the United States** or the American Idea of Religious Liberty and its Practical Effects with Official Documents. New York and London, 1888. (Reprinted from *Papers of the American Historical Association,* Vol. II, No. 4.)

Smith, Horace Wemyss. **Life and Correspondence of the Rev. William Smith, D.D.** Philadelphia, 1879, 1880. Two volumes in one.

Spalding, M[artin] J. **Sketches of the Early Catholic Missions of Kentucky;** From Their Commencement in 1787 to the Jubilee of 1826-7. Louisville, 1844.

Steiner, Bernard C., editor. **Rev. Thomas Bray:** His Life and Selected Works Relating to Maryland. Baltimore, 1901. (Reprinted from *Maryland Historical Society Fund Publication,* No. 37.)

To Win the West: Missionary Viewpoints, 1814-1815. New York, 1972.

Wayland, Francis and H. L. Wayland. **A Memoir of the Life and Labors of Francis Wayland, D.D., LL.D.** New York, 1867. Two volumes in one.

Willard, Frances E. **Woman and Temperance:** Or, the Work and Workers of the Woman's Christian Temperance Union. Hartford, 1883.

F